Gardenia Sunrise

Where Love Prevails

A Novel

by

I0319967

Sherry Ann Miller

Published and Distributed by:

Granite Publishing and Distribution, LLC
868 North 1430 West
Orem, Utah 84057
(801) 229-9023 • Toll Free (800) 574-5779
Fax (801) 229-1924

Cover Design by: Steve Gray
Cover Art Work by: Jennett Chandler
Page Layout and Design by: Myrna Varga • The Office Connection

Library of Congress Catalog Card Number: 2001091571
ISBN: 1-930980-33-7

Gardenia Sunrise

is dedicated to Marcelle,
who spent hours sharing her memories
of growing up near Chinon, the Loire Valley,
and St. Gilles Croix de Vie.
Also to Shanda, for her kind and generous
assistance with the French language,
as well as for her resources regarding
the city of Nantes,
where she served while on her mission.
May you each have the opportunity to visit
France again . . . and stay as long as
your heart desires!

Gardenia Sunrise

is also dedicated to Tara,
who lost her battle with liver cancer,
and to those who still miss her.
Tara left a legacy of faith
and hope in eternal life.
She held her toddler's hands for
only a short time,
but their hearts
. . . forever!

*I*n her dream, Brandje read a book of scripture that filled her heart with a profound and unexpected comfort. Never before had she heard such compassionate and inspirational narratives of the Savior, Jesus Christ. Hoping never to lose this peace and serenity, she realized that her spirit had been parched, as if from a pernicious drought. The scriptures quenched her thirst beyond measure as she continued reading:

> *"And it came to pass that when Jesus had made an end of praying unto the Father, he arose; but so great was the joy of the multitude that they were overcome.*
>
> *"And it came to pass that Jesus spake unto them, and bade them arise.*
>
> *"And they arose from the earth, and he said unto them; Blessed are ye because of your faith. And now behold, my joy is full. And when he had said these words, he wept. . . ."*

–3 Nephi 17:18-21

Chapter One

The Normandy style, two-story villa stood atop a large, craggy bluff, with a southern exposure that overlooked the small fishing village of St. Gilles Croix de Vie and the Bay of Biscay in western France.

Ferocious Atlantic waves pounded relentlessly against the granite cliffs nearby, but she no longer heard them, nor was she aware of the mist lingering near her face as it filtered through the window screen. The crunching of tires on the brown cobblestone driveway below her bedroom window, failed to awaken her.

She remained in a deep, undisturbed sleep, completely unaware when a stranger removed a key from above the outside door frame. As he unlocked the front door to the villa, she slept soundly upstairs in the bedroom, oblivious of his presence. The man entered the villa, turned on the living room light, then stepped back outside.

The invigorating smell of salt spray, mingled with the scent of gardenia blossoms, filled his lungs and he savored the moment. A smile brightened his face as he inhaled the heavenly fragrance. Planted by the villa owner years earlier, the dark green foliage and pale, creamy flowers grew abundant, almost wild, as they draped across the towering cliffs like billowing curtains.

He felt a deep gratitude at his return. To spend two months in France by the restless sea was the highlight of his year. It was a time for renewing both body and spirit, a time for rejoicing at the majestic creations of God.

"It's too bad Tante Nicole didn't come with you," said a younger man who removed suitcases from the trunk and placed them inside the villa. "Grandmaman was looking forward to her visit."

"Mother will undoubtedly make the trip later on," Nathan replied. "I don't believe she'll tolerate my father keeping her under his thumb for long."

While Frederick placed the remainder of Nathan's belongings on the woolen rug, Nathan removed a heavy box from the trunk, carried it into the villa, and put it on a large mahogany desk in the living room. In doing so, he failed to notice a woman's sweater resting upon the back of the sofa nearest the stairs.

When they returned to the car, Nathan said, "Be sure to remind my mother about my horse. Dorsett gets fidgety without attention."

"I will straight away," Frederick responded, reaching out to shake his cousin's hand. "Grandmaman will probably telephone her this evening with news of your safe arrival. Uncle Charles said your car will be ready within the week."

"Good," said Nathan.

The two men shook hands once again. "Goodbye then," said Frederick. "I'll tell the rest of the family you've arrived."

"Thanks," Nathan said as Frederick got back in the car and closed the door. Frederick coasted the car down the cobblestone driveway. Soon it whisked across the countryside and disappeared behind a hill.

Grateful for the French roots he'd inherited from his mother, Nathan marveled over the moonlit view of France from his vantage point.

The villa stood atop a bluff that faced south, overlooking the Bay of Biscay, yet it sloped gently downhill on the north. At the foot of the hill, a narrow road parted, rambling both southeast and northwest. To the north, grape vineyards, dairy farms and alfalfa fields stretched as far as the eye could see. To the southeast lay the small seaside village of St. Gilles Croix de Vie, with its tiny fishing port and sandy beaches. Northwest nearly fifty miles lay the bustling city of Nantes, well known for its spacious antiquated buildings and magnificent bridges. Tourists to France normally visited Paris or the French Riviera. However, those who truly knew France chose out-of-the-way places, like Croix de Vie, not only for its seventeenth century charm and picturesque atmosphere, but for the unspoiled beaches away from the Mediterranean crowds, as well.

Nathan inhaled deeply, as though drinking it all in. The stars sparkled like a million crystals against a velvet backdrop. The full moon gleamed more luminous than he could ever recall seeing it before. Sunrise would soon awaken the sleeping villagers, yet he doubted dawn could make the day any brighter. The landscape between the villa and Croix de Vie, more than two miles away, was illuminated with a silver, almost ethereal glow. Even the straight spaces between the lush green vineyard rows revealed few shadows at rest under the watchful night sky.

He had much to be grateful for, Nathan mused to himself as he went back inside the villa and opened the box he'd put on the desk earlier, failing once again to notice the woman's sweater draped over the back of a sofa.

His proselyting duties as a Stake Missionary back in Rochester, New York, were as rewarding as the two years he'd spent near Paris, where he'd served a full-time mission.

He wondered at how quickly the time had passed since his college graduation from Rochester University, as he realized he'd been out among the working class for seven years. Though he didn't consider doing what he loved best as working at all. Nathan loved writing and had several novels published, some with phenomenal success.

His future appeared bright and secure, except for one tiny detail: Nathan had no companion with whom to share his life.

Although he'd looked for a suitable wife, Nathan hadn't found anyone he could truly love. Relationships in the twenty-first century were certainly difficult. Either he would find a woman who had all the qualities he wanted in a wife, except for faith in the Lord; or he would find a woman with absolute conviction in the Lord and few, if any, other qualities to charm him.

Nathan's list of prerequisites was fair, he thought to himself, as he unpacked the box and arranged a few reference books, his scriptures, a laptop computer and a small printer upon the desk. First and foremost, she must love the Lord and have a strong testimony of the gospel of Jesus Christ. If she didn't have these qualifications, he usually didn't look any further.

In addition, he didn't want a woman who would be easy to coerce. She must be able to stand up against him if she felt it was warranted. He wanted a woman who wouldn't let his anger rage out of control, who simply refused to put up with it. She would have to be strong willed to live with him, that was certain.

She should have some sense of logic because that was an area in which he felt sadly lacking. A totally creative person, Nathan had little room left for logic. His future wife should have strengths that he did not, thus they would complement each other, like two weights balanced to an equal measure.

The woman of his dreams must want and be kind to children. Nathan loved children and loathed the idea that, even in America, children were neglected or abandoned. He also wanted someone who could be as neat and tidy a housekeeper as he was, though she needn't be a great cook. He could manage the kitchen, if necessary, but she should want to share the household responsibilities with him.

A sense of humor was a must. Any woman who married him would have to be able to laugh with him, and at him, when justified. And last, but not least, it would be a bonus if she enjoyed the sea as much as he did, and could at least fish or sail.

Of course, he had also asked the Lord if she could be attractive and trim, but he was no fool to think he was such a catch himself. He had a cowlick at the crown of his head that was totally unmanageable, and no matter what he did to make it lay flat, he always had a nubbin of hair that stood straight up. He'd tried every concoction suggested to him to get the unruly hair to cooperate, to no avail. At his hairdresser's encouragement, he'd once been given a permanent. When even that failed, he was informed that he was destined to appear as Alfalfa, from the Little Rascals, for the rest of his life, except that his hair was sandy brown.

His visual acuity was great for distances, but close up work necessitated his wearing glasses. This he disliked, but the glasses he'd chosen didn't make him appear less appealing.

He sighed. Surely these imperfections wouldn't prevent a woman from loving him. He contemplated a moment, then he shrugged and decided. No, he wasn't an unattractive man.

Nathan considered himself a rugged, well-mannered fellow, one who liked a good joke, and could tease his family unmercifully.

He was a man with few vices, except for his quick temper. If he knew how to control it, he would. He had to admit that it was particularly difficult trying to find a woman who was willing to tolerate his irritability. In a recent interview with his stake president, he'd been asked to fast and pray for the Lord to send him a woman who could love him regardless of the short fuse connected to his anger ignition center. Worse, he was asked to bring his temper under control in order to become the kind of man that a worthy woman would want.

Excess baggage, the stake president called it. Everyone has something within them that needs an extra push or shove. He wondered what excess baggage the stake president had, but could think of none. He'd obviously already conquered it.

When Nathan was satisfied with the order of the desk, he put the box in the kitchen, then picked up two suitcases. At the bottom of the stairs he turned on another switch that lighted the stairwell completely. Then he carried the suitcases upstairs.

The villa had a new and pleasant aroma today, not the usual musty scent of years gone by. Perhaps the last tenant had just vacated, or perhaps the housekeeper had changed cleaning solutions.

He reached the landing and turned left, intending to enter the larger of three bedrooms. Pushing the door open with his foot, he stepped inside. As the door opened, the light from the hall illuminated the room brightly. What the light enabled him to see, made him stop abruptly and drop the suitcases on the floor.

A woman, lovely and petite, slept soundly in the queen-size bed, entirely unaware of his presence! He looked at her for several quiet minutes, puzzled that he had found such a vision as this. His heart raced inside his chest and he felt an overwhelming sensation to care for her, to protect her. She was, without doubt, the most beautiful woman he'd ever seen.

He gulped as he realized he had stumbled into a situation that could potentially change his life forever. Completely unnerved, Nathan panicked, picked up the suitcases and backed out of the room.

Something was terribly wrong, he decided, and he wondered if the error was an omission on his part. Had he confused the arrival date?

Once outside the bedroom, he put the suitcases down, then pulled the door closed until it was ajar only an inch or two, to protect the woman's privacy. Although the woman was completely covered up to her neck with a soft, puffy comforter, he didn't know what she wore beneath the bedding, and he had no intention of finding out.

Nathan reached into a back pocket and brought forth his wallet, then secured a slip of paper from within. He scanned the writing on it and sighed in relief. His reservation was confirmed for July 1st through August 30th. Today was the second of July, plenty of time for the former tenant to have vacated, and the villa to be prepared for him. Whatever the problem, he still had his reservation confirmation and payment receipt.

He pondered the situation carefully as he nudged the door open again with the toe of his shoe. A woman was sleeping in his bed. *His* bed! His reaction changed from surprise to anger, which frustrated him even more because of his struggle to conquer his quick temper. She had no right! He'd rented the villa legally and she would have to go! That was plainly evident!

He watched her a few minutes while she slept, and swayed emotionally between indignation and infatuation. The woman was exquisitely beautiful in a fragile sort of way, with honey gold hair that surrounded her face and covered the pillow completely. A wisp of a smile rested upon her lips, as though she were enjoying some secret dream. The thought made Nathan smile unexpectedly. He was surprised and pleased to discover that anger had departed, at least for the moment.

Had he been fresh from the mission field, he would have fled the villa by now, his skin crimson from head to toe, and never returned. But he was ten years beyond his mission, a man who'd already made his way in the world. Besides, he was undeniably curious about her, and honest enough to admit it.

Considering the situation, he evaluated all the reasons why another tenant would be staying at the villa during his reserved time.

He had to admit that this was one of those moments when a man has to weigh all the possibilities. He and a beautiful woman could share the villa together for two months along the west coast of France, but what would his Stake President say? Nathan sighed. *Scratch that thought off my mind*, he thought ruefully.

One of them would have to leave, but where else could she go? He had no doubt that he would be the one to stay. He had the law on his side. And the sea, a major component in his inspiration for writing, had enabled some of his success during the past six years. This villa was his writing retreat, his time to spend working on his latest book. He had a publisher waiting and a deadline looming. What was he to do? He couldn't very well throw the woman out, could he?

A better solution occurred to him almost immediately, and he smiled as he thought about it. The idea might even be fun, he mused to himself. But first, he needed to determine what this woman was about, and why she was here. Perhaps while trying to keep his temper at bay, he should allow a little levity to the situation.

Then Nathan grinned mischievously and arched an eyebrow. This might prove a very interesting situation, he decided at once. Very interesting, indeed!

His decision made, Nathan stepped into the bedroom, turned on a lamp, removed the woman's bathrobe from the foot of her bed, then held it out in front of him. He turned his eyes toward the door, and with as much noise as he could, he cleared his throat with a loud, "Ahem!"

The woman opened her eyes and blinked sleepily, then bolted to her feet, grabbed the robe, and backed away from him as she screamed, "Who are you? And what are you doing in my bedroom?" Her shrill voice sounded both fearful and angry.

Nathan had frightened her more than she had shocked him, and he felt remorseful, if only for a moment. While averting his eyes to give her time to put on the bathrobe, Nathan tried to keep an edge of hostility out of his voice as he replied, "Since this is supposed to be *my* bedroom,

I was about to ask you the same question."

When he turned around to face her, he was relieved to see that she wore not only the robe he'd given her, but cotton pajamas as well.

Her hair caught his attention next. She had exquisitely beautiful hair, like golden strands of honey that stretched all the way to her waist.

Nathan felt awkward as he silently considered how lovely she was. Then he realized she was waiting for an answer. "Ahem," he said again, this time really clearing his throat. "My name is Nathaniel Duncan, the Third. I apologize if I frightened you, but . . ." he hesitated only for a second, then asked, "May I inquire about your name?"

"My name?" she shrieked, her voice filled with indignation. "What on earth are you doing in my home?"

"Your home?" he demanded, his voice sharpening in retaliation. "I've rented this villa for two months, beginning yesterday, and I have legal proof!" He held out his copy of the reservation receipt and was glad that she didn't yell at him any further as she read it.

She nodded, gave him a contemplative frown and said, "I'm Brandje Fulton. I own the villa and I gave notice some time ago that I would be spending the rest of the summer here."

"Brandy?" he asked, emphasizing the long *'ee'* sound, while letting her name roll off his tongue like spun silk. "Like the alcoholic beverage?" He arched an eyebrow. "An unusual name for a girl, isn't it?"

Brandje glared ominously at him.

Nathan's black-brown eyes swept over her smooth, creamy skin, fine straight nose and high cheekbones. They rested momentarily on her full, pouting lips, parted slightly in exasperation.

She pulled a stray lock of golden hair off her shoulder. It fell down her back where it caressed her thin waist.

This action did not go unnoticed. Nathan not only inspected the length of her lovely hair, but also the narrowness of her waist, her slim hips and small-boned ankles just visible beneath the rose colored robe.

When he had thoroughly finished inspecting her petite, five-foot frame, he smiled, hoping to disarm her for a moment.

She arched her shoulders rigidly, before answering his question. "My name is spelled B-r-a-n-d-*j-e*, if you must know. But for you, Ms. Fulton will suffice!"

"Well, *Ms.* Fulton," he said, emphasizing the Ms. He felt disappointed to call her that, since Ms. didn't indicate whether or not she was married. Though why that should have mattered to him, he couldn't imagine. For a brief moment his temper returned, but with some effort, he was able to subdue it. "I've rented the villa every July and August for the past six years. My reservation was confirmed when I left here last summer."

He could tell he had surprised her when her eyes opened wide and her chin dropped. "I told the rental agent to cancel all reservations until fall," she insisted.

"They didn't cancel mine," he persisted stubbornly.

She tilted her head proudly as though taking control of the situation. "I'm sorry to disappoint you, Mr. Duncan. Since I own the villa, I'll have to return your investment and insist that you find other, more suitable accommodations."

The fragile look she gave him enhanced the delicate features of her face, which seemed to force his anger away. Nathan softened and gave her a crooked smile, unable to prevent it from escaping onto his face. "I doubt that would be possible," he said. "At this late hour, every villa, apartment, hotel and campground will be booked through at least November."

"Nevertheless," Brandje insisted, apparently unaffected by his smile. "You cannot possibly stay here. I'm . . ." she hesitated for only a moment. Then with a hint of reluctance in her voice, she said, "I'm alone."

"Not anymore!" He shrugged his shoulders and hoped he appeared nonchalant, because his heart was pounding with great fury inside his chest. "I'll use one of the other bedrooms." He turned and went into the hall where he picked up the two suitcases, then entered a bedroom across the landing from hers.

Does he have any clue how much he frightened me? Brandje shivered. Then, pushing her fears aside, she walked over to the doorway and glared at the intruder as he dropped his suitcases on the bed across the hall. She could not physically throw him out of the villa, not with his six-foot, broad-shouldered body. She stood in the doorway and leaned against the frame, contemplating the situation. Legally she couldn't force him to leave. His reservation had obviously been confirmed for months. Besides, he was American, this much she'd discerned immediately from his accent. He'd no doubt come all the way from America to stay here and she felt an obligation to at least find him other accommodations. He seemed reasonable enough. Perhaps if she could locate another apartment for him, he would leave. She exhaled in dismay.

Within minutes, Nathan returned. He was so tall, and she so short, that he seemed to tower above her. *He is handsome*, she admitted to herself. His sandy brown hair waved across his forehead like a gentle ocean swell, with a twig of hair at the crown of his head that wanted to stand straight up. *Stubborn, just like him*, she thought ruefully. Nathan's dark eyes and well-chiseled face contrasted with his hair, and she wondered if his parents were from separate cultural backgrounds.

"Mrs. Fulton," Nathan began, "if —"

"Miss!" she corrected sharply. Then, realizing he had tricked her into revealing her marital status, she glared at him with contempt.

"*Miss* Fulton," he amended with a satisfied smile. "If you've nothing better to do than lounge around in your pajamas, I suggest you begin breakfast. I've not eaten since noon, yesterday."

"I most certainly will not!" she snapped. "You're not staying here!"

"Hmm, I thought we'd settled that," he teased. "Oh, well. When you finally see the light of day —"

"The light of day!" she yelled, growing more impatient with him by the moment. "It's still dark outside!"

"That may be." He glanced at his watch. "But it is almost five in the morning, your time. Do come down. I'll prepare breakfast for both of us."

Brandje gave him an icy expression she hoped would plainly reveal how despicable she considered him, but he gave her a mischievous grin in response, then turned and went down the stairs. She whirled around and stormed back into the bedroom, slamming the door behind her.

Her first instinct was to cry, but she refused to give him the satisfaction. She was too stubborn for that. Besides, when she cried her face reddened and her nose dripped ceaselessly. She didn't want him to know he'd emotionally trounced her.

Worse, she didn't want him to realize she hadn't any hope of finding him another place to stay.

Chapter Two

randje walked over to the dresser to stare at her reflection in the mirror. "It would be my misfortune," she said in a soft whisper, "to have some intruder disrupt my solitude." How desperately she needed that solitude, Nathaniel Duncan would never know.

Even now, Brandje could scarcely believe it herself, but she had come to France with one solitary purpose: to prepare herself in mind and spirit for a time not far distant when her life would end prematurely.

"Oh, that horrible night!" she said to herself with all the misery that permeated her soul. Her vision blurred as she wandered back through her memory to a night only two short weeks ago. She had just returned from the hospital to her brother's farmhouse, where they both lived, not too far from London.

Fresh, raw memories flooded over her as she recalled that her brother, Martin, had retired around nine o'clock and was likely already asleep. He'd been working long hours to keep up with both the farm and housework since her stay in the hospital.

She had silently slipped out from under a flannel blanket, and left her robe hanging in the closet, fearing the squeaky door would awaken Martin in the bedroom next to hers.

Her stomach rumbled with hunger as she made her way down the hall to a curved mahogany stairway leading to the main floor for a snack.

Although she descended the stairs with caution she could still feel her muscles twinge in agony from her recent appendectomy. She halted abruptly on the bottom step, waiting for the momentary pain to subside.

Suddenly the telephone rang noisily beside her.

Brandje cringed. Disregarding the pain, she rushed down the narrow corridor to the kitchen. She knew Martin would be furious with her for getting out of bed. Just as her bare feet left the lacquered wood and halted on the cool linoleum of the kitchen she heard his heavy footsteps descending the stairs. She stepped aside from the open door and stood next to the kitchen wall, where Martin could not see her from the hall. Curling her waist-length hair unconsciously around her fingers, she listened to the telephone ring once more before Martin retrieved it.

"Fulton here!" he growled. "It's rather a poor time to ring, don't you think?!"

Her eyes widened in surprise and she stifled a chuckle. Martin hated to be awakened from his sleep unjustly.

Then Martin said, "Oh! Dr. Graham." His voice became anxious. "Yes, I apologize. I didn't realize it was you."

There was a long pause. Then the wooden chair next to the telephone groaned as Martin sat down upon it.

"Then it's true?" he questioned, his breathing ragged and labored. "You're absolutely positive?"

Brandje held her breath, her stomach tightening with apprehension. What was her brother talking about?

"She has only six months left to live?" her brother asked, his voice a mixture of dismay and anguish.

Exhaling silently, Brandje leaned against the papered wall for support. Her mouth opened unconsciously and she placed a trembling hand against her dry lips.

"I see," Martin choked. Then, "How can I possibly tell her?"

Tears welled up in Brandje's eyes, spilled over and dripped effortlessly down her face. Oblivious to the pain, she bit her forefinger in an effort to prevent crying out in shock.

"No, she doesn't suspect a thing," Martin continued. "I haven't wanted to believe it. I've been hoping you were mistaken. I suppose I must face the facts now, mustn't I?"

Feeling as though she'd been kicked in the stomach, Brandje stifled another moan. *What had they discovered? What would end her twenty-third year of life?*

Martin's weary voice interrupted her thoughts. "I can see the wisdom of that. Yes, thank you."

She heard the click of the receiver, then intense, suffocating silence.

Finally the chair squeaked in relief as Martin stood up. His heavy footsteps shuffled against the wooden floor as he walked toward the kitchen.

Don't come in here, Brandje silently entreated. *Martin, please!*

As though in answer to her plea, Martin hesitated in the hall just before reaching the open kitchen door. "Come on, old boy," he said to himself. "You've suspected this for a week now. You promised yourself you wouldn't break down." He placed his forehead against the corridor wall, his hands knotted into tight fists on both sides of his head. "Dear God," came his choked whisper of a prayer. "Why do you have to take her? She's just a child! Why couldn't it be me? Why?"

Then, to prevent awakening Brandje with his outburst of anguish, Martin turned and fled from the house, his long legs descending the front porch steps in one leap.

Six months would mean December at the latest, Brandje calculated quickly in her mind. Then her thoughts riveted to Martin.

She stepped into the hall and over to the front door, left open by her brother. She watched in dismay as his lean body raced down the driveway and then across the pasture, until he reached the fence on the far side, four acres away. His head arched backward as he cursed the Heavens through anguished tears of bitterness. She sank wearily to the floor to weep for him, as well as for herself.

Poor, dear brother! While at the tender age of sixteen he stood by their mother's deathbed consumed with grief. Mother and son were tenaciously close, and he never recovered losing her. Twenty years later, when he was thirty-six, their father passed away, a victim of cancer. Martin was left with bitter memories, profound grief, and a twenty-year-old sister whom he adored. Now Brandje would follow the footsteps of their parents, leaving Martin to carry on alone.

Bringing her thoughts back to the present, Brandje shook herself from the awful memories and studied her reflection in the mirror. Her azure blue eyes were bright and clear, her complexion peaches and cream. She noticed nothing that seemed out of the ordinary. She didn't look at all like a woman who was going to die by Christmas.

Brandje glanced at the open window. Dawn began to break forth in all its splendor, casting a golden hue against the curtains as they danced with an early morning breeze. Suddenly a gust of wind pushed the curtain high into the air, then departed, letting the fabric fall limp against the screen. The morning air grew silent. The chiffon hung lifeless from the metal rod, a potent reminder of Brandje's future.

After removing her pajamas, she slipped quickly into a pair of slacks and a cotton sweater.

If she'd known she would have to deal with this new situation, the man downstairs, she would have listened when Martin tried to persuade her not to go to France. After she let her brother know she would not relent, he'd put up a silent barrier, refusing to voice any further opinion on the matter. That he was troubled in spirit was evident by the painful look on his face, an expression that still made her tears flow.

Martin had never divulged the secret between Dr. Graham and himself. It was just as well. Brandje never told Martin about her secret visit with Dr. Graham, who confirmed her medical prognosis. Rather than confront Martin, Brandje fled hastily to France, the one place where she could be alone, to prepare her mind and spirit for the inevitable trials that loomed ahead of her.

In her youth, she'd brought all her problems to the villa, to the sea and its majestic waves. In the past, each time she left the villa, her problems had melted into oblivion, never to be remembered. Perhaps it was the continual wearing away of the granite cliffs. Perhaps the salt water, crushing against stone, had also crushed her mountainous difficulties into nothingness. Perhaps it was the soothing fragrance of the gardenias she loved so well that calmed her fears. She only knew that the villa was her escape, her stronghold from the trials of the world.

But for now, her biggest obstacle came in the form of a handsome, somewhat confident stranger. She would deal with him first.

After he was ousted from her property she would have the time she needed to prepare herself for what lay ahead, for the day she would close her eyes and fade away to that unknown world called death.

Brandje felt more composed when she descended the narrow stairs thirty minutes later. Her honey blonde hair, pulled away from her face with a rose-colored ribbon, cascaded down her back like a waterfall. The cotton sweater she wore matched the ribbon and contrasted with the off white slacks that hugged her hips in just the right places. Her ivory-tone sandals clicked noisily against the bare wooden steps.

The smell of aromatic onions and green peppers filled the kitchen as she entered. Buttered toast, stacked on an ironstone plate, sat next to a delectable, steaming omelette. Nathaniel Duncan evidently had culinary skills better than her own.

"The toast is still hot," Nathan said, not taking his eyes from the stove. Masterfully he swirled the pan, then made a quick upward flipping motion. The omelette turned over in midair, all in one piece, and landed back in the skillet. Nathan topped the eggs with grated cheese, sautéed onions and peppers, then he folded the omelette in half. "I'll have to restock your refrigerator in payment for breakfast," he offered.

Brandje did not reply. Reluctantly she sat at the table and watched with resentment as Nathaniel Duncan slid the omelette onto a plate, turned off the burner, and put the skillet in the sink.

He slid the plate in front of her but she pushed it back. "You should eat something," he persuaded.

She took one slice of toast and nibbled at it.

"You're positive you only want toast?" Nathan asked. "My omelettes are a treat you may regret missing." He rested his tall, muscular body on a wooden chair opposite her and forked into his eggs hungrily.

Although the breakfast he'd prepared had visual appeal as well as tantalizing aroma, Brandje would not acquiesce. "Toast is sufficient," came her stiff response.

Her eyes searched his for some sign of tenderness, but she was distracted by his rugged, well-chiseled face. He was handsome, and he had some magnetic quality about him that she found difficult to resist. Under normal circumstances, she would have lost herself in his gaze with abandon. However, in her condition, she knew she had no choice but to ignore his captivating brown-black eyes that seemed to reach into her very soul, his sensual lips that beckoned hers to come closer, ever closer. How he accomplished this while eating his breakfast, Brandje did not understand.

Shaking her head in dismay, she hoped Mr. Duncan would assume this gesture referred to his omelette offering. She forced a calmness she didn't feel, and steadily returned his quiet gaze.

For a brief, fleeting moment, she wondered what it would be like to have one romantic fling before Christmas arrived. After all, she'd never been intimate with a man before, and from the hungry look in his eyes, she wondered if opportunity had presented her a perfect setting to do something she wouldn't live long enough to regret.

Brandje smiled to herself, realizing how silly that thought had been. She was not the type of woman to enter into a casual relationship, no matter how attractive it might seem, even in the face of her pending death. She shook her head for the second time, chasing such undesired thoughts away, silently hoping they would never return.

Nathan's bright smile changed her mood and she looked at him squarely across the table. "Mr. Duncan," she began formally. "There are extenuating circumstances that I am not at liberty to discuss. I cannot leave the villa and you may not stay. I would be extremely grateful if you would realize it is impossible for you to remain here."

"What circumstances?" he asked, ignoring her request altogether.

"I cannot divulge that!" she snapped, unable to quell the emotion stirring inside her. She wasn't certain what bothered her more, her anger at his stubbornness, or at herself because she hoped more could come from their untimely meeting. Stiffening, she said, "In any case, I'll ring

Bagley's office first thing this morning and insist that he find you other accommodations."

"You forget," he informed with more reprimand than sarcasm. "Your estate manager spends his summer on the Riviera. By this time of year he has all his rental properties leased out, and consequently, has no need to remain near Croix de Vie."

Brandje frowned. "Then I shall ring other property managers. Surely someone has a room you can sublet."

The idea was unacceptable to Nathan. "I reserved and paid for this villa for a reason, Miss Fulton. This is where I do my best work. I've been here every summer for six years and I have no intention of leaving. I received no notice regarding a cancellation in my reservation. I've paid for the villa for two months, and I intend to stay. Since I am also an amiable fellow, I have no objection to your staying as well, provided you don't get underfoot."

"But this is *my* home. I own it! I have the right to say who stays in my home and who does not!"

"Yes, but you retained Bagley and Associates to rent the property out for you, which they did. To me, I might add. Even if you pursue this matter in civil court, by the time all the legalities are sorted through, my two months will be long past and you can go back to being alone."

Brandje frowned. Tears gathered thickly in her blue eyes as she realized this stubborn, irresistible man would no doubt spend the rest of the summer with her. The way she had arranged her schedule, she was due to return back to England in mid-September. By then she would have had only two short weeks to herself, instead of the eleven weeks she had planned. She dreaded even contemplating the next nine weeks she would spend squashing emotions that were already running rampant within her. The last two weeks she would have alone, come September, would have to be spent unwinding from the nine weeks previous!

Brandje would have no opportunity to come to terms with her own mortality. It was more trial than she could bear. She couldn't understand how God could demand this much from her at a time when she felt so vulnerable. She put the toast down, then brought her hands up to cover her face and leaned her elbows on the table. She couldn't inform this perfect stranger that she had less than six months left to live and would need the solitude to prepare herself. Shuddering, she felt betrayed by her own emotions. She doubted her tears would have any impact upon Nathaniel Duncan the Third. Feeling absolutely miserable, Brandje whimpered.

She didn't hear him leave his chair. When she felt his hand upon her shoulder she looked over the top of her fingertips to find him bending over her.

Nathan moved her hands completely away from her face and gazed curiously into her bold blue eyes. He grabbed a napkin from the table and wiped away her tears.

"Someone's hurt you. That's why you want to be alone?" he guessed, a keen note of concern in his once obstinate voice.

Although he was completely inaccurate in his assumption, Brandje offered no denial, allowing him to draw his own conclusions. Perhaps he would soften his rigorous position and go away.

"Then I'm the answer to your problems," he insisted.

"How so?" she asked, with some confusion as to his motives.

"The worst thing you can do at this point is lock yourself up here all alone and brood over a broken romance. I'm good company. You'll find I'm reasonably tolerant, and not too temperamental, unless crossed. If you decide you want to talk the problem out, I'll be here. A friend in need, and all that."

Brandje shook her head. "You won't even attempt to understand," she complained. "It's not just that I want to be alone, It's . . . well, it's even more personal and I simply cannot discuss it."

"You're pregnant?" he wondered as a frown wandered across his handsome face.

"Absolutely not!" She glared at him with unbridled fury.

"Then what?" Relief was evident in his tender voice.

"I'm not at liberty to say!" Brandje pivoted back in her chair, pulled her hand from his light grip and resumed nibbling her toast, though she had no appetite for it.

It would not help to cry in front of Nathaniel Duncan. He would not leave the villa until she could find him other accommodations. Since Mr. Bagley was no doubt unavailable, she would have to accomplish the task herself.

"I'll clear," she said stiffly, her voice edged with anger. She stood and removed her half-empty juice glass and partially eaten toast.

Nathan stood also, then stretched and yawned. "Good," he agreed. "There are a few items I must attend to, as well." He turned and went into the living room.

Brandje filled the stainless steel sink with water and poured in dish soap. The morning sun filtered through the window, bathing her in golden warmth. She was busy drying the few pieces of stoneware when she heard the familiar sound of an internet connection via a computer modem in the living room.

Stepping to the curved archway, Brandje noticed he had put on a pair of bronze-framed reading glasses. She stared belligerently at him before asking, "What are you doing, Mr. Duncan?"

"Picking up my e-mail, surfing the web," came his immediate response.

"I can see that," she returned, rolling her eyes in dismay. "That's just what I need, an internet junkie sharing my villa with me."

"Since it is how I earn my living, you'll have to get used to it. I'm on the Internet every day, sometimes all day." He arched an eyebrow and gave her a quick smile, as though she amused him.

"Then how am I supposed to use the telephone?" she demanded, feeling both frustration and anger at the impossible man.

"Either wait until I'm done, or put in another line," he suggested.

Brandje swallowed the lump that had risen in her throat. An enormous amount of friction would develop between them before she ousted him from her property. A sense of weariness etched across her face. "I suppose you're an internet telemarketer, or some such thing?" she asked dryly.

"Not at all," answered Nathan. "The internet is one of the greatest research tools at man's disposal. In my profession, that's a plus."

"Research for what?" she asked.

He smiled before he said simply, "I'm a writer."

Although she was intrigued by his admission, she wouldn't allow him to learn of her curiosity. "What exactly do you write?" She shrugged to indicate her disinterest.

"Things," he said, giving her no explanation at all.

Futility threatened any response, and she returned to the kitchen to put away the last of the dishes. Afterward, she went upstairs to rest. An hour of tossing and turning still found her sleepless. Finally Brandje sat up and dangled her legs off the bed. Although exhausted, she brushed her hair, grabbed a handbag and went downstairs.

Nathan glanced up from the computer. "Going somewhere?" he asked.

"For a newspaper," she answered crossly. "The sooner I find another place for you to stay, the better!"

"I'm not leaving!" he said with a dangerous scowl. "If anyone goes, it'll be you. I have a legal right to the villa until the end of August."

"We certainly cannot live here together!" Brandje complained.

"It's agreeable with me," he insisted. "You're the only one offering objections. Perhaps you should find another place."

"But I own *this* property!" she protested, pushing a strand of golden hair behind her ear.

"It would never hold up in court. Legally you have no right to stay here without my permission." He retrieved a sheet of paper from the printer and studied it as though the conversation had ended.

"I can't stay here with *you!*" Brandje yelled. "It's indecent and . . ." she hesitated in abject futility before she continued, ". . . and ruinous to my reputation!"

Nathan pulled his reading glasses down to the tip of his nose and glanced at her over the frame. "To say nothing of mine," he mocked sardonically, his dark eyes flicking over her delicate curves in a teasing gesture.

"You're impossible!" she snapped.

"So noted," came his cool response.

Brandje sighed, then walked across the living room to the front door, and opened it.

"Shall I fix lunch?" he asked casually, as though nothing in the world concerned him.

"No!" she yelled. "I'll eat in town!"

"As you wish," he shrugged.

When she left the villa, Brandje slammed the door shut so hard the dishes in the china cupboard rattled.

After Brandje left, Nathan sighed. "Whew!" he whispered to himself. "And I thought I had a bad temper." Of course, he had antagonized her. Still, he wasn't sorry. He had a right to stay at the villa and she would have to accept that. But not without someone else to chaperone them, which had been his first and final resolve all along.

He wondered for a moment if he was carrying his ruse a bit far, but he wasn't sure how she would respond to the real solution he planned to offer later in the day. He'd better keep up the ploy until his aunt and uncle arrived. He didn't quite know how to tell her that he'd telephoned them while she was still upstairs, and they'd agreed to become his house-guests for a week, if need be. With the number of relatives he had scattered all over France, not to mention the Latter-day circle of brethren and sisters, he could offer a weeks lodging to any number of couples and still not run out of chaperones before the end of the year. Of course, this would put a major kink in his writing, but it would also give Brandje a sense of security that she may appreciate.

For himself, he realized that having live-in chaperones at the villa was probably the only way he could keep his covenants undefiled. The thoughts that had beset him from the moment he first saw Brandje asleep on the bed upstairs made his head spin. He'd always been sensible where the fairer sex was concerned. But that was before he met Brandje.

He decided to telephone some of his other connections to see if he could find more suitable accommodations, although his chances of success in that arena were probably less than one in a thousand.

Regardless, in his heart he knew that if push came to shove, he would go back to New York before he would force Brandje to leave her own home.

The rebel in him almost revolted at that realization. He loved his two months at the villa, and if that meant he had to have three other people sharing it with him, so be it.

Besides, the book he was writing had crucial components that needed his descriptions of the waves crashing against the granite cliffs, and all the other sounds of the ocean. He needed time spent near the sea, to listen to its rhythm, and incorporate that particular cadence into the chapters he'd waited to work on during his two month stay at the villa. Should he give all that up without a fight?

Reluctantly, Nathan closed the internet connection and picked up the desk phone. His research, and perhaps his book, would have to be put on hold for a while.

Chapter Three

*T*he sun glared brightly as Brandje walked down the cobblestone driveway and headed toward the medieval little village. Her villa was one of the few structures along the granite bluffs northwest of Croix de Vie. The nearest home to hers was half a mile away. She doubted she would find a single vacancy anywhere along the Atlantic coast, and certainly none in the small, ancient fishing village of St. Gilles, called Croix de Vie by the local inhabitants.

Within the hour, Brandje saw the brown tile roofs of the limestone houses that lined the sea front. A few fat fishing boats were harbored near the breakwater pier, the salt water licking at their bellies with white-tipped tongues.

By the time Brandje passed the wharf, her abdomen ached, presumably from the recent appendectomy. At least she hoped the stabbing assault of an invisible knife below her right rib cage was not an indication that the disease was progressing faster than expected.

She pushed through a small group of people gathered in the local pharmacy until she reached the newsstand. She paid the clerk for a newspaper and a telephone card, then proceeded toward the telephone booth.

Seventeen calls later, Brandje felt totally discouraged. The only available housing within fifty miles of Croix de Vie was a studio apartment subletting the fifteenth of August, which, she was told, had an offer pending.

Next, Brandje tackled the rental apartments found in the telephone directory. An hour later, she came to the sad realization that she had only one final option. Although she hated the idea of involving her only living relative besides Martin, she dialed a long distance number a hundred miles southeast of her, in Bordeaux, and waited patiently for an answer.

"*Maison de Limos*," came a crisp, feminine voice.

"*Mai je parle avec ma Tante Geraldine?*" Brandje asked.

After securing her aunt's promise to search for suitable housing from Nantes to Bordeaux, Brandje hung up. She had not disclosed her present living arrangements, fearing the dear woman would not understand. Then she started the long journey home.

Brandje walked back past the harbor along the winding road that stretched almost two miles before she reached the driveway that ascended uphill to the villa. She hesitated before attempting the strenuous climb up the steep slope. In addition to the pain in her stomach, she had walked farther that day than at any other time since her surgery.

Feeling exhausted, she decided it would have been better to hire a taxi for her return journey. Or perhaps she should have eaten some of Mr. Duncan's omelette earlier, instead of blindly refusing it. Now she felt faint with hunger, and she wondered if she would make it up the hill at all.

To make matters worse, the pain in her right side seemed to increase at an alarming rate. She winced every time she put one foot in front of the other.

Gritting her teeth in determination, Brandje began the ascent. By the time she reached the top of the hill she could scarcely stand. Beads of perspiration broke out on her forehead and chin. Her complexion took on a whiteness that was unlike the peaches and cream farm girl who'd been raised near London.

Brandje turned the knob and stumbled through the front door, barely maintaining her balance as she did so.

Nathaniel Duncan glanced up at her from the desk as she faltered at the open doorway. Immediately he dropped the telephone and rushed across the living room to catch her before she fell. He supported Brandje at both her elbows, concerned that she might faint completely. "Are you ill?" he asked, alarm evident in his voice. He lifted her up into his strong arms like a gentle father cradling a sick child.

"I'll be fine in a minute. I'm just winded. Please, Mr. Duncan, put me down," Brandje gasped.

Ignoring her plea, Nathan carried her up the stairs and into the bedroom where he placed her tenderly upon the queen-size bed. Removing her shoes, he asked pointedly, "This is the 'something personal' you refused to tell me?"

"Yes," Brandje sighed. "I'm here to recuperate from an operation. I expected to have peace and quiet for a while." She hoped he would take the less than subtle hint.

"What kind of operation?" he questioned, a puzzled look on his face.

Why does he have to be so attractive? she wondered to herself momentarily, then brushed the thought aside. "It's really none of your business!" she snapped, angry with herself for being attracted to him.

"Should you be climbing up and down that steep hill unescorted, or walking several miles into town and back?" he asked.

"The doctor told me to walk some every day. Really, Mr. Duncan," she insisted, propping herself up with an elbow. "I'm perfectly capable, I'm just a bit weak today. After all, I was awakened at the crack of dawn by a perfect stranger standing in my bedroom. The day's activities have exhausted me, that's all."

"Don't you think, since we'll be spending the next two months together, that we should dispense with the formality of Mr. and Miss?"

"Absolutely not!"

Nathan gave her a mock smile, one that assured her he intended to use her given name from that moment on. "Did you eat lunch in town?" he questioned, as though she'd not rebuffed him at all.

"No," she admitted with a defeated sigh.

"And you're here to recuperate?" he scolded. "I had no idea I would have to play nursemaid to a senseless child!"

"Mr. Duncan!" Brandje protested. "You don't —"

"Call me Nathan!" he warned dangerously, his eyes glinting sparks of irritation at her.

She couldn't blame him for being annoyed with her. She had acted foolishly, walking all that distance in a vain effort to oust him from the villa. Her mouth dropped open and she winced.

He softened a little, then asked, "Will a cheese sandwich be enough? You hardly touched your toast this morning."

"Yes," Brandje answered with more resignation than she wanted.

Within a few minutes Nathan returned with a sandwich and a bowl of creamy tomato soup. He watched every mouthful Brandje ate. His brown-black eyes so unnerved her that she envisioned him spoon feeding her if she offered any protest.

When she finished eating, he took the soiled dishes from her.

"I'm well enough to wash those," she told him, although her voice quivered. If Nathan didn't quit gazing at her she would melt completely.

What would it be like to have him take me in his arms and hold me while I drift blissfully off to sleep? she wondered. She did not feel uncomfortable, rather she felt a tingling sort of tenderness pass between them that needed no explanation. Although she couldn't explain why, she knew that Nathaniel Duncan was one man who would never hurt her, and that thought gave her comfort.

"After what I've seen today," he replied, "I doubt you're well enough to make it down the stairs."

Too tired to disagree with him, Brandje leaned back against the pillow and pulled the comforter over her shoulders. Within minutes she was sound asleep.

Voices laughing downstairs awakened Brandje from a deep and peaceful slumber. She slipped from the bed and glanced at the clock on the dresser. It was already seven in the evening.

Irritated, Brandje went into the bathroom where she washed her face and stared at her reflection in the mirror. Her skin had a paleness to it that she hadn't noticed this morning. What a foolish thing she'd done, walking into Croix de Vie! Silently she scolded herself.

It had been less than three weeks since her appendectomy. Although the scar was only two inches long, due to the remarkable capability of modern medical science, her abdomen still hurt in the upper right portion. The operation itself was supposed to be an outpatient procedure. Instead, she had been detained at the hospital for three days while a battery of tests were performed. At Martin's insistence, she'd only been told that there was an abnormality in one of her blood tests, and she would need to be examined further. Dr. Graham, the family physician who delivered Brandje, was eager to wait, as Martin had suggested, until all the test results were back, before sharing the information with her. Had she not visited him after his telephone call to Martin, Dr. Graham may have waited for Martin to tell Brandje the truth about her illness.

She sighed as she heard, once again, the sound of voices ascending from the living room. Irritated, she dried her face, brushed her hair, and went downstairs.

Nathan glanced up when he heard Brandje's footsteps on the stairs. He wrung his hands, and nodded to the couple opposite him at one of the two living room sofas. "Here comes Brandje," he said as he stood to introduce her.

"What now?" Brandje asked cautiously as she stepped into the living room.

"Brandje," Nathan beamed. "We were beginning to think you'd sleep until tomorrow."

"Not hardly," she said, finding her voice unnecessarily crisp. She gave him a weary smile, and waited for him to make the introductions.

Nathan nodded. "I'd like you to meet my Aunt Marcelle and Uncle Henry Fayard." He gestured toward his relatives as Henry stood up beside him.

Brandje reached out and shook the elder man's offered hand.

"Are you feeling better?" Henry asked.

"Yes, thank you," Brandje admitted.

"We thought we'd awaken you hours ago," said Henry, "but Nathan assured us that you're a very sound sleeper."

Brandje blushed. "I must be."

Henry continued, "Nathan also mentioned how lovely you are, Miss Brandje, but he understated the facts, I see."

Brandje smiled. "One of his shortcomings, I suppose," she said. Turning to Marcelle, she offered a handshake. "Glad to meet you Mrs. Fayard."

"Please, call me Marcelle. You're among friends whenever you're with us," Marcelle insisted.

Nathan waited until Brandje sat down on the sofa, then he sat beside her.

Brandje studied the couple cautiously. Marcelle, a delightful woman about fifty years old, had large round eyes, an oval face, and dark hair streaked with silver highlights.

Henry Fayard, slightly older than his wife, had a mass of thick gray hair, like a bush, about an inch long, that stuck out in all directions. *It's a strange way to wear it!* Brandje thought with amusement. It also attracted so much attention when one looked at him, that little else of his soft features and fawn brown eyes were appreciated.

Nathan cleared his throat. "Tante and Uncle may have solved our problem about proprieties, Brandje," he grinned. "They've agreed to stay with us until Saturday, as our house guests. Afterward, they've located another couple whose house is under renovation for at least six more weeks. They're staying with their son and his family in a house full of grandchildren, sleeping on an uncomfortable sofa bed. It's crowded, and they've no privacy. I've asked them to come stay in the spare bedroom upstairs, and they've agreed."

"Do you even know these other people, Nathan?" she asked, trying to ignore the fear knotting in the pit of her stomach.

"Well, I haven't met them yet, but we can do that before they arrive, if it will make you feel more comfortable."

"You've invited total strangers to come stay with us at the villa?" she asked, her voice shrill with concern. She could scarcely believe her ears, yet she didn't want to create a scene in front of Nathan's relatives.

Although she tried to keep the sharp edge out of her voice, she failed miserably at it.

"They were recommended by our stake president," said Henry persuasively. "Jean-Luc Rousseau was the bishop at Nantes for several years. He was recently released, and his new calling as the gospel doctrine leader will only require his Sundays in service right now. Their home is less than an hour north of here, on the outskirts of Nantes. This will be a good opportunity for them to have a little break."

Brandje interrupted momentarily, "I didn't know bishops were allowed to marry."

"They're not Catholic, they're Mormon," Nathan explained.

Brandje blinked in surprise.

Nathan confessed, "I'm a third generation Mormon. More formally, we are members of the Church of Jesus Christ of Latter-day Saints. Our congregations are presided over by men of the highest moral character."

"I didn't realize Mormons had bishops," she said.

"Then you've heard about us?" asked Marcelle with a hint of excitement.

"A little," Brandje hedged, wondering how much to reveal. "A couple of young men from your faith passed out literature in our area a few years ago."

"And?" Nathan prodded.

"And . . . ," she hesitated. What exactly did Nathan expect her to answer? Cautiously, she said, "I never heard anything bad about them. I believe they were quite good at soccer, though they would only play on Mondays. The rest of the time they were supposed to be tracting, whatever that means."

Nathan smiled. "We'll have to explain it to you sometime. Meanwhile, Tante brought a basket of boiled eggs, cheese, french bread and berry juice. Are you hungry? You've slept almost six hours."

"I shouldn't be," she admitted, "after the large lunch I ate. But I am totally famished." She smiled at Marcelle appreciatively while hoping the older woman hadn't considered Brandje too rude.

They gathered on the back patio where they could watch the sunset.

Sitting on the patio furniture with paper plates on their laps seemed an adequate way to dine as they nibbled away the evening, and chatted amicably until after dark.

Nathan didn't say much, and neither did Brandje. She just sat back and let nature take its course. It wasn't long before Henry and Marcelle won Brandje's affection. She laughed at all of Henry's jokes, and in just the right places. She also swapped pastry making tips with Marcelle, and offered to teach Marcelle how to crochet, a project they hoped to begin the very next day.

By the time Henry suggested they say goodnight, Brandje was genuinely pleased to have spent the evening in their company, for more than one reason. The Fayards were fun to be around, laughed often, and had a great knack for enjoying, and perpetuating, good, decent humor. They led interesting lives and Brandje was captivated by their stories and adventures. More importantly, they enabled her to focus on someone other than Nathan, and that alone was worth the inconvenience of having other guests staying at the villa.

They cleared up the dishes together, then went indoors. After they put things away, Nathan went into the living room and sat down at the desk where he opened the laptop computer and turned it on.

Meanwhile, Brandje walked to the stairs with Henry and Marcelle. "I hope I didn't offend you, when I first came downstairs this evening," she said to them. "This whole situation threw me out of balance and I was a bit on edge."

"You feel better now, though, don't you?" Marcelle asked.

Brandje smiled. "Yes, thank you so much for coming. You're both good therapy for me."

"Glad to hear it," said Henry. To his wife, he added, "This old man is past exhaustion, Marcelle. Visit if you'd like, but I must go to bed."

"I'm coming straight up," said Marcelle, anxious to please her husband.

"Goodnight, then," said Brandje. "Tomorrow I'll teach you how to crochet."

Marcelle nodded in agreement.

Henry winked and said, "Brandje, you've made this old man feel young again."

"You're such a flirt," Marcelle teased, pinching his shoulder. She gave Brandje an affectionate kiss on the cheek. To Nathan she said, "Goodnight, nephew dear. I hope we didn't interrupt your writing too much."

Nathan smiled at her from the desk. "Not at all," he admitted. "I enjoyed your company."

After Marcelle followed her husband up to the third bedroom, Brandje went back into the living room where she straightened the cushions on the sofa, then headed toward the stairs. The telephone interrupted her footsteps. She turned to answer it, but before she could reach the desk, Nathan removed the receiver and stretched the cord across to her. "It's undoubtedly for you," he said.

"Brandje Fulton here," she said into the receiver as she cradled it to her ear.

"Was that a man's voice I heard?" asked her Aunt Geraldine, chuckling with a familiar tremulous quality.

"Yes, Tante. I had dinner *guests* this evening." Brandje hoped she had emphasized the plural form of guests loud enough that her aunt received the correct impression.

"*Ce est-ce qu'un intermede romantique est?*" her aunt asked.

Geraldine Limos had misunderstood, as usual. Brandje knew from past experience that nothing she said now would change her aunt's mind. Disregarding the question, Brandje said, "About my request, Tante." She hoped to swing her aunt away from the topic of Nathan.

"I'm sorry to disappoint you, Brandje. I could find nothing."

Brandje sighed. She didn't know whether to be disappointed, or relieved. "You're sure you've checked everywhere? What about those new condominiums at *Bassin d'Arcachon?*"

"Those have been reserved for ages, dear. I am sorry."

"And at *Etang de Carcons?*"

"Nothing there, either. Do you want me to continue?"

"I suppose. If you do come up with something, you'll let me know straight away?"

"Of course. Will you bring your gentleman friend over sometime?"

"I'm not sure how long he'll be here. Perhaps."

"An old woman needs humoring. Do bring him?"

"I'll try, Tante. *Merci. Au revoir.*"

Brandje returned the receiver to Nathan who replaced it in the telephone cradle on the desk.

"Still trying to get rid of me?" he asked.

She detected an edge of uneasiness in his voice, and it saddened her. "There's nothing available from here to the Riviera," she said softly.

"I could have told you that," he admitted. "While you were in town this morning, and while you were sleeping this afternoon, I probably made a hundred phone calls trying to find another place. There's nothing out there, not even a studio apartment."

She smiled. "At least you tried," she offered. "It means a lot to know you tried."

"I didn't want to," he confessed. "But it just didn't sit right with me, spending time alone with a woman, overnight, in her home."

"Fortunately," said Brandje, "I've learned you have some strengths I hadn't detected at first. Otherwise, I don't know what I would have done with you."

"Had I found another place to stay, even if it were inland, Brandje, I would have gone there," said Nathan.

His eyes locked on hers and a feeling passed between them that almost made Brandje feel that he could read her thoughts.

Tempted to linger, to gaze into those dark eyes and caress that rugged face, Brandje quelled the emotion and walked toward the stairs. When she turned back, it was to give him an almost impish grin as she said, "I guess I'm stuck with you."

"And is that bad?" he bantered.

"That, Mr. Duncan, remains to be seen."

Chapter Four

*B*randje awakened early the following morning in good spirits. She couldn't identify why her mood had lifted, nor did she try to do so. She only knew that she was glad to be alive, and she wanted to make it a full, useful, and productive day. After dressing quickly, she hurried down the stairs.

Henry and Marcelle were in the kitchen eating breakfast.

"Did we wake you?" asked Marcelle when Brandje joined them.

"Not at all," said Brandje. "I slept so long yesterday that I probably didn't need much more."

"You barely caught us," said Henry. "Marcelle was just going to drive me into town. I've reserved a spot on a fishing charter this morning. With any luck, we'll have fresh fish for dinner tonight."

"Would you like to go with us?" asked Marcelle.

"No, you go ahead. The shops aren't open yet, so there's really no point. I wanted to clean the back patio this morning, before the sun reaches it." Brandje gave them both a bright smile and followed them outside where they got into their car and drove down the cobblestone driveway.

It didn't take Brandje long to clean the patio. When she finished sweeping, she took a stiff brush and a bucket of soapy water, and washed down the lounge chairs, the table and benches. Then she used the garden hose to rinse everything down, in preparation for the sun to magically dry them. The night before, she'd noticed that the patio furniture had been neglected, and she hoped no one else had paid any attention. At least if they had fresh fish tonight, she would have a clean grill outdoors to cook it on, and clean furniture waiting for them.

Sometime during her duties, Brandje heard the Fayard's car return and she assumed that Marcelle went inside the villa. It was nearly eleven in the morning before she felt satisfied that the chaise lounges and chairs were clean enough to suit her. Only then did she go indoors.

Reclining on one of the two sofas, Marcelle read from a book that looked like a Bible, yet it didn't say Bible on the cover. It was encased in a white, zippered, leather pouch, and was probably twice as thick as a Bible should have been. Brandje didn't ask about it, feeling that it may be improper for her to make such an inquiry.

Marcelle closed the book and glanced at Brandje as though trying to decide whether or not she should arise and help somehow.

"Don't get up on my account," said Brandje. "I'm going to take a quick shower."

"Did you still want to teach me how to crochet?" asked Marcelle.

"Of course," Brandje gave her a warm smile.

"When you're done, why don't we girls slip into town and buy some yarn and things? I want to treat you to lunch."

"Marcelle, you don't need to do that," began Brandje.

"Nonsense, need has nothing to do with it. I usually do as I please," the older woman winked.

"What about Nathan?" asked Brandje.

"If he's awake by then, we'll invite him along. If not, we'll leave him a note," Marcelle smiled affectionately. "He's a big boy. I think he can fend for himself."

Brandje nodded. "I won't be long."

When she arrived at the top of the landing, Brandje wanted to nudge Nathan's door open to check on him, but she dared not. She hoped he was feeling well after all the worry she'd put him through yesterday.

As she stepped into the shower and felt the water pour over her, she suddenly felt content with her station in life, almost fearless. For some unexplained reason, she had no qualms whatsoever today about

Nathan's staying through August. It was a feeling she tried to analyze. She supposed it came from his unexpected willingness to make her feel comfortable with him around by providing chaperones for them. Although neither needed chaperones, they were both adults. It was just the idea that he felt it important for her peace of mind. She couldn't remember a time when a man had been so considerate of her.

Yet, he'd been ornery and irritable yesterday morning. They were at each other's throats from the moment they met, it seemed.

After she nearly collapsed in his arms, he'd completely changed. It seemed as though he had a Jekyll and Hyde personality. Fortunately for her, the pleasant part of him seemed to blossom when he was around his family.

How she wished Marcelle and Henry would not have to leave at week's end, for she still had a few misgivings about the Rousseaus, Jean-Luc and Karen, who would be coming on Saturday. Marcelle, in particular, had reassured her last night about trusting the "priesthood leadership" in the church. Brandje had to admit that she couldn't understand how someone could have such blind faith in complete strangers. But all three of them felt that a recommendation from a stake president, and the fact that Mr. Rousseau was a former bishop, made his right to absolute trust on their part automatic. *It seems rather naive*, she thought to herself. Still, Marcelle didn't seem the least bit perturbed or worried for her nephew. Brandje instinctively felt if there was anyone she could trust, it was Marcelle.

By the time Brandje had showered, dressed, and French-braided her long, golden hair, it was noon. She tiptoed downstairs, worried she would wake up Nathan.

"Do you think Nathan's all right?" she asked Marcelle when she met up with her in the kitchen.

Marcelle was wrapping a sandwich she'd made for Nathan. "He's catching up from jet lag," she said with assurance. "Believe me, I know." She put the sandwich in the refrigerator and a note on the kitchen table.

Brandje hadn't considered that possibility. Immediately she felt a twinge of guilt. No wonder Nathan was cranky yesterday morning. He probably hadn't slept in thirty-six hours, possibly more. Perhaps he had napped while she was sleeping yesterday afternoon. That would explain why he was in better spirits last evening.

"Have you been to Croix de Vie before?" asked Brandje as they got in the car and headed toward the village.

"Only by the waterfront," said Marcelle. "Henry loves to fish, you know."

"Then I'll give you the grand tour," said Brandje as they whisked along.

Approaching from the west, they came first to the older part of town, with its limestone buildings lining the waterfront. Nearly all the roads in this section of Croix de Vie were paved with cobblestone right up to the doors of each building.

"This part of town," Brandje explained, "was once called St. Gilles, after a famous Catholic Priest of the thirteenth century. It has always been a fishing port, regardless of its size. In the past hundred years or more, it has also become well-known for its oyster beds. There is always the smell of fish in the air here. Up the hill is St. Gilles Cathedral," she said, pointing up a side street. "The bells are rung every day at noon, and twice on Sundays. We rarely hear them at the villa because we're too far away."

"This area of France is predominantly Catholic, isn't it?" asked Marcelle.

"Yes," Brandje admitted. "And proud Catholic at that."

When they crossed over a quaint, cobblestone and granite bridge, Brandje continued. "This is the River Vie. As St. Gilles grew, it became readily apparent that the river was the staff of life here. Those people who settled across the River Vie, called this side, *Croix de Vie*, meaning the Cross of Life. It was eventually consolidated into one city and one name: St. Gilles Croix de Vie. The locals call the village Croix de Vie, as do I most of the time."

The southeastern portion of Croix de Vie was much more modern than the older section, with bright, freshly painted buildings and newer shops and stores. "I think the population is about 11,000," Brandje suggested. "Though you mustn't quote me. Those figures change from day to day, it seems."

"Where is the beach I've heard so much about?" asked Marcelle.

"On this side of the river," Brandje explained. "Go two more blocks, then turn right."

Marcelle complied and soon they found themselves facing a long, wide beach where tourists were already camped for the day. The focal point, a huge carousel trimmed with gold paint and brightly colored baubles, twirled slowly while children and parents rode on the painted wooden horses. Street vendors lined the roadside with merchandise of all kinds, from t-shirts to chilled raw oysters, ready to be purchased should anyone desire to do so.

"When I was a child," Brandje explained, "there was no carousel at all, and no merchants along this drive. The beaches were enjoyed mainly by the local villagers. But in an effort to improve the economy, the city managers decided to make the beach a public attraction. Now it is far busier than when I was young."

"That's progress," said Marcelle.

For lunch they dined at a quaint little restaurant in the older section of town, called DeMerite's. They filled themselves with croissant sandwiches stuffed with sprouts and white cheese. Brandje ordered a glass of wine to accompany her lunch, though she was surprised when Marcelle requested apple juice.

At the dry goods store they purchased cotton yarn, which Brandje thought was an excellent choice for a beginner's first crochet project. Cotton dish cloths were quite a novelty to Marcelle. They examined some that were on display, then Marcelle bought several colors of yarn to match the decor of her kitchen back in Le Mans.

Afterward they went over to the open air food markets and bought fresh produce from the local vendors.

By the time they arrived home, Nathan was awake and involved at his normal routine, pounding computer keys with a passion. He stopped long enough to help them carry in the groceries.

"Sorry if I'm not too entertaining this afternoon," explained Nathan, "but a writer writes, always."

"Don't worry about us," Brandje assured him. "Marcelle and I are going out under the shade of the willow tree my grandfather planted. We plan to crochet in tune with the rhythmic ocean waves."

Nathan gave her a weak smile, as though preoccupied with the words he wanted to create in his book, and disregarded the two women completely as he returned to the computer.

Fortunately for Brandje, Marcelle was a quick study. It didn't take her long to figure out how to chain, double crochet and turn the piece so that she could add on another row. When she'd finally completed her first dish cloth, Brandje taught her how to form a border around it by single crocheting, putting triple singles in the corners, and tying off. Then Marcelle began her second piece while Brandje worked on an afghan she was crocheting for Martin.

By the time Henry arrived home, having caught a ride from another fisherman, but little else, Marcelle had shared with Brandje the first quarter century of her personal history.

Supper was a light affair: a tossed salad with sliced chicken breast, white cheese and tomato wedges, complimented by hard rolls, honey butter and milk. Of course, they would have had fish, but Henry had failed to provide for them, and they teased him unmercifully about it.

By the time it grew dark outside, they had laughed often, sometimes so hard that their sides hurt. It was a joyous time and Brandje savored it. Even Nathan was on his best behavior, and added much to the conversation, though very little of a personal nature.

Brandje offered no personal information about herself, and like trustworthy house guests, no one asked questions of her that would make her uncomfortable. They didn't ask about her operation, or the broken romance that Nathan still assumed she was escaping from, nor yet about her family. It was just as well. Brandje didn't have to pretend to be anyone whom she was not. For the most part, she was content to sit back and listen to them banter remarks across the patio.

Marcelle carried most of the evening's conversation, sharing stories with them that she had heard or seen in the past few decades.

When they started talking about events that had happened within the confines of their religion, the words and phrases they used seemed rather strange to Brandje. They spoke of a ward, which Brandje thought meant a large room in a hospital or orphanage where several beds were available for patients or children. They laughed at her analogy, but her questions were answered quickly about that. She learned that a Mormon ward was a geographical area on a map in which lived a group of Mormons, a congregation, as it were. She learned of a Relief Society made entirely of women, and Brandje could see the wisdom in that type of organization, especially since men were usually the recipients of such relief, as Marcelle teasingly pointed out to her. Still she didn't understand what a Priesthood Quorum was, or an Elder, but it was interesting to Brandje to associate with real Mormons and learn a little of their idiosyncracies.

At no time did the conversation turn to doctrine, usually because Nathan would change the subject if doctrine were touched on in the slightest, and for this, Brandje felt grateful.

Later that night, when the others, like her, were in bed, Brandje stared at the ceiling in her bedroom and thought on the companions with whom she'd enjoyed her day.

She hoped she would like the Rousseaus as well as she did the Fayards. Her mind was still a bit troubled about allowing two total strangers into her home to live with her, but she refused to dwell on that tonight.

In her analytical mind she tried to categorize things she'd noticed about Nathan, his aunt and uncle, that might be attributed to their religion, or that might be a family characteristic.

One thing she had noticed was that none of them drank wine. She had suggested serving it with the salad tonight but they'd all stared at her in horror, as though she'd asked them if they wanted her to serve up a plague. Then Nathan said, "I'm a milk drinker," and the other two had chimed in to match his statement. She'd heard that some religions didn't drink wine. Perhaps the Mormons were one of those.

Another thing that had attracted her to these three Mormons was their absolute refrain from using profanity, or using God's name vainly in their conversation. So many of her friends, both when she was growing up and associates she'd known at the university, used fairly crude language, which had always been a source of embarrassment for her. Brandje's father had taught her differently, and never permitted foul language of any kind to cross his children's lips. She felt refreshed to associate with someone who didn't use profanity.

Who were these Mormons, she wondered to herself, *who never tell nasty jokes, only good, clean, fun ones? They never smoke or drink wine and they don't use improper language.*

She'd also noticed that they loved to tease, but she doubted that was a religious characteristic. More likely, the whole Duncan tribe were from the bantering stock.

Nathan had done her a great service by inviting his aunt and uncle to stay with them. Not only had they been a refreshing change from her self-imposed isolation, they had also been able to make her laugh, something she hadn't done in quite a while.

Brandje worried whether it was proper to laugh in light of all that remained for her to face. She hoped God had a sense of humor.

Her family had not belonged to any one particular faith, but her father read the Bible to them every morning after breakfast, from the time she was able to sit on his lap to the day he was taken back to the hospital for his final journey. After her father passed away, Martin had been too busy keeping the farm to bother reading scriptures with her, and she had neglected them entirely the past three years.

In her heart, Brandje believed in God, and in His son, Jesus Christ. She prayed almost constantly, recalling the prayers she had memorized in her youth. Her prayers were recited with fervor these past few weeks. Still, she felt that something was sadly lacking in the prayers that she offered. It seemed to her that she couldn't even make her words reach the ceiling. Would she ever feel that she had gained the attention of Almighty God in Heaven, whom she'd learned to reverence?

She recalled that Jesus had been resurrected after His crucifixion. The sound of her father's voice as he read those passages about the Savior's appearance to Mary, after He'd come forth from the tomb, still touched her heart when she thought on it. She felt a sad homesickness inside her and wondered if she should splurge on a Bible of her own to read while at the villa.

The week with Nathan and the Fayards flew by quickly, and Brandje felt disappointed when Saturday morning arrived. The Fayards had been good companions for her. Although each member of the household had their own duties, as they'd agreed upon that first evening, they had also spent many happy hours together.

Nathan spent most of his days writing on his latest novel, directly after a brisk morning run.

On Saturday morning, Brandje arose early to watch sunrise from a chaise lounge on the patio. As soon as the sun climbed over the eastern horizon and scattered sunshine across the patio, Brandje noticed a honey bee determined to land on her sandal. Quickly she grabbed the hose, turned the spigot on, and sprayed cold water at the pesky creature. When it circled about her, she feared that she had angered it. Just as she whirled around, hose in hand, to see if the annoying bee intended to attack her from behind, Nathan stepped outside from the kitchen door. To her dismay, Brandje ended up spraying water all over him before she realized he was there.

"Aha!" Nathan grinned. "A water fight! Uncle! Tante!"

Marcelle and Henry became eager participants as they helped Nathan catch Brandje. She screamed gleefully and sprayed them all down with fervor. They laughed so hard they could scarcely get the hose away from her. When Nathan finally pried her fingers from it, he was drenched and so was she. Henry and Marcelle were also soaked, but they seemed happy about it, regardless.

Right after lunch, the Fayards left for Le Mans. The villa seemed empty without them. Nathan went back to his computer, and Brandje headed for the stairs.

"Going to take a nap?" he asked.

"I think so," she agreed.

"You seem to be feeling better," he suggested.

"I am. My naps seem to help."

"Would you like to walk down to the beach when you wake up?"

She smiled. "Yes, I'd like that very much."

Chapter Five

*B*randje noticed Nathan glance up from his computer when she came downstairs a few hours later. She had brushed her honey-blonde hair until it sparkled, then parted it on the side. Framing her face were shorter, feathered curls that blended with the longer hair.

Nathan folded a sheet of paper he had removed from the printer, inserted it into an addressed envelope, sealed it, stuck a stamp on the outside, then placed it on the mantel.

"For Monday's mail?" she asked.

"Yes," he replied with a smile. "My publisher likes me to give him a periodic update."

"It must be challenging to be an author," she observed.

He nodded his head. "Are you ready for that walk?" he asked, changing the subject. "Supper will be ready in a couple of hours."

"I could have prepared it," she scolded. "Why didn't you wait until I was awake?"

"You and Tante spoiled me enough already," he insisted. "Now, about our walk?"

"I'm ready," she agreed.

As they left the villa, he took her by the hand and headed toward the cobblestone driveway.

Brandje stopped and gave him a puzzled expression. "Which beach are you going to?" she asked.

"The only one there is," he answered.

She smiled. "There's more than one when the tide is out. Come on, I'll show you."

Gripping his hand, she led him behind the house, across the expansive lawn toward a hedge of hydrangea bushes near the edge of the bluff. Where the last bush in the long row stood, drooping heavily with pink blossoms, she stepped around the bulky foliage.

Behind the hydrangea was a brick wall and a narrow path, nearly overgrown with fragrant gardenias, that led along the edge of the granite cliff. Along the way, Brandje picked one of the creamy gardenia blossoms.

"I helped my grandfather plant some of these," she told him, "when I was just a child. It took years to get them established, but as you can see, his labors were well worth it."

As she inhaled the sweet fragrance, a honey-gold lock of her long hair swept across her face, lifted by a fresh ocean breeze.

Without saying a word, Nathan took the gardenia from her hand and tucked it into her hair, sweeping the stray lock behind her ear in the process.

When she looked up at him, she felt a strange longing within her, as though something warm and tender had passed between them. She blushed and lowered her eyes.

Nathan slipped his hand beneath her chin and lifted her head, giving her no choice but to look at him.

As she gazed into his dark brown eyes, she marveled at the emotions she felt, and wondered if this was infatuation, or something more permanent.

"Picture perfect," he whispered.

Brandje smiled wistfully. She took his hand and turned back around, then led him along the pathway a few more feet. When she stepped aside to let him see what he'd missed the past six summers, she was not surprised to see his mouth drop open and his dark brown eyes widen.

Chiseled stairs, worn smooth by wind and waves, descended all the way from the top of the cliff to the bottom, nearly a hundred feet below them. The first few posts and chain banister were covered completely with gardenia plants, obscuring any proof that the stairs were there at all. Along the entire outside edge of the steps, all the way to the bottom, stretched a heavy bronze chain fastened to sturdy, waist-high poles that had been tapped into the strong granite. The effective banister protected visitors from falling off the edge of the steps. Below them spread a cozy inlet with its own private beach.

"Six years I've come here," he confessed, "and never once did I discover this."

"For a writer," she teased, "that's not very observant."

He smiled sheepishly.

"Of course," she reported, "you have to watch the tide tables closely because twice a day there is no beach at all. But since we've about an hour left today, we're pretty safe. I would hate to be out on the sandbar at high tide."

She pointed to a brown strip of wet sand that stretched out through the water to a large gray boulder standing some fifty yards out. The massive rock stood twelve feet tall. "Huge waves crash over Timbal's Point, sweeping everything into the sea," she explained. "The tide rushes in with a fury here, reaching the top of Timbal's Point quickly, sometimes in less than an hour or two. When we were children a sea lion got caught unaware and was thrown against the cliffs from the point." She shuddered with the memory.

Nathan put an arm around her shoulder, drawing her to his side. The casual embrace did not go unnoticed by Brandje and she felt the same sensation of tenderness she had experienced on their first day together, when he'd carried her up to the bedroom, after she'd collapsed in his arms. Much to her surprise, she enjoyed the pleasure of his arm about her. Unfortunately, it was a position that made it impossible to descend the steep stairs. When he released his arm and placed her hand in his, leading her all the way to the bottom, she wished her grandfather had chiseled the steps wide enough for two people to descend side by side.

"My grandfather chiseled these stairs the year after he built the villa," she explained on the way down. "Since the bluff has a southern exposure, it's one of the few places in all of France that you get a fantastic view of both sunrise in the East and sunset in the West."

"And the gardenias?" Nathan asked. "How did your grandfather ever get them to grow here?"

"Years and years of patience," said Brandje, smiling with the memories. "He lost every plant within the first three years. Then he learned that gardenias need a protective barrier to shelter them from the northern winds. That was when he built the ledge and the wall, and planted the hydrangeas to hide the wall from view of the villa. Then he planted gardenias once again. He had to cultivate and protect them during the winter for years afterward, but his efforts finally paid off. Even now, the gardener covers them every winter with large clear tarps. The black wall and the tarps keep them warm enough in winter to survive."

Nathan helped her down the last few steps, then turned around to smile at her. The past few days with Nathan and his relatives had strengthened their relationship and she was glad to have some time alone with him. In a wistful sigh, she wished the Rousseaus were not coming to the villa at all.

"You miss your grandfather?" Nathan suggested when he heard her sigh.

The question brought her back to reality. She would not tell him why she'd really sighed. Instead, she nodded and gave him a warm smile in response, then removed her sandals at the foot of the cliff. After she rolled up her pant legs, Nathan did likewise. Then she picked up both pairs of shoes and put them several steps up the granite cliff. "Trust me," she said, "this is safer."

For a while they splashed in the waves that rushed against their ankles. Afterward they built a huge sand castle by scooping wet sand into an enormous mound and patting it all down. Brandje dug a tunnel from one side, Nathan dug from the other side.

"I haven't done this since kindergarten," he told her with a grin. Laughing, she challenged, "I'll beat you to the center!"

"Never!" Nathan accepted with a shake of his head.

With renewed effort, Brandje dug wet sand out of the tunnel, over and over again, until she felt exhausted.

When their hands finally met, Nathan grabbed hers unexpectedly and she was unable to free herself.

"Got you," he teased. "I've captured you and locked you away in my palace. I'll never let you go."

"Nathan," Brandje protested weakly, "you know I haven't enough strength to fight you."

"Then don't fight," he answered seductively, releasing her hand. His eyes burned across her face and rested upon her lips.

Brandje had no power, or desire, to escape his spell. As he moved up onto his knees, she did likewise. As though in a trance, she was unable to do anything but respond willingly to his unspoken demand.

His lips drew nearer, his eyes flirting with her, until she could focus on nothing but the forthcoming kiss. He paused less than an inch from her and she remained silent, returning his seductive gaze. Slowly, oh-so-slowly, his lips brushed gently against hers. When the kiss deepened, she lost all ability to withdraw.

Suddenly a wave crashed over them, drenching them both in foaming, cold, salt water, but she was oblivious to it. She didn't want to think of anything but Nathan's lips upon hers and the passion that he'd kindled inside her.

The oceans were unrepentant. Another wave, bigger this time, forced them apart. As it separated them, it broke the spell as well.

Nathan stood up quickly and pulled Brandje to her feet. "Come on," he called above the pounding of the surf. "You weren't joking about the tide."

He took her by the hand and pulled her to the stairs, huge waves crashing against their legs the entire way.

They reached their shoes just in time to rescue them from the foaming salt water. Then they hurried up the stairs several steps before they were completely out of reach of the ferocious waves. It seemed as though the ocean had a mind and will of its own. Unable to snatch the lovers from the granite steps, it became a roaring monster of foam and misty salt air, as if in protest.

Nathan's sandy brown hair dripped around his face. His one defiant lock stood straight up, refusing to mimic the other, more obedient strands.

Noticing, Brandje laughed openly.

"What?" he insisted. "I look that bad?"

"Oh, you're handsome enough," she teased. "But someone should have nicknamed you Al."

"Oh, no!" he moaned, trying in vain to rub the stubborn lock into submission. "It's no use. I'm thirty-one years old and nothing's worked yet."

"Have you tried raw egg white?" she asked with a broad smile.

"No," he admitted. "I doubt it will work, but I will try it."

Brandje laughed. "My father purchased the entire Little Rascals series on video. I used to watch them every day when I was younger. Even if egg white doesn't work, you may want to know that Alfalfa was my childhood hero."

Nathan gave her a broad grin and kissed her once again. Then he scooped her up into his arms to carry her.

"I can walk up," she protested immediately.

"I'm not risking a repeat of that first day," he warned. "Besides, you're light as a feather."

"You won't think so a hundred steps from now."

But Nathan only grinned and carried her the entire way up the cliff side staircase without any lack of endurance. When they reached the top he put her down, keeping her trim figure locked against his side with his arm.

They sat together for a while, a few steps from the top, and watched the tide roll in, but in this part of the world, the tide was anything but gentle. Raging waves heaved themselves higher and higher until they completely covered the massive boulder known as Timbal's Point. If a ship were to slip into the inlet in a storm, Timbal's Point would dash it to pieces before it ever neared the cliff walls.

As the salt spray misted around them, they absorbed themselves in the silence. It seemed to Brandje that this was the first time she'd ever found comfort in the quiet of someone who was not already related to her. Neither needed to say a word to feel the other's companionship.

Soon Brandje shivered and Nathan stood up. "Come along," he said, "I can't have you catch a chill."

Brandje inhaled the delicious aroma of roast beef the minute they walked through the kitchen doorway.

"Yum!" She inhaled once again. "What's for dinner?" She opened the oven to peer inside.

"Nathaniel Duncan specialty," he answered as he shut the oven door. Turning her into his arms, he asked huskily, "Now, shall we —"

"Let's eat!" she interrupted, worried for a moment where his line of questioning was going to take her. "I'm famished."

"You're also drenched," he reminded with a laugh. "And I was only going to suggest that we clean up before we dine."

Brandje blushed. "Why don't you use the bathroom first while I set the table? I can shower while you finish getting dinner ready."

"Agreed," Nathan said. Then he retreated to the second level.

While he was gone, Brandje wiped the excess moisture from her face and skin with a paper towel, then proceeded to set the table. She placed the blue stoneware with loving care, while humming a romantic tune. Giddy with happiness, she still felt caught up in the warmth of their first kiss. Sweet memories of his lips upon hers had not been washed away, regardless of the ocean's ferocious attempts.

A storage room beneath the stairs was locked with a combination which Brandje remembered from years of use. She unlocked it now and stepped inside. The small room was filled with boxes and crates. One, in particular, held several valuable pieces of silver service tenderly wrapped in flannel. Brandje opened the crate and searched through the packing to find two silver candlesticks that she'd remembered from her youth. When she found the heavy holders, she placed them in the hall on the floor. Then she turned back around to lock the door.

The telephone rang unexpectedly, startling Brandje. She fumbled with the lock for several moments before securing it, then she picked up the candlesticks. The telephone continued to ring noisily. Concerned that she might miss the call, she stepped quickly into the living room where she removed the receiver from its cradle on the desk.

"Brandje Fulton here," she said into the mouthpiece. A faint click on the line made her wonder about local interference.

"Brandje, it's Martin," came her brother's familiar voice.

"Hello," she said warmly. "Sorry I haven't rung yet. I know I promised, but the time slipped by me."

"I tried to telephone this morning without success," he said. "You must have been out."

"I . . . I was on the patio, washing things down a bit," she said, remembering the water fight with Nathan and the Fayards that morning.

"That's it, I'm sure," he agreed. "How are you feeling, Brandje? You're not overdoing it, are you?" Martin's voice was edged with concern.

Brandje realized his consideration was more than simple anxiety over her recent surgery. The realization struck a familiar cord within her and she wondered how she'd let several days go by without even thinking about her illness.

"No, I'm fine. I'm . . . well, I'm about to sit down to dinner." She had no intention of telling him about the tall, handsome man with whom she shared the villa. Martin, admittedly over-protective, wouldn't understand. For that matter, neither did she.

"Brandje," his voice sounded strained, anxious. Was it because the call was long distance, or were his emotions surfacing? "We didn't get a chance to visit before you left. There were some things I should have discussed with you."

"Oh?" she asked. Had he really intended to tell her all along?

"Yes, but it will wait until you return. You've been through a lot with the surgery and all. Enjoy your holiday, love. When you're home we'll sit down, and talk things over."

"I'm not sure I'm coming home, Martin," she said. She didn't want the news out in the open, as he suggested. The few days they'd spent together after she overheard his conversation with Dr. Graham were totally unbearable. She had found Martin watching her every movement, and he'd 'mothered' her intolerably. "At least not as early as I'd planned. I might not come for several months."

"Several months?" he blurted, his voice harsh. "I don't think that would be the best idea! What about Elisha? The child's been after me day and night about you. What will I tell her?"

"You were the one who said our relationship would be better cooled down," Brandje reminded, fighting back tears that his mention of Elisha brought.

"I . . . I've changed my mind," he admitted. "I miss you." He amended that remark quickly. "We miss you. I didn't realize how much like you Elisha is, high-strung and willful. Besides, we've never been apart before, except for your stay in hospital. "I . . ." His voice was husky, almost as though he were on the verge of tears. "I can't go on like this," he finally confessed.

His hesitation gave her the impetus she needed to be the strong one. "I'm sorry, Martin. My mind is made up. Perhaps I'll come home in October."

He sighed audibly. "Brandje, I feel like we've drifted apart these past few months." He paused and she realized it was difficult for him to express emotion to her, even after twenty-three years. With distress evident in his voice, he whispered, "You . . . know that I love you?"

"I know," she murmured, her eyes misting at his declaration of devotion. He rarely told her he loved her, and then only under duress. He apparently wanted her to know once more before she died. A lump arose in her throat as she whispered back, "I love you, too, Martin."

"I'll ring off then. You will write?"

"Of course," she promised, commanding her emotions to be still. It was best not to reveal everything to her brother.

After she hung up, Brandje wiped the tears from her eyes before Nathan returned.

Turning her attention to the candlesticks, she polished them until they glistened. She located two blue candles from a kitchen drawer and fitted them into the holders just as Nathan came into the dining area.

He was dressed in cream dockers and a plaid shirt, his hair was still damp, but combed neatly.

"Did I hear the phone?" he asked, but she heard a blend of dismay and disgust in his voice.

Brandje was totally surprised at the change in his attitude. She nodded and placed the candles on the table.

"Candlelight?" he asked. His eyes darkened angrily.

"I thought you might like it," she hinted, thoroughly confused by his coldness. For a moment she wondered if the evil part of his Jekyll/Hyde personality had found a way out again.

"What for?" he asked sharply. "Surely you're not expecting a romantic evening?"

"I thought —" she stammered. "No, of course not. It was a foolish idea."

"It was!" he growled, his dark expression cutting through her heart like a sword. "You're dripping wet! Go change!"

Brandje didn't need to be told twice. She rushed from the room on the brink of tears at his angry outburst. What had she done to upset him?

Once in her bedroom she removed her wet clothing and wrapped her goose pimply flesh in the rose colored robe. Shivering, she went into the bathroom, washed her salty clothing in the sink and hung them on a towel rod. Then she showered briskly, and shampooed her hair. The entire time her mind swept back through the past few hours, but she didn't have a single clue why Nathan had been so tender one moment and absolutely ugly the next. Unable to solve this new mystery, she dried off and wrapped the robe about her, knotting it firmly at the waist. Bending forward, she used a hair pick to sweep all the tangles out of her hair.

She was about to return to her bedroom when she heard Nathan call up to her. "Brandje!" His voice, excessively harsh, seemed to emphasize his contempt of her.

"What?" she asked, losing patience with his brisk manner.

"The pilot light is out in the oven. There are some matches on my night stand. Bring them down!"

It was a demand, not a request, and it made Brandje seethe inside. "All right!" she snapped and stepped briskly across the hall to his bedroom. The matches were on the night stand next to a trim brown telephone. She picked the matches up and stuffed them into her robe pocket. Her fingers brushed lightly over the telephone as she recalled that Nathan's anger had emerged right after Martin called.

Brandje picked the telephone up and followed the cord to a socket in the wall. She remembered that each bedroom at the villa had a telephone outlet, but Nathan must have brought his own telephone. She'd never installed any other phones at the villa except the one on the living room desk.

Suddenly realizing what had ignited Nathan's temper, Brandje yanked the plug from the wall with all her strength. As she did so she remembered vividly the clicking sound she'd heard on the line as she'd conversed with Martin. Intense anger flared in her blue eyes. She wound the cord around the telephone and took it with her down the narrow stairs. She didn't bother to consider that she was dressed only in her robe, nor that her only protection from Nathan was the telephone in her hand.

"You were listening in on your extension, weren't you?" she accused the minute she set her dagger bright eyes on him. This time *her* voice held contempt. She tossed the book of matches on the counter as she held up the extension phone and waited for his response.

Nathan spooned gravy over the potatoes in a roasting pan he'd removed from the oven. Ignoring her accusation, he snapped, "If you don't get dressed I'll have to put the roast back in the oven!"

"That's why you're angry!" she yelled, trembling as she recalled some of the things Martin had said to her.

Nathan yanked the oven door open and shoved the pan back inside. He snatched the matches, relit the pilot light, adjusted the burner, then slammed the oven door shut before he turned around to face her. His brown eyes were almost as dark as black ice. A muscle twitched along his well-chiseled jaw. "If I'd thought for one minute that your romance was still uppermost in your thoughts, I'd have never kissed you!" he snarled. "But you gave no indication whatsoever!"

"I don't know how much of my conversation with Martin you heard, but I want you to know that I believe eavesdropping is a most despicable act!" she shouted.

"Not nearly as loathsome as a woman who confesses love to one man while accepting kisses from another!" he growled. "What's worse, you apparently have a daughter you've abandoned! What kind of woman are you?"

The intonation of his voice felt like a ton of bricks falling against her, crushing, disintegrating her life force. If it were not for the fact that his accusations were totally false, Brandje would have fainted straight away from the tone he'd used against her.

Her relationship with Martin was totally familial, and this knowledge gave her power over Nathan. She gathered all the strength she could muster. With renewed energy, she hurled the telephone across the room at him. He stepped aside and the telephone hit a corner of the counter and fell to the floor in pieces.

"You've spent the past six days with me!" she yelled. "If you don't know who I am by now, then you have no right to know!"

Brandje turned and rushed back up the stairs and into her bedroom, slamming the door behind her. Then she threw herself upon the bed and wept in abject misery.

Suddenly there was a tight hand upon her shoulder.

Brandje froze. She had no desire to speak to Nathan again. Indeed, she had spent what little energy she had yelling at him. She had nothing left inside her with which to fight him. "Go away," she begged. "Nathan, please! Just go away!"

"Stop it!" he snapped. "Why are you so upset?"

It seemed evident that, in addition to his terrible temper, he had little tolerance for a woman's tears.

He rolled Brandje onto her back. The robe she wore slipped down to reveal most of her bare shoulder. Brandje gasped. She pulled the robe back and held it in place as she stared bitterly into his harsh, ice black eyes. Her face was red from crying, her eyes were swollen, and her long golden hair was tangled all around her.

"Why are you crying?" Nathan demanded once more. "Does the truth hurt that much?"

"You wouldn't know the truth if it jumped out and bit you!" she accused. "Martin is my brother!"

"Your brother?" he asked, as his hand released her shoulder. He sat upon the edge of the bed and trembled. Wearily he looked into her stormy blue eyes. "All this fighting because I thought he was . . ."

Brandje nodded, wiping the tears from her face with her hand.

"And the child?" he asked. "His daughter, perhaps?"

"She's an orphan," Brandje admitted. "We've been friends for three years."

Still laying upon the bed, Brandje remained taut, her right hand clutching the robe closed at her throat, her blue eyes searching his.

Nathan groaned and stretched out beside her on the bed. He gathered her into his arms, kissing her forehead, her eyes, her chin.

She remained stiff and unforgiving. /

Nathan tried again, kissing the tears from her cheeks.

She softened a little when he halted at her lips.

"Forgive me, Brandje," he whispered. "I'm sorry."

His kisses made her want him in a physical way that she'd never known before, regardless of their quarrel. She felt herself softening, yet she knew she could not give in to this almost overwhelming desire his kisses had aroused. If she did, who knew where their nearness would end? As much as she wanted him, she could never betray herself or the promise she'd made to her father years earlier.

With renewed energy, Brandje stubbornly shook her head. "You don't deserve my forgiveness," she said. "You not only listened in on a private telephone conversation, you jumped to conclusions about me that were totally false. What kind of *man* are you?"

"You have to ask?" he said in a choked whisper.

"I do," she admitted. "Because of your actions, I feel betrayed. Can I ever trust you again?"

Nathan sat up and turned his back to her. Silence hung in the air like a dense fog.

"I didn't intend to listen," he finally explained. His voice trembled as he spoke. "I picked up the phone to answer it because I didn't think you were going to, at least you'd let it ring several times. Before I could say hello, I heard a man's voice. My first thought was that it had to be the man from your broken romance. How was I to know you had a brother? You haven't shared more than a teaspoon of information about yourself this entire week. I know my eavesdropping makes me despicable in your eyes. I have no excuse for my behavior. Except to say that I . . ." He hesitated for a moment. Then he said, "I'm having feelings for you, Brandje, that I've . . ." He sighed, but he didn't complete the sentence. He concluded with, "I'm sorry, Brandje. I know I've destroyed your trust in me, but please, give me one more chance."

Brandje hesitated, wondering how to proceed. A million thoughts raced through her mind all at once. He'd treated her with such contempt she could scarcely forget it. Yet now he was tender and kind. She found she not only wanted him in a physical way she hadn't expected, she also wanted to forgive him.

If she had told him straight out that there was no broken romance, instead of letting him assume, none of this would have happened. In retrospect, she would have to accept some blame for piquing his curiosity.

She sat up beside him, straightened her robe, and placed her hand in his. "There is no broken romance," she confessed. "I didn't exactly lie to you, I just didn't correct you when you assumed . . ." she let the sentence hang, allowing him a moment to realize her part in this game of deception. In her defense, she said, "I was grasping at straws. I wanted you out of my home and you wouldn't go. I was willing to use whatever method I could to get rid of you. I didn't consider what a sin of omission would do to you. Can you forgive me?"

"If you can reciprocate," he suggested in a whisper.

"I can," she agreed.

But there was something else bothering her. Brandje knew she would have to tell him, and hope that he would be able to accept what she had to say. Unfortunately, she'd never found a man yet who would put his own desires aside for her. But it was one issue for which she had no other option. "Nathan . . . there's something else you should know."

He turned to face her. Then he put his arm around her and cradled her against him for a moment. "What?" he whispered huskily.

There was no easy way to say it, so Brandje just let it tumble out, as she had on many other occasions. "I'm still . . ." she hesitated, giving him a wistful grin. "I'm still a virgin." It was time that he knew, especially if their relationship was headed where she feared it might.

Nathan released her and stood up immediately. He turned his back to her. "I see," came his first comment.

Brandje wondered if Nathan was appalled by her confession. Silently she waited to see what reaction was forthcoming.

Finally Nathan turned back around to face her. "Confessions are good for the soul," he said. "So am I."

Her mouth dropped open in utter surprise. *What?* she thought in bewilderment. *How can that be? You're thirty-one years old!*

He smiled and she thought he was pleased at her surprised response. Then he continued, "Just because I kissed you, it doesn't mean I want to go to bed with you. Well, I may want to go to bed with you, but I won't. I've made a covenant with the Lord that I won't until I marry. I take my covenants with the Lord seriously, Brandje. That's just the way I am."

Brandje closed her mouth, unable to respond to his confession. She had anticipated that she would have to fight him off, not unlike many such occasions. Yet *he* was turning *her* down. *What manner of man is Nathaniel Duncan the Third?* she wondered.

Nathan bent over and placed a quick kiss on the tip of her nose. "Dinner will be served in ten minutes," he said. Then he left the room and went downstairs to the kitchen.

Brandje shook her head in amazement. Nathan had saved himself for the woman he would marry. He was the first man she had ever met who could make such a claim, and he also wanted her to retain that which she considered a priceless and precious gift.

She recalled the promise she'd made to her father several years before he died. In a moment of father/daughter tenderness, she'd listened with great interest as her father spoke of the joy he found in her mother, a truly virtuous woman. His words came back clearly to Brandje: "Not diamonds or rubies, not silver or gold, could have given me a more meaningful wedding gift. Remember this, Brandje, and act accordingly." Brandje's heart swelled with gratitude as she thought about her father's wisdom.

Nathaniel Duncan had allowed her to keep her promise to her father . . . and to herself.

This was a refreshing revelation regarding Nathan's true character. She began to think that Nathaniel Duncan could almost be considered the 'perfect man.' She smiled to herself. *Well, if it were not for his nasty temper, and that stubborn lock of hair that stands straight up on top of his head!*

Chapter Six

*W*hen Brandje went down to dinner, she felt a little embarrassed. She'd had time to consider their conversation. Nathan's sensitivity to such a delicate matter had touched her in a way she hadn't expected. She recalled numerous dates in the past when, if a man knew about her personal commitment, it became a challenge to him. Somehow she wanted to thank Nathan for his consideration. However, she didn't know exactly what to say.

"Do you approve?" he asked as he held out a chair.

"That you're a gentleman through and through?" she wondered aloud, sitting down as he positioned the chair for her.

"No." He smiled. "The roast beef?"

Brandje looked at the platter in the center of the table for the first time. Nathan had cubes of potatoes and carrots surrounding the roast in a tomato rich gravy. The meat crumbled apart easily with a fork and the aroma, which Brandje had failed to notice again until that moment, was heavenly.

"It looks delicious," she admitted. "You've been very kind."

He nodded, but said nothing more. Sitting opposite her at the table, he lit the candles in the candlesticks and smiled at her.

Pleased that he chose to use the candles, she smiled back. Nathan cleared his throat and asked, "Would you mind if I offered a prayer before we eat?"

Brandje was surprised. This was a first for her. She wondered why he hadn't asked her before now. For that matter, why hadn't Henry or Marcelle? But she dismissed the thought, considering that this was her home and they were guests therein. They were, most likely, too polite.

"Be my guest," she said, and bowed her head to wait for him.

To her amazement, the prayer he offered was not the usual prayer she had heard repetitively in her youth. Nathan spoke directly to God, as though He were a personal friend. He thanked Him for blessings that had come to him throughout his life; for Brandje's forgiveness toward him, and her willingness to allow him to stay on at the villa; for the Lord's intervening hand in providing them with honest, faithful chaperones; for the opportunity he'd had to meet Brandje and for their friendship; his gratitude list went on and on. Then he asked God to bless them with things she had never before considered, such as: The food which they were about to partake; the Rousseaus who were, at that very moment, en route to the villa; Brandje, that she would continue to have a forgiving heart and that her body would be healed from the surgery she'd had; himself, that he would have more patience and be less inclined to get angry. He closed the prayer with, "In the name of Jesus Christ, Amen."

Brandje whispered, "Amen," and glanced up at Nathan. "That was a lovely blessing," she complimented. "I suppose all Mormons pray as you do?"

Nathan laughed. "No! We thank and ask God only for those things which each person feels in their hearts."

"Meaning?"

"Meaning . . . if the Rousseaus were here, they may have thanked the Lord for a safe journey, for their children and grandchildren, for whatever it is that they feel thankful for. They certainly wouldn't have thanked the Lord that you have such a forgiving heart."

"Oh," said Brandje. "That's what I meant. It would be an individual kind of prayer."

He agreed with a nod of his head and a wink of his eye.

"The only prayers I've ever heard are memorized prayers, like the one from Matthew . . . how does it go?"

"Our Father who art in Heaven, hallowed be thy name . . ." he suggested.

"Yes, that's the one."

"It's from Matthew 6:9 through 13," he offered. "It's a great prayer."

"Yours seems more personal," she said softly, looking down at her plate so he wouldn't see the surprise and wonder that she felt.

"Thank you." He smiled. "Here, how much would you like?" He gave her a healthy portion of meat and vegetables.

"That's plenty," she suggested.

Nathan served himself twice what he'd given her. She noticed he had a healthy appetite.

After a few moments of eating in silence, Nathan asked, "So you have family in France?"

"My Tante, Geraldine Limos. She lives in Bordeaux. She's what one would call a spinster," Brandje answered.

"Never married, hmm?"

"She couldn't find anyone suitable, she says. Though if she were less materialistic, she would have had no problem."

"Materialistic?" he questioned.

"That may not be the best choice of words," Brandje offered. "But she takes great pride in property. When Grandfather died, he left a home in Bordeaux, with a huge vineyard, to Tante Geraldine, and he left the villa to me. Tante was furious and tried, in a court of law, to have his will overturned, but she wasn't successful. Since then she's been cordial, but still somewhat withdrawn."

"Why did your grandfather leave the villa to you?"

"No one was more surprised than I," she admitted. "At the time I was only sixteen, and Martin was thirty-one. I thought the villa should have gone to Martin. I guess Grandfather knew my Father would eventually leave the farm to Martin. I spent nearly every summer of my youth here with Grandfather. I suppose he didn't want me to be left out."

"Was he your father's dad?"

"No, Mother's." Brandje sighed wistfully. "Mother died in a tractor accident when I was an infant. After I started school, Father sent me to Grandfather's each summer, and he never let me work the farm with him."

"I'm sorry you never knew your mother," Nathan offered.

"Don't be," she smiled, reaching across the table to squeeze his hand. "My father took videos of her that I've committed to memory. And he had photos of her hanging up in my bedroom. Every night before I went to sleep he tucked me in and told me a story about my mother, things she did, how much he loved her. Sometimes he would tell me what she would have done that day, had she been allowed to stay with us. She would have kissed my skinned knee or braided my hair perfectly, or helped me pick out my first perfume. I treasured the stories he told me. He made my mother seem alive for me every evening. I have such sweet memories in the stories he shared."

"Your father sounds like a wonderful man."

"He was," she whispered, tears springing to her eyes. "Sometimes I miss him more than I can say."

"My parents are both living," Nathan said quickly. "Mother has five sisters and seven brothers. Her mother now has more than fifty grandchildren."

"There is only Martin and me," Brandje admitted. "And Tante."

"Tell me about Elisha," Nathan said, "if you don't mind."

Brandje brightened. "Elisha is such a joy!" she exclaimed. "I miss her terribly. Three years ago, when my father was in hospital during his final battle with cancer, I went to his hospital room to visit. There was a little girl standing on a step stool beside him, teaching him how to play cards. Old Maid, I think. She was only four. She had beautiful strawberry blonde hair that hung in ringlets around her little face. Father seemed pleased with her company. He'd met her one day when the nurses wheeled him to the solarium for some sunshine, and they became quite fond of one another." Brandje leaned back against her chair. "Elisha left the hospital the day before father died, and we were grateful she had not been there after that. We didn't learn until a month later that she was an orphan. Her mother passed on a year or two earlier."

"Why was she at the hospital?" asked Nathan.

"Asthma," Brandje answered. "Sometimes she gets quite ill."

"She's apparently attached to you, judging from your brother's remarks."

"I used to visit her twice a week. She became the highlight of my life. Martin and I looked into adopting her, but they wouldn't let us because it wouldn't provide her a normal environment, meaning a mother and father. I was furious! But legally, there was nothing we could do."

"So you continued your friendship, regardless?"

"Of course," she said. "But lately, another couple has taken an interest in her, and when we discussed it, Martin felt that I should step back and allow the Witherlys time to get to know her, perhaps adopt her."

"Do you want them to adopt her?" he asked.

Brandje sighed. "I love her with all my heart, so how can I come between her and the Witherlys? She needs a family."

Nathan reached across the table, placed his hand beneath Brandje's chin and lifted her head up to gaze into her deep, blue eyes. When he spoke, his voice was husky and trembled a little. "The sadness I see in your eyes seems intimately personal to you. Is there something you're not telling me?" he asked. When she didn't answer, he said, "You puzzle me. You seem frightened somehow. Won't you please share with me whatever secrets you're trying to hide?"

Brandje gasped. His assessment of her was so astute that she shivered a moment before answering. "There are extenuating circumstances that I am not at liberty to discuss, Nathan. Remember?" she asked, hoping he would let the matter drop.

"Something you cannot, or will not tell me," he sighed. "I thought that was a ruse to get me out of the villa."

"No," she said, "I didn't lie to you when I told you that."

"What is it?" he pleaded. "Brandje, please. Maybe I can help you work through it."

"You can't," she said as a tear slipped down her cheek.

"Then tell me about your operation," he insisted.

"Is there nothing in my life that I can keep private?" she asked.

Nathan sighed, but changed the subject. "Then tell me what you do for a living. Have you launched your career?"

This topic seemed safe enough to her, so Brandje answered him. "I just graduated from the University at Southampton. I majored in social psychology and minored in childhood development. Though I shouldn't say that I graduated, since I slid by rather carelessly."

He smiled. "What do you plan to do now that you've graduated?"

"I was offered a position at the orphanage where Elisha lives. They need another counselor there this fall." Brandje gave him a bright smile, hoping he would not see past her cheerfulness to the sadness his topic kindled inside her.

"Did you accept it?"

"I . . ." she hesitated. Every question he asked took her closer to revealing the truth about her future. Brandje stood up and sighed, "Oh, Nathan, suddenly I'm weary. I think I'll go up to bed."

"Is it something I said?" he asked quickly.

"No. It's not you, Nathan. I'm just tired, that's all."

"But you've scarcely eaten a thing."

"Will you get the Rousseaus settled in when they arrive?" she asked, ignoring his remark.

Nathan hesitated, then said resolutely, "As you wish."

Brandje turned and went into the living room and down the hall. As she climbed the stairs, her feet felt like they were solid lead and a hundred pounds each. Almost mechanically she changed into her pajamas and slipped under the quilt.

The nights were pleasant at the villa, even in the middle of summer, due to the ocean breezes and the moist salt spray. But Brandje paid no attention to the cool air or the curtains as they lifted and waved at her.

An intangible burden that was almost more than she could lift pressed her down against the mattress as she realized how fast the next few months would pass.

For a little while, Nathan made her forget what the future held for her. Tonight, thinking about Elisha, and about her career, knowing there was no hope for any of her goals and dreams to come true, was too much for her. The memory of her fragile existence came back like a black, ugly veil, enveloping her, suffocating the life out of her.

Finding comfort in her ability to fall asleep quickly, Brandje welcomed the world of slumber as it nudged her into forgetfulness.

Nathan stood up, stretched his arms above his head and yawned. Then he walked into the kitchen and filled the sink with soapy dishwater. He scraped the plates and put them in the sink, along with the silverware and glasses. Using a damp cloth, he washed the table.

Picking up the candlesticks, he recalled the delicate features of Brandje's timid smile moments before he'd yelled at her. A strange gnawing sensation filled his heart as her image floated through his mind. She was unlike any woman he'd ever met. Gentle, probably like her father, he mused. Her love for the child, Elisha, was definitely maternal. She would make a good mother, a considerate wife. He'd met numerous others who wanted a quick thrill, and little else, with no sense of permanency, no commitment.

Perhaps that was the reason why Brandje had not yet shared her true reasons for being at the villa. She seemed devoted to family ties, to tradition and stability. He liked these traits in her. Yet there was a sadness about Brandje that he couldn't decipher. She had a despondency that he didn't understand. He wondered if her father's death had anything to do with it.

He worried whether or not it had anything to do with the surgery, about which she refused to give any information. Perhaps she had a female problem, something to do with her child-bearing capabilities. Nathan wanted children, but if God had sent Brandje as the answer to his prayer, which he was beginning to suspect, and she couldn't have children, then there was always adoption. It wouldn't matter to him if he hadn't fathered them biologically. He loved all children. He believed he was man enough to accept any such eventuality. Why wouldn't Brandje share such a problem with him? Why keep it a secret? After all, she'd told him she was a virgin. Why not this other thing?

Nathan felt an innate desire to protect Brandje, to reverse the sadness in her life. Somehow he would find a way to bring her joy, to fill the emptiness that seemed to echo in her voice, to put sparkles of happiness in her sad blue eyes.

Other physical emotions filled him with a sense of longing for Brandje that nearly overpowered him. He prayed that these feelings would soon disperse. He'd spent the better portion of his life effectively waiting such feelings out, but with Brandje it was different. He doubted the longing he had for her would dissipate easily.

After washing the dinner dishes and tidying the kitchen, a habit he'd formed years previously when he'd served a mission in Paris, he retrieved his scriptures from his bedroom. Within moments he was stretched out on the sofa, absorbed in reading his favorite stories from the book of Ether.

He became so engrossed in reading that it startled him when he heard a knock at the front door. He jumped up immediately to answer it.

"Bishop and Sister Rousseau," he said as he opened the door to their new house guests.

"Yes!" said Bishop. "But please, call us Jean-Luc and Karen."

"Glad to meet you, Nathaniel," said Karen. "Thank you so much for the invitation to stay with you."

"It serves two purposes," explained Nathan. "But I suppose Bishop told you all about it."

"Yes," said Karen stepping into the living room. "But where is your landlady?"

Nathan chuckled at her question. "I haven't even considered Brandje a landlady type," he confessed. "You'll understand more when you meet her in the morning."

"Oh?" asked Karen.

"She retired early," said Nathan. "She said she felt tired."

"I understand that feeling," said Karen. "I'm there myself."

Jean-Luc and Nathan carried the couple's suitcases upstairs to the third bedroom. Whispering so he wouldn't awaken Brandje, Nathan said, "Brandje's room is beyond this wall. She says she's here to recuperate from an operation, and she seems to tire quite easily."

Karen whispered, "I'm a registered nurse. Though I haven't worked at nursing full-time since we married, I've put in enough hours at the hospital in Nantes to keep my license active. My children call me the family doctor. If Brandje needs a good nursemaid, I can manage." Karen's silver gray hair bobbed about her face as she nodded reassuringly.

"I hope she won't need your services," said Nathan, "but it's comforting to know you have the skills, if required." He gave her an appreciative smile. "The bathroom is at the top of the stairs, between Brandje's room on the left and my room on the right," he continued.

"Why don't you two go downstairs and get acquainted?" suggested Karen. "I'll unpack our things and get us settled in. Not to worry, I'm quiet as a church mouse."

"Thank you, love," said Jean-Luc, giving his wife a kiss on the cheek. "This might be a good time to do just that."

When Nathan and Jean-Luc were situated opposite each other on the sofas, Jean-Luc looked at the younger man with compassion, and said, "Something tells me you've a lot to say, Nathan. I'm a good listener, you'll find that's true enough."

"I'll plunge in then," said Nathan. Within fifteen minutes he brought Jean-Luc up to date on nearly all that had occurred since Nathan arrived at the villa six days ago.

"And you say Brandje hasn't told you what kind of operation she had?" asked Jean-Luc.

"Bishop, I wish I knew," said Nathan. "It's driving me mad, knowing that there's something wrong, but not knowing what it is."

"You must love Brandje very much," suggested Jean-Luc.

Nathan's head came up and he stared at the older man in astonishment. "What?"

Jean-Luc grinned. "I've seen the signs often enough in the past forty years. I'm not blind to it, you know."

"I wouldn't say that I love her, exactly," said Nathan in bewilderment.

"You're sure?" asked Jean-Luc. "Because from where I sit, you've got it bad."

"I don't know what to say," confessed Nathan. "Is it possible to fall in love with someone in six short days? I've been searching for over ten years now. Somehow I expected it to take a little longer."

"It's good you requested chaperones right off," said Jean-Luc. "If you can't even recognize the symptoms, you and Brandje could have a serious problem about now."

"You're right about that," said Nathan.

"It seems to me your biggest problem is to make a decision. Either you love her or you don't. If I'm right, and you are in love with the woman, what do you intend to do about it? Do you intend to convert her? Unless you plan to marry now and convert her later, which is still the risky way to go, you'll have no choice but to teach her the gospel. You're well beyond the age when an Elder would normally marry. Sometimes the best advice I've been able to render is that it would be better to be married than excommunicated. I trust we haven't reached that step yet."

"Of course not," said Nathan, slightly irritated. "But I'm not the one who should teach her the gospel," he admitted. "I'm afraid I'd botch that up. I think I'm too close to the situation where Brandje's concerned. She needs to learn the gospel through love, not through coercion."

"You're right. No one can be forced into the Gospel," Jean-Luc agreed.

Nathan nodded. "It isn't that I don't want to teach her, she seems receptive enough. But . . ." he hesitated only for a moment. "One thing I haven't told you is that I have a terrible temper."

Jean-Luc laughed, "We all do," he admitted. "You haven't cornered the market on that."

"Well, mine is bad enough that my stake president challenged me to try to get it under control."

"It must be bad, then," Jean-Luc agreed.

"So far I've learned that if I'm more playful, if I laugh a little more at life and don't take matters so seriously, I don't argue as much. I thought I was making some good progress until today. But before you arrived tonight, Brandje and I had an argument, and I —" He ran a hand through his hair. "I really lost it with her," he confessed. "How she ever found it in her heart to forgive me I'll never know."

"Maybe the Lord put the two of you together because He knew you needed someone with a forgiving spirit."

"There's no 'maybe' involved," admitted Nathan. "Except I'm not so sure that Brandje's the 'someone' I should get involved with. I have a difficult time saying anything to her. She takes offense easily, either that or I come off as offensive, I'm not sure which."

"May I offer one suggestion," asked Jean-Luc, "that's worked for me a number of times?"

"Sure," Nathan readily agreed.

"Whenever you first begin to feel angry about anything, withdraw from whomever, or whatever, you're mad about and go somewhere private where you can get on your knees. Talk it over with God and don't get up again until the anger is gone."

"Like Brigham Young once suggested?" asked Nathan.

"Exactly. But if I recall my history correctly, Brigham had a short fuse, too, and he was a prophet of God. I think it's safe to say there's still hope for you." Jean-Luc gave him a knowing grin.

"I hadn't expected this to turn into a bishop/ward member confession," Nathan said. "But I do feel better to have shared all this with you."

"You needn't worry about discretion on my part," said Jean-Luc. "I learned a long time ago, before I was ever called to be a bishop, that a lot of confessional material may go in, but none of it comes back out again."

"Thank you," said Nathan. "I appreciate that."

"With our living together in this house, just the four of us, it won't take my Karen long to pick up on how you feel about Brandje. She's got a sixth sense that is uncanny."

"How do you think we should proceed on trying to convert Brandje?" Nathan asked.

"One day at a time. The Lord knew what He was doing when he got the two of you together. Let him work His miracles. It's really all in His hands, no matter what we do. I'd say if Brandje asks, someone should answer her. If the spirit moves us to say something otherwise, we should obey. But somehow I expect the Lord has His hand in the pot, perhaps more than either of us realizes."

They heard footsteps on the stairs as Karen descended them. She entered the room and said, "Did you get those groceries out of the car, dear?"

"No," said Jean-Luc. "I'll do that right now. Excuse me a moment, Nathan."

"Certainly," said Nathan. "You didn't need to bring groceries," he said to Karen as Jean-Luc went out the door. "The fridge is pretty full already."

"We wouldn't think of not sharing food costs," she insisted. "Besides, perhaps we brought something you'll like."

"No doubt," Nathan grinned.

"Now," Karen asked, "do you have a set schedule of rules to follow, or . . . ?" She left the question open.

"I'd say anything goes," came the response. "During the week, after breakfast, I usually jog into town and back. Brandje hasn't done that, nor do I think she should yet. By the time I get back she's usually busy with one of her little projects. She likes to crochet in the afternoons, or nap if she's tired. I try to spend at least six or eight hours a day at the computer."

"Sister Fayard said you're a writer. You know, I believe I've read one of your books. Aren't you the Nathaniel Duncan who wrote, *Three Against The Sea*?"

He smiled, "Uh oh."

"Gotcha!" she grinned. "I thoroughly enjoyed it. Our son is reading my copy now."

"Thanks," he said. "I'm still not used to meeting up with my readers."

"But that book sold more than three million copies in the States!"

she exclaimed. "Surely you're used to praise by now."

"At book signings and publisher events," he said. "But you're the first in France to mention it to me, besides my family."

"Ah, well, several in our ward have read it," she said. "I've heard good reports from many of them."

Jean-Luc returned with a box of groceries and placed it on the kitchen counter. "There you go."

"Thank you, dear," said Karen, giving her husband a pat on the back.

Nathan followed them into the kitchen. "If you want to know where things are, just look around. We've nothing to hide in this kitchen, unless you notice Brandje's dinner wine that she bought last week." He opened a cupboard and held out the wine bottle for their inspection. "I think we quite surprised her when we announced that we were all milk drinkers that first night." He smiled, remembering. "She never opened it, and she didn't offer it anymore, either."

"See there," said Jean-Luc, "you've been working on converting her for a week now and didn't even realize."

"She seemed touched when I offered prayer tonight," Nathan told them. "With her permission, of course. We hadn't asked her to let us bless the food when Tante and Uncle were here. We felt a bit awkward, this being her house and all. But I wanted to bless the food tonight so I gathered some courage from somewhere and asked permission. To my great relief, she let me."

"Will you be going into Nantes with us to church tomorrow?" asked Jean-Luc. "Our little ward is quite charming."

"I'd planned to," said Nathan. "Usually I drive to Le Mans and attend with Tante Marcelle. But since you're here, I hoped to go with you." He paused. "Though I can't speak for Brandje."

"Well, we won't push her our first day here," suggested Karen. "These things take time."

"You're right, as always, love," Jean-Luc told his wife.

They quickly unpacked the groceries and Nathan managed to find a spot for some of it in the refrigerator.

Afterward, Jean-Luc yawned and said, "It's been a long day. I think we'd better turn in."

"Me, too," Nathan agreed. "What time does church start?"

"At ten," said Jean-Luc. "Our building is about an hour away."

"If you don't mind, I'd like to ride with you. My car was supposed to arrive by week's end, but it's not here yet."

"You shipped a car from the States, Nathan?" asked Karen in surprise.

"No," he laughed. "I store it at my Uncle Charles' place. He's a collector and dealer of antique autos. In exchange for my leaving it with him, he shows it off in displays around the country. He doesn't charge me any storage, and he keeps the car running. His showroom is southeast of Paris. But it sometimes takes a bit of maneuvering through the family to get it delivered to Croix de Vie."

"You may certainly ride to Nantes with us," said Jean-Luc. Then to his wife, "Come, dear. If we don't go to bed now, we'll spend the entire night visiting with Nathan and will be too tired for church in the morning."

"There's an alarm clock on your dresser," said Nathan.

"Goodnight then," said Jean-Luc, with Karen echoing her husband.

"Goodnight," Nathan nodded. He switched off the lights and followed his guests upstairs.

Within moments Nathan was stretched out on the bed, having read his scriptures and said his prayers. He reached over to turn on the alarm and noticed the bare spot where his extension telephone used to be. With perfect clarity he remembered everything that Brandje and he had said to one another that evening. The memory haunted him in a painful way he had not expected.

His stake president and his mother had both warned him about his temper. And they'd both been right.

Nathan nearly lost Brandje's trust because of his inability to control his temper. With grave determination, he vowed that he would never allow that to happen again.

Chapter Seven

When Nathan awakened, he turned off the alarm and hurried into the bathroom. Quickly he showered, shaved, and dressed for church in a navy, pinstripe suit that deepened his dark brown eyes.

When he arrived downstairs, Karen was sitting in the living room reading scriptures. "Good morning," he said. "I didn't hear you get up."

Karen smiled pleasantly. She, too, had clothed herself in her Sunday best, prepared for church long before they would need to leave. "I heard a noise about an hour ago," she explained. "I came downstairs to see what it was and found the wind had blown the kitchen door open. I went to close it, but then I saw a woman standing out by the hydrangea bushes. She's been there quite a while. I suspect she's your landlady."

"Is she all right?" Nathan asked.

"I suspect so," said Karen. "I didn't want to disturb her, so I left the door ajar until she came back. I was worried I would lock her out."

"I'll go check on her," Nathan said. Without waiting for a response, he went outside.

Near the bluff, looking out over the expansive Bay of Biscay, stood Brandje. Nathan walked toward her, hoping his presence wouldn't disturb her too much. She was still wearing her pajamas and rose-colored robe, but her feet were bare. Her silky blonde hair was swept back off her shoulders by an early morning breeze. The wind danced with it, making her hair wave and bend at will.

As he drew near, Nathan cleared his throat, hoping she would hear him before he arrived. She turned for a moment, gave him a brief smile, then turned back to look out over the water.

When he finally reached her, he put his hands on her shoulders from behind, leaned over and whispered in her ear, "A penny for your thoughts."

She didn't turn around to face him, she just stared straight ahead at the Atlantic Ocean. "Have you ever watched sunrise on the sea?" she asked.

"No."

"When I was younger, Grandfather would watch the tide tables for those few mornings when low tide uncovered the beach just before daybreak. We would get up while it was still dark out and go down to Timbal's Point and climb it. At first he carried me on his shoulders, but as I got older, he would pull me up with him. When we finally reached the top of Timbal's Point, he would sit down on that one smooth spot I told you about yesterday. Then he would fold his legs Indian style, and cradle me on his lap. Grandfather and I loved to watch the color changes the sea goes through at sunrise."

"I've never bothered to wake up that early," Nathan admitted. "At least, not near the sea. At scout camps in my youth we'd get up early, but I was probably too young to appreciate it."

"You've missed something special," she said as she leaned back against him.

He put his arms around her. Still, she didn't turn around to face him. She just stood there in his embrace. He could feel the warmth of her back against his chest, even through their clothing.

"You've been out here since dark?" he asked.

Nodding, she questioned, "What time is it?"

"It's nearly eight."

"Dawn arrived around six this morning," she announced. "I came about an hour earlier."

"That's what I mean, Brandje. That's three hours."

"It was worth every moment," she whispered.

He smiled. "Sometimes I wonder what goes through that head of yours."

"It didn't feel like three hours," she said. "It seemed like three minutes. I often come out here and wait for sunrise."

"Why?"

"I won't tell you."

"Why not?"

"I think you'll laugh," she whispered.

"I won't," he said. "Tell me."

She sighed. "Promise you won't laugh."

"I promise."

After a few moments hesitation, she explained, "I watch sunrise to prove I'm still here. I'm still alive. It revitalizes me somehow."

"You're sentimental," he teased, his voice husky as he leaned down and kissed her neck.

"You think that's sentimental?" she asked.

"Don't you?"

"No," she answered, shaking her head. "I think that's a part of life that few people can appreciate."

When he considered that her father and mother died far too early in their lives, he could understand the appreciation she had for daybreak, and the symbolism she devised for it.

"The water changes," she told him. "At first it's black, like a dark void where even the waves don't exist. As the sky begins to lighten, the sea changes from black to charcoal to gray. Then to a grayish pink, a whitish pink, then to a beautiful mix of pinks and lavenders. Finally the lavender changes to a gray purple, and then to a fine, pale blue. Then the sea grows bluer and bluer until it's almost a true azure, and looks like this." She spread her arms wide, as though to emphasize her point.

Nathan looked out over the sea and marveled at the beauty of it. This morning it was more azure than blue, almost the exact color of Brandje's eyes. A gentle breeze sent a wisp of Brandje's hair across his face. It had the scent of gardenias after an early morning rain.

"I like the smell of your shampoo," he said.

"Gardenia Rain," she responded. "Father said it was my mother's favorite."

"And yours?"

She nodded. "Whenever I smell gardenias, I think of her. It makes me feel like she's nearby, somehow. That's why Grandfather planted all these gardenias, and nourished them so well. He always said it was Mum's fragrance."

They stood staring out at the ocean for a few more minutes. Where the sea and the sky merged together on the horizon, the two were remarkably the same hue. It was almost impossible to tell where the azure sea ended and the blue sky began. It was a tranquil moment, a time of peace and serenity Nathan had never known before, having Brandje leaning against him, the wind caressing his face with her beautiful hair, and the breathtaking view from the bluff.

"I will never forget this moment," he finally said.

"I will remember it for the rest of my life," she whispered.

Suddenly Brandje inhaled sharply and stiffened in his arms.

"Are you all right?" he asked.

She turned around to face him, and Nathan saw both pain and fear etched plainly in her blue eyes, which had suddenly changed from azure to a gray, almost lifeless blue.

"Brandje?" he questioned as a strange and unsettling fear clawed a pathway to his heart. "What is it?"

"It hurts," she whispered. "I —" She took one deep, ragged gasp, then collapsed in his arms, unconscious.

As Nathan came toward the house, carrying Brandje, he called out for Karen, hoping she would hear him through the open dining room window.

Karen looked up from her reading just in time. "Jean-Luc!" she called upstairs. "Something's wrong, hurry!" Then she rushed to the kitchen, flung the door open, and held it until Nathan passed through with Brandje.

As Jean-Luc came down the stairs, Nathan said, "She's fainted. What should we do?"

"Put her on the sofa," instructed Karen. "Jean-Luc, get the first aid kit out of the car. Nathan, get me a cool, damp cloth."

Nathan placed Brandje carefully on the sofa. Jean-Luc, still in his robe, went out to the car to retrieve the first aid kit. By the time he got back, Nathan had located a cold wash cloth from the bathroom upstairs.

Under both men's watchful eyes, Karen placed a pillow under Brandje's head, and counted Brandje's respirations and pulse. Then she took Brandje's blood pressure and listened to her heart with a well-used stethoscope.

"What is it?" Nathan asked, his own heart pounding like a jack-hammer inside him.

"It's a little high," Karen said.

"What? Her heart rate?" persisted Nathan.

"Both her heart rate and her blood pressure," Karen explained. "Did she say anything at all before she fainted?"

"She said it hurts," Nathan answered. "She didn't say what hurts."

"Well, that would explain the quick pulse and high blood pressure," said Karen. She removed a small tubular vial from the first aid kit, broke it in half and waved it momentarily under Brandje's nose. "Smelling salts," she explained. "It'll revive her. As soon as she's conscious, swab her forehead and face with the cloth, Nathan."

Brandje moved her head, as though trying to get away from something that bothered her. Then her eyes opened. To her amazement, she found herself lying on the sofa surrounded by two strangers and Nathan. "What happened?" she asked.

"You fainted," said Karen. "Lucky for you, Nathan was right there to catch you."

Nathan placed a damp cloth against her forehead. "That feels good," said Brandje. "Thank you." Then, turning to Karen, who seemed to be the one in charge, she asked, "Why did I faint?"

"You tell us," answered Karen. "Nathan said you complained of something hurting."

Brandje searched her memory, recalling that she had nearly doubled over with pain. "It must be from my surgery," she offered. "Doctor said it would take a while to heal."

"Did you tense up with the pain?" asked Karen.

"Of course," Nathan answered for her. "How could she not?"

"If she's going to continue having pain like this, she will need to learn how to breathe," Karen stated with an air of authority.

Brandje looked at the older woman for an explanation.

Karen seemed more than happy to comply. "Fainting can sometimes be avoided. Not always, mind you. Next time you have a painful moment, try taking deep breaths and blowing the air out very slowly," she instructed. "Like having a baby, if you are in control of the pain, the pain cannot control you."

"Deep breaths?" Brandje asked.

"Yes, it's been proven useful when dealing with stress or pain," Karen answered. "How long has it been since your surgery?"

"About three weeks," said Brandje.

"What kind of operation did you have?" she asked.

Brandje looked directly at Nathan. If she told them it was an appendectomy, Karen would undoubtedly suspect something worse. Most people recover within three weeks of an appendectomy. "Are you a doctor?" Brandje asked, avoiding the question.

"Good heavens, no!" Karen gave her a warm smile. "I still have my nursing license, but I haven't worked at it for a while. I probably know just enough about the human anatomy to make me dangerous."

They laughed. It seemed a good way to avoid answering Karen's question, and it wasn't pursued further.

"We haven't been introduced," Brandje said, sitting up slowly. "I'm Brandje Fulton."

"You're sure you don't need me to stay?" Nathan asked Brandje as she reclined on the sofa.

"I don't know what more you could do for me than Karen can," Brandje answered with a reassuring smile. "I feel bad enough already with her missing Sunday services today. I won't be responsible for two of you not going."

"Now, enough of that," she heard Karen's voice from the kitchen. "You shouldn't be alone just yet, and I'm the most qualified to care for you. Besides, this will give us a good chance to get acquainted."

Brandje smiled. "She's right, you know," she told Nathan. "I'm sure I'll be fine. I'm feeling a lot better now."

He smiled and gave her a quick kiss on the forehead. "I'm off, then. Karen has the telephone number to the bishop's office. If you need me, don't hesitate to call."

"All right," said Brandje. "Now go. Jean-Luc's probably worried you'll be late."

She gave him a warm smile, then watched him slip out the front door. When she heard the crunching of tires on the cobblestone driveway as the car headed down the hill, she sighed in relief.

"I thought so," said Karen as she sat opposite Brandje on the other sofa. "You're still having a lot of pain, aren't you?"

Brandje looked at the older woman in dismay. She felt absolutely miserable, both physically and emotionally. "It shows, does it?"

"Perhaps not to the untrained eye. But something is definitely wrong with you, dear. And I have a suspicion that you know exactly what it is."

Brandje gulped, not knowing what to say. If she told Karen the truth, that confidence could be lost. If Nathan found out, it may destroy the tender, although fragile, closeness they shared last night.

"You're worried I will tell Nathan," Karen suggested. "But I can assure you that I am one nurse who follows regulations to the letter. If you don't want the men to know, they won't learn it from me."

"I–I can't —" Brandje began.

"Very well, let me tell you what I know this far," said Karen. "Then you may tell me how close to the mark I am, if you choose. Remember, however, that what I've already learned I did not share with the men when they were here, although I could have."

"What?" asked Brandje, her eyes opening wide.

In a take charge manner, Karen began, "You're suffering from something more severe than recuperation from any operation. You have pain so extreme it sends your heart rate soaring, as well as your blood pressure. It's little wonder that you fainted this morning. Your skin is pale, damp and feverish to the touch. I suspect you've something fairly serious. I've ruled out a heart problem because, although your heart rate was well over a hundred beats per minute when you were first brought into the house, it was steady and strong, and I heard no murmur or sluicing. As well as being pale, your skin is also a mite sallow. This, of course, would not be picked up by the men, since your suntan hides it for the most part. I'm inclined to believe that your liver is in trouble. Your surgical scar is in such a position that I would suspect you've either had an appendectomy, or an ovarian cyst removed. Also, I've noticed that you place your hand over the upper portion of your abdomen, a little on the right, as though that is where the pain is located."

"How did you know where my scar is?" Brandje asked.

Karen stood up, came over to Brandje and sat beside her on the sofa, where she patted her hand affectionately. "My dear," she said "When Nathan was upstairs getting a wash cloth, and Jean-Luc was outdoors retrieving the first aid kit from the car, I took the liberty of checking to find out where your incision was. My first thought was that the incision might have torn. I needed to know whether or not we should transport you to the hospital."

"Oh," said Brandje. "I see."

"What's more," continued Karen, "in my physical examination of your abdomen, I found that your liver is somewhat enlarged. In my medical opinion, I suspect you have cirrhosis or something equally as devastating."

Tears rolled down Brandje's cheeks as she buried her head against her knees and wept. "I have a malignant liver cancer," she said. "Something quite rare. My doctor says it's terminal."

Karen nodded and took Brandje into her arms. "Oh, my child, I am so sorry."

Brandje finally gave in to an uncontrollable, furious siege of tears, and it was several minutes before she could catch her breath. When she'd spent all the tears she had harbored inside since first learning the medical prognosis, the events of the past month came tumbling out of her. For more than an hour she was the only participant in a one-sided conversation about her medical condition, her brother, father and mother, and the orphan child, Elisha.

Karen sat patiently, listening to Brandje confide in her as though she was the young woman's mother.

The conversation soon turned to Nathan when Brandje said, "After I left London and came to Croix de Vie, I hoped to have some solitude. I thought that's what I wanted. I was here only ten days before Nathan arrived and insisted on staying. I felt responsible for him. After all, he'd had the villa reserved and paid for months earlier. And though we both tried to find him other accommodations, we failed."

"That's when he called his Aunt Marcelle," Karen responded, "who called the stake president, who referred our names to her."

Brandje nodded. "You can't tell Nathan about this Karen. You promised," she begged.

"I would never break a promise," assured Karen, as she moved a wisp of Brandje's golden hair away from her face and helped her lay back down on the sofa. "But if you love him, as I suspect, then he'll have to learn the truth from you sometime."

"Nothing escapes your scrutiny, does it?"

"Very little," admitted Karen.

Brandje hesitated for a moment as she thought about Nathan and what he had come to mean to her in the very short time she'd known him, especially since yesterday. "He's a good man," she admitted, "with a terrible temper. But then, I match him tooth for tooth when it comes to anger." She sighed, then brightened long enough to say, "But you're right. I do love him." A tear of joy slipped down her cheek as she realized it. "I love him with all my heart."

"It appears to me that the feeling may be mutual," observed Karen. "At least I've never seen a man so distraught as he was when he brought you through the back door this morning. His concern was not motivated by kindness or compassion. It was motivated by love."

"He almost told me as much last night," Brandje remembered. "But he hesitated, and didn't continue. I suppose he's waiting to see how I feel about him."

"I should think he'd find that rather obvious," Karen suggested.

Brandje smiled. "I hope so," she said, "and yet at the same time, I don't want him to fall in love with me. I can only hurt him. Can you imagine what this information will do to him?"

"Has the doctor considered chemotherapy, or a transplant?" Karen asked. "I understand they're having great success in the States with liver transplants."

"Chemotherapy won't work on this kind of cancer," Brandje admitted. "And my blood type is quite rare. The possibility of finding a suitable liver donor is less than one in ten thousand. I told Dr. Graham not to put me on the donor list. Then I came here."

"I wouldn't delay telling Nathan the truth if I were you," Karen suggested. "If he feels as strongly towards you as I suspect, it may be kinder to give him some advance warning, before we have to rush you to the hospital in a coma, or worse."

"I can't," Brandje insisted stubbornly. "Do you know how hard it was just to tell you?"

"I already knew," responded Karen. "At least I knew most of it. Nathan doesn't have a clue. He thinks you're here to recuperate from your operation. He has no idea you're here to gather the courage you'll need to face your own death."

"Still," said Brandje, "he's thirty-one years old and hasn't married yet. It seems that marriage isn't part of his game plan. At the end of August he'll go back to New York, having had a pleasant time with a woman he may have had feelings for, perhaps hoping to keep up a correspondence and determine if she's someone he should pursue next summer. When he's gone, I'll stay here. By the time I . . ." She hesitated, swallowed, then continued. "By Christmas he'll have forgotten all about me."

"You know very little about love," said Karen. "You think that what he's feeling will diminish with time and distance, but from what I know of love, absence doesn't make it go away."

"Absence makes the heart grow fonder?" Brandje asked with a whisper, knowing the truism was penned with good reason.

Karen nodded. "While it's refreshing to find someone as self-sacrificing as you are, refusing to tell Nathan the truth is not in your best interest, or his," she insisted. "Believe me. I've spent almost forty years learning that trust in any relationship is the very foundation upon which that relationship is built."

Brandje moaned. "I can't! How can I watch his feelings turn to pity or worse?"

"Is that what you think love is all about?" asked Karen.

Brandje thought about the question for a moment.

But Karen intruded into her thoughts to bring up other questions. "You claim to love Nathan with all your heart. What if your roles were reversed? What if he were dying? Would you love him less? Would you pity him?"

Brandje shook her head vigorously. "No!" she exclaimed. "I could never feel like that!"

"What makes you think that Nathan would?" Karen asked.

Then she patted Brandje's hand. "I'll not tell him of your illness," she promised. "But I strongly feel that you should . . . and soon."

Karen stood up and walked around the sofa. "I'm going to put a pot of stew on for when the men return. Would you like to rest?"

"I think I'll go upstairs," Brandje said, "and take a nap. I was up terribly early this morning."

"Do you need some help?" asked Karen.

"No. I can manage," Brandje said. "I think the pain medication you gave me helped some."

"We should call your doctor in the morning and tell him about the pain. He may want to prescribe something stronger for you."

"I will," said Brandje, "but it will have to be at a time when both men are away from the phone."

"I'll send them into town to run errands for me," suggested Karen.

"I doubt Nathan will go," Brandje said. "He spends hours at the computer every day."

"We'll come up with something to get him out from underfoot," said Karen. "I think you'd feel better if you could avoid these attacks of pain."

"You're probably right," said Brandje. "Please wake me before they get back. I'd like to take a shower and clean up."

"Very well," said Karen.

Within a few moments Brandje was curled on her bed, deep in thought. She watched the curtains dance with the wind, and considered the things Karen had suggested. She realized fully that she loved Nathan more than she dreamed it was possible to love. Although she ached for him, it was not just a physical aching that she experienced. She ached in her soul, in her heart, and in her mind, as well. The realization made her feel restless and unsettled. She had much she wanted to accomplish in the short time God had allotted her.

She tried to imagine what it would be like if their roles were reversed. If Nathan were making his funeral plans for Christmas, and Brandje was not, how would she feel? Such thoughts loomed up impossibly before her, as grave and unbending as the granite cliffs that faced the pounding waves nearby. The task was unachievably difficult, one for which she had no ability. The thought consumed her, drained her. She concluded that if she were to learn such a thing about Nathan, it would devastate her more than that horrible night when she overheard Martin talking to Dr. Graham on the telephone, when she learned the truth about her own impending death.

If Nathan loved her, as Karen suggested, which still hadn't been resolved in Brandje's mind, how could she tell him something that would shatter his heart and his life so completely?

Chapter Eight

Brandje awakened to hear someone whistling downstairs. She rolled out of bed and looked out the bedroom window. Jean-Luc's mini-van was already in the driveway, which meant the men had returned from church.

She hurried to the bathroom to take a shower. Her abdomen felt better and the pain that had initiated her fainting spell had dissipated completely. She studied her reflection in the mirror, but couldn't see the swelling that Karen found earlier. Perhaps it would only be discerned by a physical examination, such as Karen had performed.

Karen had, in a very short time, become a dear and treasured friend to Brandje. She was gentle, kind, trustworthy, and intuitive. *However,* Brandje mused to herself, *I thought I asked Karen to wake me up before the men came home from church!* Vaguely, she remembered Karen sitting by the edge of her bed, patting her hand and putting a cold compress on her forehead. Perhaps Brandje had been too tired to wake up. No matter. She was awake now.

After her shower she dressed quickly in blue jeans and a yellow knit shirt. She rolled the pant legs up to mid-calf, and put on a pair of blue sneakers. Then she brushed her blonde hair until it hung like a sparkling, golden waterfall down her back.

When she went downstairs all three house guests looked at her curiously. "Feeling better?" asked Karen.

"Yes," Brandje said, "much better."

Nathan came from the kitchen. He wore an apron over a pair of levis and a casual shirt. "It's about time," he said with a puzzled frown. "Are you all right?"

"What are you so worried about?" she asked. "It was only a little nap."

"My dear," said Jean-Luc, "it is Monday afternoon. Nathan is cleaning up dishes from our noon meal. We have spent more than twenty-four hours worrying about you."

Brandje looked at her watch. The date read Monday, July 9th. Her mouth dropped open in surprise. She looked at Karen for some kind of explanation. She didn't understand how she could have slept so long.

The elderly woman put down her tatting and said, "I tried to wake you before they came home from church yesterday, but you sleep very soundly, my dear. I checked your vital signs and everything seemed normal so I let you sleep."

"Yes," said Nathan, "and we've sent her up to check on you frequently since then."

"Yes," Karen nodded. "I've been up and down those stairs a dozen times today." She gave Brandje a knowing wink. "They wouldn't believe me that you were fine, but as they can plainly see, you just needed some extra rest."

"I'm sorry I worried all of you," Brandje said to the three. "But I'm feeling much better, and I'm starving."

"And well you should be," said Nathan. "Come on in the kitchen and I'll make you something to eat."

"I'm not helpless," she retorted.

His dark eyes glistened and narrowed. "Don't even start!" he warned. "You're going to be pampered around here for a while. You'd better get used to it."

Brandje sighed and followed him into the kitchen. Karen gave her a knowing smile and Jean-Luc returned to reading the newspaper.

Nathan prepared grated potato pancakes and shirred eggs. It was better than any she'd ever tried, even in a French restaurant.

"Where did you learn French cuisine?" Brandje asked, impressed with his talent.

"I told you my mother is French," he answered, sitting across from her at the kitchen table.

"No, your Aunt Marcelle told me that your mother is French," she reminded.

He grinned. "That's right," he agreed. "Mother and Father lived here in France, near Narbonne, for several years after they married. Later they moved to New York state where I was born, their first and only son after three daughters. With four women in the family, I've had no choice but to learn along with the others. It's been to my benefit. I've never hired a cook or housekeeper. Mother taught me all her skills and Father did likewise with my sisters. They can hunt, fish and repair automobiles right along side me. My parents are a liberated couple quite unlike anyone you'll probably ever meet. They have allowed us many opportunities others may not have considered."

"How many relatives do you have living in France?"

"It would be impossible for me to count them all, but Grandmaman will know. She's going to live forever, I think. She's eighty-seven now, and as spry as when I was a child."

"It must be nice to have so many relatives."

Nathan laughed. "It has its disadvantages. One summer I had thirteen cousins, all female, who wanted to visit me here at the villa. That is, they wanted to have a big slumber party, with me as their chaperone. I didn't feel that was appropriate, regardless that they are my cousins. I tried to persuade otherwise, but three of them burst into tears, which you'll recall, has a tendency to anger me."

Brandje almost winced with the memory.

"I threw them all out and sent them home. To this day I am called the ogre of the family."

"How long ago was this?" she asked.

"Four summers, I believe."

"And they still call you that?"

He nodded. "My family is a forgiving sort, but they never forget."

Jean-Luc walked into the kitchen. "I just picked up the mail," he said as he placed two envelopes on the table, one for Nathan and one for Brandje.

"Thank you," said Brandje.

Nathan opened his letter first. "It's from my mother," he said, skimming over it briefly. "She says that a cable arrived from Bagley and Associates saying that I will have to make other living arrangements while I am in France."

Brandje laughed gleefully. "Oh, my!" she exclaimed. "What on earth will you do?"

Nathan grinned. "She says Grandmaman will have a spare bedroom empty in a few weeks, but for only one night. If I'd like to stay there then, I should call Grandmaman right away and let her know."

"That ought to help," Brandje laughed. "You should write and tell Bagley and Associates thank you for the timely notice, and warn them that the cobblestone streets of Croix de Vie are lumpy to sleep on."

He smiled. "And your letter?" he questioned, handing it to her.

"It's from Elisha," she responded, as she opened it. "Shall I read it to you?"

"If you'd like," Nathan encouraged.

Brandje read the letter aloud.

> *"Dear Brandje;*
> *I'm sorry I was naughty when you said goodbye. Matron*
> *says you are still not good from your operation. Do you*
> *still love me? I still love you.*
> > *Your friend, Elisha."*

"Dear, dear Elisha," Brandje whispered, "Of course I do."

She looked up at Nathan, who was studying her closely. "If you love her this much," he said, "there must be something we can do to adopt her."

Brandje lowered her eyes, and felt her skin blush beneath his watchful gaze. Was he suggesting what she thought? She prayed with all her heart it wasn't so.

Jean-Luc interrupted them again. "The tide's almost out," he said.

"Did you still want to go fishing?"

"Yes," said Nathan. "Would you like to go with us?" he asked Brandje.

"Is Karen going?" she hesitated, thinking about what Karen had said yesterday. Brandje needed to telephone the doctor sometime today.

"She's a little tired," Jean-Luc replied. "And she doesn't care for it like I do."

"Why don't you two go on ahead?" asked Brandje. "I'll join you in a little while."

"Fair enough," Jean-Luc nodded. Looking at Nathan, he asked, "Shall we?"

For a brief moment Brandje noticed the hesitation in Nathan's eyes. It was evident that he wanted her to join him. Hoping to encourage, she said, "You go ahead, Nathan. I have a few things to do upstairs. I'll come down later on."

Nathan took the hint. "As you wish," he said with resignation.

When the two men left, Brandje stood by the kitchen door and watched until she saw them disappear behind the hydrangeas. Then she dashed upstairs, retrieved her personal phone directory, and returned to the living room. "Will you keep watch for me?" she asked Karen.

Karen put down her tatting and nodded. She went to the back door and said loud enough for Brandje to hear, "There's no sign of them."

Brandje dialed the number to Dr. Graham's office. Within a few minutes she'd managed to convince the nurse that she needed to speak with the good doctor personally. Moments later she heard Dr. Graham's voice on the other end of the line. She explained what had happened to her yesterday morning. He was relieved to hear she had a nurse staying with her and asked to speak with Karen regarding some instructions for her care. Then he agreed to call an associate he knew in La Roche sur Yon, capitol of Vendee, who could prescribe what Brandje needed and arrange for the prescription to be filled at a pharmacy in Croix de Vie.

When the call ended, Karen turned to Brandje and said in a matter-of-fact tone, "You have a primary carcinoma called neuroendocrine. It's a very rare tumor that is entirely confined to the liver. It doesn't normally metastasize to other parts of the body. Usually, cancer begins somewhere else and spreads to the liver. Do you understand what this means?"

Brandje nodded. "That I have an excellent chance of recovery if a donor can be found," she said. "Dr. Graham told me this already."

"Then why not go on the waiting list?"

"I told you. My blood type is too rare."

"Your doctor says you are the only person, right now, who would need a liver from someone with that blood type. He's checked with his colleagues in the States and they are hopeful they might find one for you."

"Did he tell you the odds?" Brandje asked.

"Yes, it's a remote possibility," agreed Karen. "But it is still hope, and that has to be worth something."

"Why?" asked Brandje. "So they can put me in a hospital and keep me sedated, with paraphernalia sticking out of me everywhere, hoping to sustain me long enough? Hoping that one accident in ten thousand might have a person involved who has my blood type? My father died in hospital waiting for hope, but he wanted to die at home. I'm not going to let that happen to me."

Karen sighed. "He says you may begin experiencing some delirium as the tumor progressively destroys the liver. He's going to prescribe something for pain, and morphine for you to use if the first prescription doesn't help enough. He's also prescribing another drug to help with the delirium, should it present itself." Karen hesitated. She squeezed Brandje's hand. "I think you had a little delirium last night, Brandje. It was all I could do not to call for an ambulance. You seemed better if I bathed your forehead with a cold cloth. It was most difficult keeping this from the men."

"Thank you," said Brandje. "As a nurse, you must have strong desires to do what you think is best for the patient. But even in Europe there are 'Do Not Resuscitate' laws. Thank you for respecting my wishes in this."

"I don't agree with you." Karen gave her a quick hug. "But I will do whatever you ask of me."

"If I succumb to delirium or cannot, otherwise, make the decision for myself, have me airlifted back to London with instructions to keep me at home. I don't want to die in hospital, Karen. Please."

"Very well," said Karen. "If it comes to that, I'll go with you and care for you."

"I can pay you," said Brandje. "My father left us a healthy life insurance policy."

"I wouldn't consider payment for a service of love that I am able to render to a dear and treasured friend," said Karen.

Brandje hugged her. "Thank you," she whispered. "I'll never forget this."

"Neither will I," said Karen wistfully.

"I'd better go check on the men," said Brandje. "I feel better than I have in quite a while."

"That's good," Karen said. "I'll return to my tatting. And there's a program I want to watch on the television. Enjoy yourself, just be careful and don't overdo it."

"I promise," said Brandje.

Within minutes she stepped across the yard and behind the hydrangeas. Nathan was out on Timbal's Point while Jean-Luc was fishing west of Timbal's Point, in the eddy of a tidal bank that emptied into the wide Atlantic Ocean and the Bay of Biscay.

Nathan glanced up and saw her on the top step. He motioned for her to wait for him, which she did. Within a few minutes he climbed down the Point, across the sand bar, and up more than a hundred steps to Brandje's side.

"Ever fish?" he asked with a quick smile.

"Not since before Grandfather died," she said. "I don't know that I'll remember how."

"Would you like a willing teacher?"

"Only if you promise we'll catch something."

"We'll catch something, all right," he said. "But it will probably be each other."

Brandje smile as she considered the implications of his statement.

Without further comment, Nathan turned and sat down on the third step below her. "Climb on my shoulders."

Brandje protested with a quick frown. "I can walk!"

He scowled ominously. "Not today," he stated. "That wasn't a request. Karen gave us strict orders to make sure you didn't get over-tired, regardless how much you object."

Brandje sighed. She put one leg, and then the other, over Nathan's broad shoulders. He took hold of her legs and pressed them against his chest as he stood up.

"Careful!" she squealed. "Nathan, I haven't ridden like this since I was a child."

"You still are," he mocked. "You weigh all of . . . what? Ninety pounds?"

"Ninety-seven," she informed him. "In the buff."

"Hmm," he grinned.

Regretting her rash statement, she playfully put her hands across his mouth before he could comment further.

Not until he had descended the steps and scaled Timbal's Point, did he help her swing down. Then he caught her in his strong arms, as though she weighed nothing at all.

Nathan baited the line with a strip of squid and cast it out for her. Then he gave the pole to Brandje.

"Where's your pole?" she asked.

"You're holding it."

"That's not fair to you."

"It's plenty fair. This way I get to keep my eyes on you, and not on the line!" He arched an eyebrow and gave her a smile which, Brandje interpreted, said more about his feelings than words could have.

The roaring of the waves pounding against the outer rocks was deafening. They almost had to shout to hear each other. Brandje yelled, "I thought fish only bite when the tide ebbs."

"It's not a hard and fast rule," he yelled above the thundering waves. The unrelenting water crashed against the south side of Timbal's Point where a sheer drop-off could only be seen at low tide. Almost as an after thought, Nathan grinned mischievously and yelled once again, "The best catch of my life was when the tide was coming in two days ago."

Brandje blushed at his reminder as she spooled the line back on the reel. She was grateful he stood behind her and could not see the color in her cheeks.

Nathan replaced the inefficient lure with a small herring and recast the line, then gave her the pole once again.

She looked across the sand to Jean-Luc, who was reeling in a surf perch too small to consider keeping. She raised her hand and waved at him. He held up his tiny fish, then cast it back with a shrug. Brandje laughed, as Jean-Luc baited and cast his line once again.

She turned her attention back to her line. The late afternoon sun beat down upon them relentlessly and Brandje was beginning to think that she would never catch anything. Then she felt a tug on her line.

She jumped with excitement. "I've got something."

Nathan wrapped an arm around her and helped her set the hook. Staying in position, he taught her how to feed line and reel back, feed line and reel back, over and over until her arms ached. After several minutes she trembled so much that she couldn't control the pole and the reel at the same time.

Nathan gently took the pole from her. "Lean against me," he said. "I'll bring it in for you."

Brandje did as he instructed, grateful to have his warm body to lean against and protect her.

"Must be something big," he said.

"Don't lose it!" she insisted. "What kind of fish do you think we caught? With my luck, it's probably a shark."

"It's no shark," he answered. "I think it's a skate, the way it wants to stay on the bottom."

"A skate? Really? I've never caught one of those."

Before he could respond, the large fish was flung from the water and up onto the beach.

Nathan helped her down the back of Timbal's point and they ran over to where the strange-looking creature lay. It was flapping its big gray wing-like fins as if it could just fly away.

"It looks like a manta ray," she said.

"No, it's a skate. They make delicious eating."

"They do?" she asked with a wide grin.

"Yes. They taste just like scallops."

"Oh, I love scallops," said Brandje.

Jean-Luc sauntered over. "Showed us up proper, didn't you Brandje?"

"Did I?" she teased.

"As if she didn't know," said Jean-Luc. "Oh, Bother!"

His disgruntled exclamation made both of them laugh. Afterward, Brandje held the skate up and Nathan took photographs.

When they were done, Jean-Luc said, "I used up all my bait. Do you have any left?"

"Sure," said Nathan. "Use mine. I'm going to take Brandje back up. She's getting tired."

Jean-Luc nodded, then climbed Timbal's Point to retrieve Nathan's gear box.

Nathan killed the skate, cut off both wing-like fins and deposited them into a mesh net that he fastened to his belt. Then he tossed the remains into the sea. "Let's get you topside," he told Brandje. "I don't want you fainting again."

"I'm feeling fine," she insisted. "I just got tired trying to reel in that skate."

"I know," he said. "But I'm not taking any chances."

He scooped her into his arms and carried her up the granite steps.

With both hands full, he was unable to use the bronze chain bannister her grandfather had installed years earlier.

Brandje was surprised when he made the ascent, and he wasn't winded in the least when they reached the top.

He stood her up and circled his arm about her shoulders, then surprised her by whispering in her ear, "I'd like to check the tide tables and see when we can watch sunrise together from Timbal's Point."

"I'd like that," she said, giving him a wide smile.

He pulled her close and held her tenderly. "I hope you're going to tell me sometime soon about your operation."

Brandje stiffened and pulled away. She had no intention of telling him anything about her health concerns. *He should have realized that!* she fumed to herself.

Gently he rubbed her shoulders. "Brandje, don't be angry when I ask you these questions. Do you know what I've been going through the past twenty-four hours? I care about you more than I can say. I want to know what's going on."

His unexpected confession softened her. She stepped closer and snuggled right next to his warm, muscled chest. "I'm not ready," she said. "But when I am ready, I'll tell you. I promise."

"How long will that take?" he questioned.

"I don't know."

She felt, rather than heard, him sigh.

His unheard expression seemed to echo her own feelings. Although Brandje enjoyed the closeness they shared, she also worried over how quickly their relationship was growing. She hadn't wanted to fall in love. Not now, not like this. If Nathan felt the same way about her, the only thing he would remember in the years to come would be his grief.

I'm not what he deserves, she thought miserably. *He deserves someone healthy who can bear his children and grow old with him.*

He put his hand under her chin and gazed down at her, as though studying the contours of her face and the blue in her eyes. "Such a somber expression," he observed. "Anything I can do or say to change it to a smile?"

She looked into his dark brown eyes, thinking how easy it would be to get lost in them. A smile began at the corners of her mouth as her eyes traveled down his face and settled on his warm and sensual lips.

He arched an eyebrow, obviously surprised at the emotions she allowed him to see upon her face. "Hmm," he whispered huskily. "Is that the secret to making you smile?"

His question made her smile even more. Taking her lead, he bent his head down toward hers, his breath caressing her cheeks as he planted tender kisses in a line that led straight to her mouth.

That one tantalizing kiss seemed to last forever, yet was over all too soon when Nathan drew back. "Brandje," he said raggedly. "I . . ."

Quickly she placed her fingers over his lips to prevent him from saying that which she both dreaded hearing, and wished she could hear. She gave him a wide, flirtatious smile. "Could you teach me how to cook these things?" she asked, lifting the net that was attached to his waist.

He smiled and gave her a quick wink. His mood changed to playfulness. "Thanks for having the courage to stop me," he teased. "I needed to have cold water thrown in my face, or a fish, since that was all you had handy."

She laughed with him, surprised at his candor.

"Come along," he said as he stepped away, then took her by the hand and led her back to the villa.

When they entered, Karen was no longer in the living room. "She must have gone up to her room," said Brandje.

"She probably needed a nap," he explained. "She was up half the night checking on you. It was all I could do not to check on you myself."

He placed the skate fins into the sink, and rinsed them thoroughly. Then he got out the cutting board. Within a few minutes he had the tough skin removed. Using a round, mini-sized cutter, he punched circles out of the wing-like fins, as though making miniature cookies.

"How are you going to prepare it?" she asked.

"It's great on the barbecue," he said. "I'll take these round chunks and marinate them in lemon juice with garlic and herbs. Then I'll wrap them with bacon strips and stick them on skewers with some zucchini, cherry tomatoes and mushrooms."

"What are you going to do with all these little scraps of meat left over?" she asked, indicating the small pieces that remained after he'd punched all the circles out.

"I'll chop them up fine and use them in a delicious skate chowder tomorrow," he answered, as though he'd prepared skate many times before.

"You've had some experience at this, haven't you?"

"Actually, I'm faking it," he explained. "The truth is, I've read about skate, and eaten it a few times. But this is my first attempt to cook it myself."

"You're doing a good job," she complimented. "If you hadn't told me, I'd have thought this was your fiftieth time."

"Amazing what a little acting ability can do for you," he said.

"You act?" she asked in surprise.

"Not since college," he admitted. "But I want to make a good impression where you're concerned."

She gave him a shy smile. "You needn't worry about that," she suggested.

Chapter Nine

*A*fter they finished dinner preparations, cleaned the kitchen and set the skate to marinate in the refrigerator, they retired to the living room. Jean-Luc had not yet returned from fishing, and Karen was still upstairs taking a well-earned nap.

Brandje gathered her yarn and crochet hook and sat on the sofa, ready to continue crocheting the afghan she was making for Martin.

Rather than sit beside her, Nathan sat at the desk and turned on his computer. *It's safer there*, he thought to himself. If this longing and desire that he had for Brandje kept escalating until August he was going to be one desperate man. Either that, or he was going to marry her before it was too late. The thought sobered him immediately. Was he already thinking about marrying Brandje? Did he really love her? A deep aching inside told him the answers. However, he rationalized, she wasn't a member of the church, and he'd promised the Lord he would only marry in the temple. Silently, Nathan said a prayer that the Lord would guide her to the gospel, not for his sake, but for hers. He was worried she would join the church just to please him, and that thought concerned him a great deal. Besides, was he ready to commit his heart to this woman? He glanced up at her over the computer and inhaled sharply as the full impact of his feelings settled upon him. He doubted he could ever live without her now. Somehow she had worked her way into his heart, without him even realizing, and had become his reason for being.

For more than a dozen years he had assumed that, because it hadn't happened to him, love wasn't what the Lord had planned for him. He had thrown his life into his writing, into helping his parents research their family lines, into serving in the gospel in whatever capacity the Lord wanted him. But love, marriage, children and family were obviously for someone else. Weren't they?

Then it struck him with full force as he continued to glance over the top of the computer monitor. Brandje was the woman whom God intended Nathan should marry! He said a silent prayer, asking if the feelings he had for Brandje, and his hope to marry her, were from the Lord. To his utter joy and delight, a warm tingling swept over him, beginning in his heart and radiating outward, until there could be no doubt in his mind any longer. Brandje was the one!

That only left one barrier: her church membership.

Someone would have to convert her to the Church of Jesus Christ of Latter-day Saints. He hoped it wouldn't be him. He was too close to the situation. As much as he wanted to teach her the gospel, if she didn't understand a principle the way that he did, would she get upset with him, or would he get upset with her? He couldn't risk it.

Silently, Nathan prayed again, this time asking the Lord to find another avenue to convert her, for he doubted his ability to do so. He wanted her to have her own testimony, not his. The basis for a lasting, eternal marriage, was that both parties would be able to stand on their own beliefs, complementing one another, helping one another. Their marriage would never last if she joined simply because she loved him, or because she thought her conversion would please him. His heart poured out in earnest as he silently begged for the Lord's assistance.

"Are you awake?" Brandje asked.

He raised his head. "Yes, I am."

"I thought you'd fallen asleep for a minute," she said. "Perhaps you need a nap."

"No, I'm fine. I . . . was just thinking about you."

"I wonder if you'd like to tell me what those two brown books are on the desk," she suggested.

"Books?"

"The ones with the zippers."

"Oh!" he exclaimed. "My scriptures."

"That's all?" she asked with a mischievous grin. "No long, elaborate, religious discussion with, what was it called again, *The Golden Question*?"

His eyes widened in surprise, and he almost stammered, "H–How do you know about the Golden Question?" He picked up the scriptures, walked over to Brandje, and sat beside her on the sofa.

She smiled. "I used to go to school with a girl who always called me her Golden Contact. The only trouble was, every time she asked me if I wanted to know more, I told her no. It got to be a standing joke."

"I see," came his dismayed response. "Then I won't ask you the Golden Question. Fair enough?"

Brandje nodded and gave him a faint smile.

He placed the scriptures on the sofa between them, then returned to the desk in utter desperation.

"I thought all Mormons were dying to spread the truth and convert the world," she whispered.

"Hmm?" he asked in a daze. He hadn't heard her question because he was lost in a silent prayer. He'd been telling the Lord that he didn't consider His sense of humor very good at the moment, getting Nathan's hopes up, then dashing them like that.

"Nothing," she answered.

Brandje returned to her crocheting. She was clearly irritated, and if Nathan had only glanced in her direction he would have seen that for himself. Apparently Nathan wasn't dying to convert *her* to Mormonism. Perhaps he didn't think it was possible that she could ever believe the way he did. Perhaps he didn't want her to become a Mormon because that may obligate him. Perhaps she was reading more into their romance than he was. She sighed in abject misery.

Brandje jabbed the crochet hook under each single crochet and dug the yarn back through, creating single crochet stitches all the way across the afghan. When she finished the entire row she realized she'd skipped all the double crochets that created the pattern of a Navajo motif. "Bother!" she muttered to herself, having adopted Jean-Luc's expression without even realizing it.

She removed the crochet hook from the main piece. Then she pulled on the yarn where she had removed the hook, until the entire row unraveled and she could start over once again.

Nathan, apparently deep in thought, hadn't even looked up at her since he left her side. His eyes were closed and she wondered for the second time if he would feel better by taking a nap.

She set the afghan down and picked up Nathan's two books of scripture. Unzipping one, she read the words, *Book of Mormon*. Nathan hadn't bothered to open his eyes, but he surely must have heard her unzip it.

Gathering courage, Brandje read aloud from the first page. "The Book of Mormon. An account written by the hand of Mormon upon plates taken from the plates of Nephi."

Finally Nathan opened his eyes and looked at her. He smiled and a sense of peace seemed to come over him that she hadn't noticed before.

"If you're determined to read it," he said, "go ahead."

"You won't mind?"

"Of course not. It's my favorite book in the entire world."

"It is?"

He nodded.

"Why?"

He shrugged. "I wonder if you can figure out why."

"You don't think I can?" she asked.

He shrugged again. "Maybe . . . maybe not."

"You're on!" Immediately she regretted having accepted the challenge. She wouldn't have consented at all if Nathan hadn't been so smug about it. He acted as though it would be impossible for her to figure out why the Book of Mormon was his favorite.

Nathan stood and stretched. "I'd better go check on Jean-Luc," he said. "I don't want him to get caught out on the sand bar when the tide comes rushing in."

"Good idea," she agreed. As soon as he left she dumped the afghan, crochet hook and yarn back into the basket.

Sometimes Nathan irritated her so much she could scarcely stand it! On the other hand, sometimes he charmed her so easily that he made her tremble inside. She didn't know whether to smack him, or kiss him . . . which, she realized as she calmed herself, was exactly the same thing!

Nathan went out the kitchen door and was halfway across the bluff before he allowed a smile to spread across his face. "I won't ask you the Golden Question," he whispered to himself, thinking about his conversation with Brandje just moments earlier. "But I'll bet you'll ask me."

When he was hidden from view of the villa behind the hydrangea bushes, he looked down at Jean-Luc, who was still fishing, and waved at him. But Jean-Luc, intent on the task at hand, did not look up. Nathan sighed in relief.

Having determined that he now had a little privacy, he knelt down upon the ground atop the granite bluff, and offered up a prayer of gratitude, humbled to the core.

The following morning Brandje awakened early and prepared breakfast for her house guests. She had a list of things she wanted to do that day, and she was anxious to begin.

Karen was the first one to arrive downstairs. "Smells delicious," she said as Brandje served her hot porridge with cream, and melon wedges with strawberries.

"Thanks," said Brandje. "My prescription should be ready today and I'll need a ride into town."

"We'll need to get some potatoes for that skate chowder," said Karen. "Would you like to go right after breakfast?"

"I wanted to clean out the storage room first," Brandje said. "When

I'm feeling well, I like to tackle one project each morning, then rest in the afternoon. Maybe we could go to lunch after I get done."

"Sounds good to me," Nathan said, walking into the kitchen.

"I didn't hear you get up," said Brandje, hoping he hadn't heard her mention the prescription.

"Me too," said Jean-Luc, following Nathan.

"I don't want breakfast, though," said Nathan. "Too much skate and fried potatoes last night."

"You ate three servings," teased Jean-Luc.

"Right," said Nathan. "But this morning, I'm going to run it off." He gave Brandje a quick smile. "You won't be offended?"

"No," she answered. "It's just porridge and melon."

"Good," he said, kissing her forehead. "I'll be back later." Then he went outside. Brandje watched him do his stretching exercises as she dished up Jean-Luc's porridge.

"He's a good man," Jean-Luc said. "I'm glad we came."

"I am, too," said Karen. "The salt air feels good in my lungs. I believe that cough I had all winter is finally going to clear up out here."

"Good," Brandje interjected. "Because you've both become dear friends to me."

"Likewise," said Jean-Luc affectionately.

When Nathan returned from his run, he went straight to the computer where he wrote for several hours, while Jean-Luc went for a long walk. Brandje spent the morning cleaning the storage room and organizing it. With Karen's help, she was done in record time.

Shortly before noon, the Rousseaus took Nathan and Brandje into Croix de Vie in their minivan. Brandje asked that they drop her off at a small toy shop. She wanted to pick out a gift for Elisha.

Karen suggested she accompany her because she wanted to buy some toys for the grandchildren.

Nathan said he needed more printer paper, and Jean-Luc wanted to pick up a golf club and some balls. He'd decided that the expansive back lawn at the villa would be a perfect place to practice.

They agreed to meet at DeMerite in an hour for lunch.

After the two women waved goodbye to the men, and watched the car until it turned the corner, Karen said, "Interesting how close this toy store is to the pharmacy."

"Yes, isn't it?" Brandje agreed with a giggle.

They entered the toy store and looked around for a while but Brandje just couldn't seem to decide on anything. Karen had no such problem and purchased a small arsenal of toys for her grandchildren. "These will make nice birthday gifts," she explained. "We have three in August and four in September."

Just as they were about to leave, Brandje looked down at a small shelf near the front door. Perched on the bottom stood a handmade, twelve-inch, porcelain doll, a close replica of Elisha, with long, strawberry blonde ringlets. She wore a forest green dress drenched in tiny pink rosebuds. Brandje picked the doll up and carried it to the counter. "Do you have a box for this doll?" she asked the salesman.

"*Oui, Madame*," came the quick response.

After she made her purchase, Brandje followed Karen out of the toy shop.

"The pharmacy?" asked Karen.

Brandje nodded. "As much as I hate to admit it, yes."

They walked across the street and into the pharmacy where Brandje quickly paid for her prescriptions. In addition to the morphine Dr. Graham had prescribed, she was also given a milder pain medication specifically designed to cause no drowsiness, as well as some pills for delirium, to be taken as needed.

As they were about to leave the pharmacy, Brandje hesitated. Walking toward them was a man she disliked intensely. She whirled around and said to Karen, "I do NOT want to run into Pierre today."

Karen looked behind Brandje and saw a tall, thin man sauntering toward them. "The back door?" she suggested.

"Quickly," Brandje agreed.

The two women headed toward the back of the store. Just as they went through the doorway, they heard an annoyed Pierre call out, "Wait! Mademoiselle Brandje, is that you?"

"Keep going and don't look back," Brandje suggested under her breath.

They continued walking, then stepped through the open back door of a bakery down the alley. Brandje stood behind the door as Karen asked the baker, "Do you have croissants today?"

The baker led her to a display case filled with fresh croissants. Brandje remained behind the door and watched from a crack near one of the hinges. Pierre looked inside, but seeing only Karen, he shrugged, turned around and left. Brandje sighed in relief.

Karen, having purchased a bag full of baked goods, scolded Brandje. "What is all this cloak and dagger stuff?" she questioned.

"He's an insufferable man," Brandje explained. "Fresh, insolent, a man with positively no manners."

"I see," said Karen. "You and he were friends once?"

"He thinks so," Brandje answered, "only it's not true. I've loathed him from the first time I met him."

Karen sighed. "For a moment there I thought you were going to tell me he murdered your grandfather or something."

Brandje laughed. "No, no. But if he'd found me, he would have slobbered all over my hand trying to kiss it. He would have announced to the entire village that I am the love of his life, and in an intimate manner that I detest. We would never be able to keep our luncheon date with Jean-Luc and Nathan, and we would have spent the rest of the day trying to get rid of him."

Karen smiled. "Is he that bad?"

"Worse!" Brandje complained.

"I think he's gone now," said Karen. "Perhaps we should go to the restaurant."

"We're still a little early, but under the circumstances, I can see no alternative. Do you mind if we take the alley? I saw him head back out toward the street after he left here, and I don't want to take any chances."

Karen nodded. "I'll humor you," she agreed.

Within a few minutes they reached DeMerite, a delightful little restaurant with bright blue curtains at the windows and small, cozy tables. To their surprise, Jean-Luc and Nathan were already there.

"Guess you win that bet," said Jean-Luc. "They're here before the hour is up."

"Wagering again?" Karen teased her husband. "Really, Bishop!"

"Not for money," Nathan defended.

"It's a good thing," Karen bantered. "Otherwise I'd have to report you to the stake president."

"Sorry," said Jean-Luc. "But it was just a harmless little bet."

Brandje laughed. "Then gambling is another thing the Mormons frown upon?" All three pairs of eyes looked in her direction. She could plainly see the concern her comment brought, so she added quickly, "It's a good thing!"

The others laughed and the awkward moment was soon forgotten as they sat down to enjoy a delicious lunch.

They were just finishing when Brandje heard a familiar voice behind her that made her cringe in disgust. Karen picked up on it immediately and looked over her shoulder to see the man named Pierre, whom they had so desperately tried to avoid, walking toward their table.

"Mademoiselle Brandje! Mon amour, j`ai longtemps attendu!"

Brittle with caution, Brandje turned in her chair to face him. "Pierre, what a . . . surprise." She forced herself to be polite, regardless whether she wanted to or not.

Pierre had changed little over the years. His black hair was slicked away from his face with heavy tonic. His straight nose protruded between small, button-brown eyes. How she hated those eyes that now swept hungrily over her petite figure.

"I thought it was you earlier," he said with a toothy smile, "at the pharmacy."

Brandje inhaled sharply at his mention of the word "pharmacy," and a piece of sweetbread stuck in her throat, causing her to choke. She coughed, clearing her airway, but she felt totally embarrassed and betrayed by the wretched man.

"Are you all right?" Nathan asked, offering her a drink of water.

"Fine, thank you." Her eyes did not meet his and she looked up with a poisonous expression flung in Pierre's direction. Then, remembering her manners, she said, "Pierre Lobrouge, this is Nathaniel Duncan, Jean-Luc and Karen Rousseau." The men shook hands while Karen kept her hand in her lap, unwilling to offer it to Pierre.

Pierre pulled a chair away from another table and joined them, uninvited.

It was obvious that Pierre only had eyes for Brandje. He was practically drooling when he asked, "Why do you not tell me you are coming from England? I would be happy to be your escort."

"As you can see," she suggested, "I have plenty of people to escort me."

"Ah, but it is not always so!" the thin man proclaimed. "And the villa?" he queried, dismissing the subject. "You have not sold the villa, have you, *mon amour?*"

"I told you long ago that I have no intention of selling."

"You have not changed your mind?" he persisted.

"The lady said she had no such intention," Nathan intervened, obviously displeased with the other man's lack of manners.

Belligerently, Pierre took Brandje's hand and kissed the back of it with great flourish, leaving it wet and sticky.

Brandje shuddered.

"*Mon amour,*" he said in a husky, intimate tone, "do not let this be offensive. I have made no secret that I am fond of you. Let us now return to the ways of the past. Let old disputes be forgotten."

"Pierre!" she admonished. "This behavior is most inappropriate, especially in front of my escorts."

"Then I will telephone later. We will have lunch. It is a promise?"

"Perhaps," Brandje agreed, willing to say anything at that point to be rid of him.

With her word practically guaranteed, Pierre left them, a satisfied smile plastered upon his small, pinched face.

Brandje glanced at her friends around the table to discern how they had reacted to Pierre's intrusion.

Karen seemed genuinely relieved to have the man leave. Jean-Luc was somewhat amused, but Nathan glared at Pierre's back as though ready to commit the man to an early grave.

"I suppose *that* was an ex?" Nathan asked, his voice edged with anger.

"No," replied Brandje.

"What disputes have you had in the past?" Nathan demanded.

Jean-Luc shook his head ever so slightly, as though warning Nathan not to use this approach.

"He wants the villa, not me," she answered.

"I'd say he wants both and doesn't care in which order," was the crisp reply. Again Nathan asked, "What disputes, Brandje?"

She blushed, ashamed of the memory. However, she knew Nathan well enough to realize he would not let the matter drop. "Pierre became a little too forward at a River Park Celebration we attended one September a few years ago. Martin ended up tossing him into the river. It was the most embarrassing evening in my life and one that I would rather forget," Brandje explained with a steady gaze. She hoped her nonchalance would put his fears to rest.

"He's lucky he didn't have a repeat performance today," Nathan grumbled, apparently unconvinced.

"Water under the bridge," Jean-Luc suggested.

"Right," said Karen. "Speaking of bridges, Jean-Luc and I took the Loire River road part of the way here. The bridges are quite extraordinary. It's really a beautiful drive."

Within minutes, Jean-Luc and Karen had them both laughing.

Brandje was grateful the awkward situation with Pierre had passed. However, she was completely aware that, because of Pierre's intrusion, Nathan's anger was kindled once again.

When they finally arrived back at the villa it was nearly three in the afternoon. Brandje was surprised to see an antique Mercedes Benz convertible parked in the driveway. The classic automobile was painted a pale yellow, with brown fenders and lots of chrome, and it obviously belonged to Nathan.

"At last," said Nathan as Jean-Luc set the brake. He got out of the car and headed straight for the beautiful Mercedes.

"Puts ours to shame, doesn't it, love?" asked Jean-Luc wearily.

From around the side of the house stepped a young woman with cling tight clothing and high heels that accented her shapely legs. To say she was a voluptuous woman, Brandje decided, would be a negligent understatement, though she suspected the woman may be much younger than she appeared.

"Nathan, darling!" the woman exclaimed with a silky French accent that seemed to drip with invitation.

"Isabelle," Nathan gushed, giving her a big hug.

For a moment he glanced in Brandje's direction, but he made no effort to introduce her to Isabelle.

"I brought your car as quickly as I could get away," Isabelle announced. "But I cannot stay in Croix de Vie today. You must take me straight back to Nantes."

"Gladly," he responded. "Do you mind?" he asked the Rousseaus, ignoring Brandje completely.

"Go ahead," said Jean-Luc. "We can keep things under control here."

Nathan held the door open for Isabelle, then hopped in the car and drove the antique Mercedes Benz convertible merrily down the hill.

Brandje felt utterly bewildered and betrayed. A twinge of jealousy sparked her anger the rest of the day. Although Jean-Luc and Karen tried their best to keep her spirits up, by seven in the evening Brandje was furious. While Brandje and Karen washed the supper dishes together, Jean-Luc read the evening paper at the kitchen table. Unable to control her temper any longer, Brandje lashed out, at no one in particular, "Four hours! It doesn't take four hours to drive to Nantes and back."

"He's an honorable man," Karen tried to soothe. "You'll see."

Brandje sighed. "You'd think I own him the way I'm feeling," she admitted.

Jean-Luc smiled. "I'm glad my name isn't Nathan."

"So am I, dear," laughed Karen.

"Oh, you two!" Brandje snapped. Then she realized how harsh those words left her mouth. "I'm sorry," she apologized. "I'm terrible company tonight. I think I'll go out and watch the sunset."

"The tide's coming in," warned Jean-Luc. "And those steps. Really Brandje, do you think that's wise?"

"Don't worry," she said, "I'll be very careful."

"What if you faint again?"

"Should I handcuff myself to the chain?" she asked with a smirk.

Karen pinched his arm. "Brandje's a big girl," she scolded.

"Oh, all right, have it your way!" he exclaimed.

Brandje went to the closet and grabbed her sweater.

"It's not cold," Jean-Luc reminded with a frown.

"No, but I've been chilled all afternoon."

Karen looked up quickly from the dish water, but Brandje gave her a warning glance. She had no desire to tell Karen about the abdominal pain she'd felt most of the afternoon, ever since the meeting with Pierre. The sharp, knifing sensation had made her forehead bead with perspiration more than once. Fortunately, if Karen noticed, she did not mention it. An hour earlier, Brandje took her first pain pill, and now, though she felt chilled, the abdominal pain had subsided.

She slipped the sweater over her shoulders and stepped outside, grateful to be away from the Rousseaus for a brief time. Brandje regretted that she'd been poor company all afternoon. How could one man make her feel so vulnerable and angry all at the same time?

Soon she sat perched a few steps from the top of the cliff, watching the waves bury Timbal's Point far below her. The gardenias filled the air with such a heavenly fragrance it lifted her spirits and she felt a little less irritated.

Out on the Bay of Biscay, a fleet of small fishing boats advanced toward the Port of St. Gilles. Their hulls rested heavily in the water after a good days catch. Far to the south she could see the ships go by, some large, some small, but all with bellies full.

She considered the events of the day, totally confused by what had occurred. *What a hypocrite I am!* she said to herself. *Do I want Nathan to love me, or don't I?* If she didn't want him to love her, then it shouldn't matter that he chose to spend his day with a young, beautiful, voluptuous French woman. And if she did want him to love her, she would have to tell him about the cancer. It would be the right thing to do. She shrugged in absolute bewilderment.

Did Nathan love her? If he did, as she had assumed before today, he wouldn't have deliberately ignored her and gone off with another woman. The only explanation for his behavior was that he didn't love her at all. Her intuition had been wrong, as had Karen's and Jean-Luc's.

If he hadn't fallen in love with her, there was nothing to gain by telling him that she loved him. Brandje concluded that Nathan needn't know about her illness, nor about her feelings concerning him, regardless how much she wanted to share her love with him.

Let Nathan have a carefree summer! Brandje decided with bitter finality that he would go back to New York at the end of August unencumbered with information regarding her health, and completely unaware of her love for him!

Chapter Ten

randje heard Nathan come in around midnight. She'd been reading from the Book of Mormon for several hours, but she just couldn't seem to maintain her concentration. The words seemed vaguely familiar to her, but she had no reason to account for the feeling. It annoyed her, and she wanted to understand why a book so totally foreign to her should also be so familiar.

By three in the morning Brandje finally fell asleep, but her dreams were disjointed and muddled. Part of the time she dreamed she was falling off the bluff that overlooked Timbal's Point, but no matter how far she fell, she never reached the bottom. The other dreams had to do with her running away from someone or something, but she could never quite tell who, what or why.

Much later that morning she was awakened by the telephone ringing downstairs. Then she heard someone coming up the stairs. There was a knock at her door.

"Yes," Brandje answered, rolling over on the bed.

"You're wanted on the telephone," came Nathan's voice through the closed door.

"I'll be right down."

Quickly Brandje slipped on a robe, brushed her hair and went downstairs. Nathan was at the laptop computer, writing as usual. Jean-Luc could be seen through the open window, practicing some golf strokes, and Karen was at the dining room table writing letters.

She picked up the receiver and spoke into the mouthpiece. "Brandje Fulton here."

"It is Pierre Lobrouge, *mon cheri*," came a sickening familiar voice. "Pardon the interruption but I had in mind an idea about your property and I would like to discuss it over lunch on Monday. Will this suit you?"

Still irritated that Nathan had taken nine hours to return Isabelle to Nantes, Brandje said, "I don't know, Pierre." She hoped Nathan had heard her use Pierre's name. "I'm really not interested in selling the villa."

"Perhaps we can discuss a completely different approach that would be satisfactory to everyone," he persuaded.

Brandje sighed. She didn't want to meet this man anywhere. He was oppressively obnoxious.

On the other hand, Nathan hadn't been in best form since yesterday afternoon. She was still seething about his disappearance with Isabelle, and his late return. But he had no claim on her affection, she reminded herself, and she had not promised him anything, either.

"I don't know," she said again. "I —"

"Oh, please, *mon amour*. It is a matter of life and death that we speak together. My mother is ill and I promised her I would not fail her in this quest."

"I'm sorry to hear that," said Brandje, suddenly feeling guilty for refusing him. It was just a business meeting, after all. "I suppose Monday will be all right."

"May I pick you up around noon?" he asked at once.

"No," she hesitated. She did not want to be alone with him in a car. "I'll meet you at DeMerite at noon."

"But I would be most happy to drive —" he began.

Brandje cut him off. "Pierre, if you want to meet with me to discuss the villa, I will. But it will be on my terms. Is that understood?"

"*Oui, mon cheri*. Strictly business, I assure you."

"All right," said Brandje, "until Monday."

She hung up the phone and turned to go back upstairs.

Nathan stood and followed her up. She turned into her bedroom and attempted to close the door, but he wouldn't allow it. He followed her inside, leaving the door open.

"You're going to lunch Monday with *him*?" he hissed.

"He wishes to discuss some arrangement about the villa," she answered, her eyes squaring off with his. "I told him I would meet him."

A muscle twitched along his jaw and his eyes darkened angrily. "I thought you weren't going to sell," he pointed out.

"I won't sell," she said stubbornly. "But Pierre said he had some other idea, and wanted to discuss it at lunch."

"Whatever he offers, I'll pay double!" he snapped. "Call him back and cancel."

"But you don't want to buy the villa," Brandje protested.

"Maybe I do," he said. "You won't get a better offer from anyone."

"Nevertheless, I must meet him for lunch. I don't know how to reach him otherwise. I don't know where he lives, and I have no telephone number for him. I can't be rude and not show up."

"You can!" he insisted. "Better still, I'll go for you! I'll tell him I've already purchased it and get him off your back!"

"That's not fair," she argued. "I don't even know what his offer is."

"You *want* to go?" he asked, giving her a tart frown.

Feeling threatened, Brandje retaliated. "It would be nice to get out from underfoot for a while. I feel like an intruder when you're working, trying to be quiet and not disturb you." A note of despair crept into her voice and she twisted a strand of her hair nervously with her fingers.

"I've never asked you to be quiet!" Nathan snapped.

"I know that, but it must take a great amount of concentration to write a book."

Nathan sighed. "What am I to do with you?" he asked.

Brandje heard the weariness in his voice, but she remembered all too well his abandoning her yesterday so he could spend his time with Isabelle. "Nothing," came her cold response. "Absolutely nothing."

For a moment he looked deep into her eyes, but she allowed no sign of softening to emerge. Finally he shrugged and turned away.

After he went back downstairs, Brandje shut the bedroom door and curled up on the bed like a little child who'd just been sent to her room. Even though they hadn't yelled at one another, she thought it was their worst quarrel yet. She felt more miserable today than yesterday. She didn't understand why she permitted herself to be hurt so easily by a man who apparently didn't care about her.

Nathan didn't like Pierre, but Brandje didn't like Isabelle. Nathan could go out and spend almost nine hours with Isabelle, without even introducing her to Brandje. But Brandje wasn't supposed to spend one hour with Pierre for a business luncheon. *Something is definitely wrong with this picture!* she fumed.

Pierre didn't want to buy the villa, and she wasn't going to sell it, anyway. She just wanted to hear Pierre out. Perhaps he only wanted to lease the villa privately, which would save her all the cleaning, gardening and managerial fees that she now paid to Bagley and Associates.

Maybe Nathan was just trying to guarantee that he would be able to come here each summer. If he leased the villa permanently, he could sub-let it through Bagley's, and guarantee himself a spot each summer, without his landlady living with him.

The more Brandje came to know Nathaniel Duncan, the less she understood him. He could be charming and polite, tender and persuasive, angry and hostile. He could also be gentle as a morning rain, and protective as a granite cove. He was an enigma. She would never comprehend his many moods.

Brandje shrugged. It was futile to try to understand him. In a few weeks they would separate, never to see each other again. That thought depressed her even more than the upcoming luncheon engagement with Pierre.

After a while she rolled off the bed and onto her knees. She hadn't prayed much as a child. But she needed to find God, she reasoned, before she died.

With clarity, she recalled Nathan's prayer, and how he had spoken to God as if He were right beside him. She bowed her head and began with a soft whisper, "O God, the Eternal Father, I know you're there, and can hear me. I don't know what to do anymore."

Tears tumbled from her eyes but she made no effort to wipe them away. "I have fallen in love at a time when I shouldn't give my heart to anyone. I have cancer destroying my liver and the doctor told me that I will die soon. I don't want to die yet." She pressed her face against the quilt upon her bed and wept silently.

Finally Brandje lifted her head and wiped away her tears. Then she bowed her head once again and continued. "I accept whatever you have in store for me, dear Father. I have little choice in the matter. I am willing to accept death, if that's what you want for me. I've always believed you had a plan for everyone, and I have to accept that my cancer must be part of your plan.

"I don't like pain, dear Father. If you could take me without allowing me too much pain, I would appreciate it. The doctor says I may get delirious. That frightens me. I don't want to lose control of my mind. If you could see your way clear to agree, I'd like to forgo the delirium also. If I had a choice, I'd rather just slip into a coma and sleep, completely unconscious, until the time I die.

"This is a terribly selfish prayer, Father. I'm focused inward, and I apologize. It's just that, I've never prayed like this before, and I'm facing some big obstacles right now. I want to learn to know you like Nathan does. I want to be able to tell you all the feelings in my heart, and I want to trust that you will hear me, and answer my prayers.

"Nathan talks to you as though you were his own beloved father. From what I have learned from my reading in the Book of Mormon, you are my father, as well.

"About Nathan, Father. I didn't mean to fall in love with him. It just happened. I don't know what to do about it. Earlier I thought he was feeling the same way about me, but I'm not sure anymore. Please guide me. Help me to know what to do. Help me to know what to say to him. I don't want to hurt him. But I don't want to be hurt by him anymore, either.

"I do believe in you, and in your son, Jesus Christ. I feel in my heart that you both live. Help me to understand that which I will need to know about you before I die.

"I ask for these blessings in the name of Jesus Christ, Amen."

When she was finished she stayed on her knees for several long minutes, during which time she was filled with a sweet, warm tenderness that she couldn't explain. For the first time in her life, she felt that her prayer had gone beyond the ceiling, and was on its way to Heaven.

Afterward, she thought about the feelings she'd had, and realized that God had already answered her prayer by giving her that warm and wonderful experience. Her great sadness was that she wanted to share her experience with Nathan. But right now, that was impossible.

Karen was a great help to her through the rest of that week. They walked together in the mornings, and talked about life and the futility of it. Karen had a different perspective on life than Brandje had ever heard before. She believed that all the terminal sickness in the world was just one more evidence of God's power. "He has to call us home somehow," she told Brandje one day. "Everyone can't suddenly die in an accident, or in their sleep. That might get pretty suspicious after a while."

Brandje laughed. "I guess you're right," she agreed. "But what about illness that doesn't end in death, or at least, not right away?"

"You mean like a heart condition that lingers for years, or epilepsy, things like that?" Karen asked.

"Exactly."

"I can't explain all sickness," Karen began. "But there are a few things I think I understand. Sickness can help a person draw closer to God, if they allow it. In your own experience you know that's true. Would you be here at the villa, seeking answers from God, if you were not ill?"

Brandje shook her head.

Karen continued, "In cases such as Alzheimer's, perhaps the families of those persons need to learn sacrifice, service or compassion by having to care for the afflicted."

Brandje could see that a lot of what Karen told her made sense.

Karen had a knack for always having just the right answer on the tip of her tongue.

Where Nathan was concerned, however, no one had any answers. Nathan arose each morning, ran for almost an hour, then retired to the living room where he pounced on the computer keys most of the day, rarely stopping, even for lunch. During the entire week, his verbal communications to Brandje had been clipped and sparse. He wasn't good company for anyone else that week, either.

Jean-Luc, apparently frustrated with Nathan's withdrawal, drove daily to Nantes to check on the progress of their house remodeling, and returned each evening.

Brandje spent the week tackling one new chore each morning, then reading the Book of Mormon or napping in the afternoon, depending on how she felt. Fortunately, she had no more abdominal pain the rest of the week. In the evenings, she and Karen did handwork and watched television with Jean-Luc.

On Sunday the Rousseaus and Nathan went to church in Nantes, but Brandje stayed at the villa to rest. She had the luncheon engagement with Pierre tomorrow, and that was more stress than she felt capable of dealing with at all.

On Monday Jean-Luc went to Nantes early in the morning, so Nathan volunteered to take Brandje into Croix de Vie for the luncheon with Pierre. When they arrived, he put his hand gently upon hers.

"What time should I pick you up?" he asked wearily, as though he had no strength left within him.

"I can't imagine it will take any longer than an hour."

Nathan nodded. "You're sure you want to meet him alone?"

"I'm a big girl," she defended. "I know how to handle Pierre if he gets out of line."

"You wouldn't want me to come in and sit at another table?"

She frowned. "Absolutely not!"

He sighed. "I'll be back in an hour."

"Thanks," she said, slipping her hand out from under his, and getting out of the car. She waved as he drove off, but he saluted her, as though she were his drill sergeant. The gesture annoyed her, and what she didn't need right now was another irritation to ruin her day.

Pierre was patiently waiting for her at the reception desk.

"*Mon amour*, we meet again," he said with great flair, taking her right hand and kissing the back of it in his usual manner.

"Pierre," Brandje nodded her head slightly.

He offered her his left arm, but she sidestepped him and took his right instead. Then, while they were walking toward the table, she wiped the back of her right hand vigorously on her skirt, hoping no one would notice.

Pierre held out a chair for her at a table he'd earlier reserved. A waiter brought them cold water and menus.

"How long will you continue to punish me for my poor behavior that September?" Pierre asked boldly while Brandje studied her menu.

"As long as it takes you to realize I'm not interested in a romantic interlude," Brandje stated with equal boldness. This time she would not let him gain the upper hand, she vowed to herself.

He frowned, but was unable to comment because the waiter interrupted them. Brandje selected *coq au jus* while Pierre decided on *boeuf bourguignonne*. Returning to Brandje's statement after the waiter left, Pierre said, gazing at her thoughtfully, "Neither am I interested in a short season of romance." His voice had a seductive tremor that sickened her. "Contrary to popular belief, the French prefer permanent relationships."

"This was supposed to be a business luncheon," Brandje reminded hastily. "I will not spend this time discussing personal matters."

Pierre frowned momentarily, then changed his expression quickly to a broad smile. "But of course, *mon cheri*. Business first, pleasure later," he hinted.

Before Brandje could protest further, he said, "I have come upon a plan whereby I would lease your villa on a five-year contract, with the exception of the time that you or your brother occupy it."

"I can't make any agreement with you until I've conferred with my brother," Brandje told him with polite brevity. "I trust you understand."

"But you have the final authority, therefore, it is you who must consider my offer," Pierre pleaded, mentioning an enormous sum far exceeding the amount she was presently receiving. Suddenly his expression changed to grave seriousness. "This lease, *mon amour*, is of vital importance to me."

"Why?" Brandje questioned. "Does the villa bring you so much pride that you would rather live apart from your vineyards?"

"C'est ma Maman," he reported sadly. "She is ill! The doctors insist she must live near the crisp salt air. Your villa is only an hour drive to my vineyards. I could continue my business while providing for my mother's health. You understand?"

Brandje smiled, not certain whether she should believe the scoundrel. Fortunately the waiter appeared with a plate of chicken cooked in broth with rice and herbs for her, and a thick beef stew for Pierre.

"C'est delicieux," Brandje complimented while the waiter stood by, waiting for this customary response. When Pierre indicated that his meal was also perfect, the waiter left them alone once more.

Brandje forked hungrily into the chicken, hoping to avoid further discussion. She realized that if she approached Martin with Pierre's offer, he would undoubtedly encourage her to accept it. But the final decision, of course, would be hers. Martin made it clear early on that the management of the villa was entirely in her hands. When she stepped out of the picture, Martin would certainly benefit from such an arrangement.

"My suggestion is suitable, *non?*" Pierre asked, interrupting her train of thought.

"I will write to my brother and ask his advice," she said. A frown crossed over her face and she bit her lip in apprehension.

"There is a complication?" he guessed, as he watched her expression.

"I wouldn't be able to give you possession until later in the year. I have a," she hesitated, wondering how to word what she needed to say. "I have a health problem of my own, and I will be at the villa for several months yet."

As Pierre studied her, a silent tear spilled down her cheek. "This matter of your health?" he asked solemnly. "It is significant?"

Brandje nodded, all color draining from her face.

He inhaled sharply, then lowered his eyes to the dinner plate, as though considering her answer to his question. He remained silent for the remainder of the main course.

"This is why you avoided me at the pharmacy?" Pierre questioned when dessert was served. "You did not want me to know?"

Again Brandje nodded, knowing that her assent was not entirely truthful, but willing to pretend, regardless.

Pierre seemed to brighten afterward, as though disregarding what she had told him about her health. His mood became playful, as though he hoped she would now acquiesce to his desires.

When they finished, Pierre escorted Brandje toward the entrance. He apparently wasn't content with tucking her arm in his, so he coiled an arm around her shoulders and pulled her close to him, whispering seductively in her ear, "*Mon amour, J`ai longtemps attendu pour —*"

"Really, Pierre!" Brandje admonished, interrupting him. "I'm not interested in romance of any duration." She tried unsuccessfully to extricate her body from his tight embrace.

"Do not disappoint me, *mon cheri*," he cautioned, while pushing the door open so they could both exit. "Now that we have discussed business, we must not let pleasure slip by us easily."

He slid his hand to her cheek and turned her face towards his, leaving an imprint with his fingers. When she realized he was going to kiss her, she began to protest. His mouth covered hers. She clamped her teeth together to prevent his prolonging the embrace.

Pierre frowned and released her.

Brandje was immediately relieved to see Nathan's car sitting in front of the restaurant. Unfortunately, Nathan was not in it.

Pierre walked ahead of her and turned abruptly so that they were face to face. He placed both hands on her shoulders and Brandje sensed he was going to try again.

"Pierre," she reprimanded sternly. "Stop this immediately. It can lead nowhere. The reason you cannot lease the villa until later on is because I have a terminal illness. I shall be put in my grave by the end of the year!" It was the only thing she could think of to discourage him completely.

Pierre dropped both hands to his sides. He stared at her incredulously, his face changing from a steamed pink to pale lemon in a matter of seconds. "*C'est vrai, mon cheri? C'est vrai?*" he demanded.

"It's true enough," said a familiar voice behind them.

Brandje whirled around to see Nathan standing with his arms folded across his chest, acting as her security guard. She gasped and placed a hand over her mouth to prevent a cry of anguish from escaping. Nathan had overheard!

Nathan gave her a knowing wink and said to Pierre, "What other reason would persuade Miss Fulton to allow a registered nurse and two male assistants to live with her?" He gave the Frenchman a glare of solid ice. Then he took Brandje's hand and led her over to the Mercedes.

"I'm so sorry, *mon cheri*," Pierre muttered as he leaned wearily against the side of the building as though he'd been winded by a severe blow.

Nathan assisted her into the car, whistled his way to the driver's seat, and drove away. When they were several blocks from the restaurant, Nathan burst out laughing. "That was the finest performance I've ever witnessed. He actually believed you!"

Brandje felt immediately grateful that he had mistaken her grim declaration for sheer fabrication. She tried to respond equally amused, but she couldn't bring herself to laugh at the prospect.

Nathan did, however. He leaned his head back and laughed for all he was worth. "That's even better than telling the guy to drop dead!"

He thought the whole idea that she might die was one great big ludicrous joke. It made him laugh. How could she ever tell him now that she was not acting, that she made the confession in grave seriousness?

"You should have seen your face! The grim reaper! You missed your calling entirely, Brandje. You should have been an actress. You were marvelous!" he laughed.

Soon tears filled her eyes and slipped down her cheeks. She turned her face into the wind so he would not notice.

Nathan maneuvered the car off the side of the road and set the brake. "Will you ever stop crying?" he demanded. Turning her around to face him, he pulled her across the seat and onto his lap.

Brandje remained silent under his command. She shook her head, buried her face against his shoulder and wept. Nathan would never know that she'd finally found someone she loved more than life itself, nor would he ever guess that her words to Pierre were true.

When she calmed down enough to answer his questions coherently, Nathan lifted her chin, forcing her to look at him.

"Why all these tears?" he asked in total frustration. "Did Pierre harm you?"

Brandje shook her head.

"Then what?"

"You were angry with me all week long," she sniffed. It was a simple excuse, and not untrue.

"Silly girl! You should know why," he accused.

"No! You never even hinted that you wanted to buy the villa until last week."

He gave her a wry, crooked smile. "You are absolutely blind!" he exclaimed. "Sometimes I wonder if all Heaven doesn't dash about protecting you. You're far too sensitive. And vulnerable. You're like an injured bird learning how to fly. Somewhere along the way you've forgotten how, and I'm the only one around to pick you up and show you the way again."

Brandje's blue eyes widened in surprise at his analogy. "Do you mind?" she asked timidly.

He pulled her tight against his chest and stroked her honey blonde hair. "I doubt you'd know my mind if I told you."

Chapter Eleven

The rest of the week Nathan was in good spirits. He still jogged in the morning and worked on his book for six to eight hours each day, but in the evening he visited amiably with Brandje, Jean-Luc and Karen as though nothing out of the ordinary had ever occurred the week before.

Brandje was the only one who noticed any differences between two weeks ago, and that week. He'd made no attempt to kiss her, nor had he given her that special smile of his, the one that she felt had been created just for her. She didn't know whether to be disappointed, or relieved.

Late Friday afternoon, Nathan looked up from the laptop computer and said, "Whew! The worst is over."

"You're finished?" Brandje asked excitedly, looking up from the afghan she was crocheting.

"Well, not exactly," he admitted. "What I meant is that the first phase, what I call the creative process, is over. I can print up the book and start red-lining it."

"Proofing it?" Karen questioned.

"Ripping it apart, would be my guess," Jean-Luc wagered.

Brandje raised an eyebrow. "You've spent three weeks writing it, only to rip it to shreds?" she wondered aloud.

"I'm going to print it up exactly as it is," Nathan explained the process. "Then I'm going to take one page at a time and read it over and over again, checking each paragraph for structure, correcting each grammatical error, choosing better words that describe things more precisely. I call it red-lining because I use a red pen." He smiled affectionately at her.

Brandje's heart skipped a beat. It was the first real smile, one that openly showed his affection, that he'd given to her since before their argument over whether or not she should meet Pierre for lunch. She smiled back, hoping the one she gave him had an equal effect.

"I think this calls for a celebration," said Karen. "Brandje and I can prepare a candlelight supper, if you'd like."

"I've got a better idea," said Nathan, disregarding Karen's suggestion immediately. "I'd like to take everyone out for supper. I've been wanting to try that new restaurant, Saint-Jacques, at the other side of town. Any takers?"

"We'd be delighted," said Karen. "Wouldn't we, Jean-Luc?"

"Absolutely," he grinned.

"And you, Brandje?" Nathan asked thoughtfully. "Would you like to go with us, as well?"

"I . . . would." The hesitant timidity in her voice was due to the pain inside her, but she gave him an eager smile, hoping he hadn't noticed.

He seemed to sense her hesitation, and for a moment, Brandje noticed a trace of disappointment in his expression. However, an hour later when she arrived downstairs dressed in a shimmering blue evening gown, he acted as though he was genuinely pleased to take her hand in his and lead her out to the Mercedes Benz.

Saint-Jacques, a dinner and dance hall, was created out of a renovated, eighteenth century mansion. The main floor was divided in two sections. The kitchen in the rear, was accessed through two sets of swinging doors on either end of a long bar with tall stools, where guests waited for their table while inebriating themselves.

Brandje thought little of it, since this was a customary practice in France, as well as in Great Britain. Fortunately, their reservation was early enough that they didn't have a waiting period.

The dining and dancing hall was upstairs, where the entire dance floor took the middle portion of the room, and intimate tables were interspersed all around the outside perimeter. A small stage separated the musicians from the dance floor, where even at this early hour, several couples danced closely together to a slow, sensual waltz.

After they were seated, the waiter brought them wine lists, but the three Mormons turned them down, and Brandje followed suit. She didn't mind not drinking wine with a meal, even if the waiter did look at them oddly. In France, wine is nearly always served with a meal, especially in the coastal areas of the Bay of Biscay and inland to the Loire Valley, an area known for its vineyards and excellent wine.

Soon the waiter exchanged the wine list for menus. For the French, a typical noon or evening meal consists of a first course, usually a soup or hot dish, such as a *tourtes, pates, hures* or a *souffle*, all of which demand elaborate preparation. Next in line would be a main dish, consisting of meat (often fish), and vegetables mixed in a wine, tomato or garlic sauce. After the main dish, guests are usually offered a variety of popular French cheeses, including the white cheeses, *comte* and *contel*, served with one of the traditional French wines. Following the cheese and wine, dessert was offered to those patrons hungry enough to still desire it.

Their dinner was selected on the basis of which seafood was the freshest that day, and ranged from a variety of mussels with spinach and grilled oysters, to stuffed squid and lobster in curry sauce. Many of the seaside areas in the Bay of Biscay were well known for their oyster farms, and these, of course, were rarely omitted when one dined out.

By the time they'd eaten their main course and received the cheese, served with non-fermented grape juice, Jean-Luc said to his wife, "I believe we'd better dance some of that dinner off before we continue."

Karen nodded and joined him on the dance floor.

This left Brandje and Nathan alone at the table. He looked across at her and asked casually, "And you?"

She gave him a demure smile. "I'm willing to try if you are."

Nathan took her by the hand and led her out on the dance floor. She knew immediately that this was another mistake. The nearness of him made her feel light-headed, almost giddy, and she found herself throwing caution to the wind once again. The orchestra played a fast-paced tune not unlike a polka, and Nathan whirled her around the dance floor in quick, small steps that kept her alert to his changes. After a couple of blunders for both of them, they laughed and eventually adapted to one another. Before long, Brandje was able to sense, by the pressure of his hand on her back, which direction he intended to go and how to best complement his movements.

By the time the rousing number ended, Brandje felt fatigued. However, she wouldn't tell Nathan. The orchestra began a slow and sensual waltz once again, giving the dancers a little break. She noticed that Jean-Luc and Karen had returned to the table, but she didn't want to join them just yet. She wanted this slow dance to last forever.

Although Nathan was a full foot taller than she, he pulled her close to him, allowing her to rest her head against his strong chest. She wondered if she should offer some sparkling piece of conversation, but decided against it. These silent moments were some she would savor long after he went back to New York.

Along the outer walls, three doors led outside to a balcony that encircled the dining hall entirely. Nathan led her out onto the balcony right after the waltz ended.

"It's a beautiful place to spend the evening," she said, giving him a warm smile, while thrilling to the touch of his hand against hers.

"I like it as well," he agreed.

They stopped and leaned against the balustrade. The night air was cool and refreshing. Because it was a chillier summer than normal, the often oppressive heat had not claimed the evenings. Unexpectedly, Brandje shivered. Noticing her discomfort, Nathan removed his suit coat and placed it over her shoulders.

"Thank you," she whispered, holding the front of the coat closed with one hand.

When she slipped her other hand into his, Nathan caressed it as he looked down at her. A warm sensation filled her with peace, and she wondered what thoughts were forming in his mind, to no avail.

Brandje returned his steady gaze. She didn't understand why he couldn't see the love she felt so strongly for him, written plainly in her azure eyes.

Nathan smiled for a moment and Brandje wanted to melt into his arms, but she restrained herself. The next move, she determined, would have to come from him.

"Do you think you'll feel well enough to go to Chinon with me next week?" he finally asked.

"Why?" His question surprised her.

"My grandmother wants us to visit."

"I thought she only had one spare bedroom," reminded Brandje, pleased that he'd asked her to accompany him.

"Isabelle has twin beds in her room. She said she'd be happy to share with you," he explained.

"Isabelle lives with your grandmother?" Brandje's eyes widened in alarm.

"She has a right to stay there," he answered with a self-incriminating sigh. "She's my cousin."

"Your cousin?" Brandje couldn't believe her ears. "Isabelle is just your cousin?"

He arched an eyebrow, she hoped in dismay, then he nodded. The penitent expression on his face led her to believe he regretted having deceived her by not properly introducing Isabelle.

"Why didn't you tell me?" she asked, her voice trembling.

"I was angry," he confessed. "If you'll remember, I'd just met your Pierre."

"He's not *my* Pierre," she insisted. "He never has been."

"I know that now. But the morning that Pierre called, and you accepted his invitation, I didn't know what to think."

"You might have considered that I know how far away Nantes is, and that it doesn't take nine hours to drive there and back again," she suggested, surprised at how calm her voice sounded.

He nodded, as though he finally understood. Then he explained, "Isabelle had been waiting for us to return to the villa for over two hours. By the time she and I arrived in Nantes, our cousin Frederick had already left for Chinon, and Isabelle had missed her ride, so I ended up taking her all the way to Chinon myself."

"And how was I supposed to know that?" Brandje questioned.

"Oops," he whispered with a hint of sorrow in his voice.

"You hardly said a word to me for a week," she accused, remembering the awful week before her luncheon with Pierre.

"I know. And I apologize. It's just, where you're concerned I get a little edgy," he explained.

"Why?" The question slipped out before she could think about it.

Rather than answer her question, Nathan looked deeply into her eyes, searching almost hopefully, it seemed to Brandje. Then he changed the subject without answering her at all.

"You haven't said whether or not you'll go to Chinon with me," Nathan reminded.

She felt keenly disappointed, and hesitated to give him an affirmative response. In addition to her discouragement over his refusal to answer such a simple question, she'd been in pain all day. How could she make a promise that she may not be able to keep? Finally, she resolved the issue by saying, "If I'm feeling well enough, I would enjoy it."

Nathan nodded in response. If he was disappointed by the guarded answer she'd given him, he did not mention it. "You'll love Chinon," he told her excitedly. "Not only is the Loire valley filled with medieval castles, Grandmaman lives in a huge chateau with formal gardens overlooking the Loire River. It's a beautiful place."

"Hmm," mused Brandje testily, turning away from him. "Perhaps you would have liked staying with your grandmother these past three weeks, instead of with me." She knew it was the wrong thing to say the moment the words slipped from her mouth, but she was irritated with him. She had given him the perfect opportunity to state exactly how he felt about her, and he had not cooperated.

Nathan turned her around to face him. His eyes darkened angrily and a muscle twitched along his jaw.

Brandje saw him struggle to control his temper, and this time, he succeeded. Somehow he forced himself to soften, and this pleased her. He shook his head and rubbed her shoulders. For several minutes he just stared into her eyes, as though he was trying to read her mind by what he found there.

Then, unexpectedly, Nathan's lips sought hers and she willingly allowed him to kiss her. Just as unexpectedly, he withdrew. His face was ashen, and his expression suggested that he felt as though he'd committed a grave error.

Brandje forced a pretentious giggle before baiting him. "You know," she teased, "I can't decide whether you want to kiss me or not."

"Perhaps that's because I can't decide, either," he said, completely deflating Brandje's emotions. Then he turned her toward the dining hall. "Come along, you're getting chilled." He escorted her back into the dining room where they joined Jean-Luc and Karen at the table.

"You're right on time," Jean-Luc announced. "The waiter just brought our dessert menus."

"Oh, not for me," Brandje said. "I couldn't eat another thing."

"No dessert?" asked Nathan. "I'll certainly have something."

Karen stood up. "I'll slip over to the powder room. Will you join me, Brandje?" she asked.

Brandje nodded. As she returned Nathan's suit coat, Karen said,

"You two go ahead and order. We'll be back in a bit."

Nathan sat down at the table, picked up the dessert menu, and gave them a brief nod.

When they reached the ladies room, Karen turned to Brandje and studied her for a moment. "You're pale," she said hastily. "I have some blush with me. Would you like to freshen up a bit?"

Brandje studied her reflection in the mirror. "I don't feel well," she admitted. "My liver has ached all afternoon. Dancing tonight seemed to make it much worse."

"You need to tell Nathan about the cancer," Karen insisted with an air of authority. "Otherwise, I fear you will end up comatose, and I will be forced to tell him."

"I can't," said Brandje. "Not yet. I haven't a clue how he feels about me. How can I tell him anything if our romance is all one-sided?"

"You still can't see, after all that's happened, how he feels about you?" Karen asked, her eyes widening in surprise.

Brandje shook her head. "Sometimes I think, oh that look has to mean —" She sighed and sat down on the settee. "Other times, he's so distant and withdrawn it could only mean that he doesn't want me to care about him the way I do."

"Love is blind," Karen said with a grimace. "And you got a double dose of it."

"I've given him plenty of opportunities," Brandje insisted.

"If he tells you that he loves you, will you tell him the truth about the cancer?" Karen asked.

Brandje nodded. "If he loves me, he should know right away. Maybe I would even want to fight to stay with him." Tears filled her eyes and she brushed them quickly away. "But if he doesn't care about me, like I do about him, it would serve no purpose to tell him anything . . . not that I'm dying, and certainly not that I love him."

"Why won't you fight to stay without his loving you?" Karen persisted. "Brandje, you must! At least put your name on the donor list, that's all I'm asking. If a liver doesn't become available before you go home, you'll be able to say to God that you tried. You've got to do at least that much."

Brandje sighed wearily. Karen just didn't understand. Though Brandje cherished the sweet friendship the two women had developed, she couldn't be persuaded to fight for her life. Not without Nathan. Finally Brandje looked at the older woman through her tears and said, "God's plan for me doesn't include fighting to live. If it did, He'd give me a reason."

"You have plenty of reasons. You have family and friends who all want you to stay."

"It's not about *want*," Brandje sniffed. "It's about *need*. I have no one who really *needs* me. Martin has managed thirty-six years on his own. Without me, he will be free to look for someone. I've always felt that he gave up his life to raise me, to take the place of my mother, to work as a team with my father in caring for me. Now that Father's gone, Martin thinks he has to act as both parents to me. He deserves a life of his own, and a wife and children. I have no other family but Tante Geraldine, and she needs no one. Most of my friends are married now, many of them with children. I'm alone. Without Nathan, I have no reason to continue. Can't you understand? Oh, Karen," she sobbed, "I need you to understand. Please try."

Karen held Brandje in her arms as a tender mother would hold a beloved daughter. She stroked her hair and soothed, "There now, Brandje. I'm sorry. I'll try to understand. I will."

Later Brandje washed her face and applied fresh makeup to hide the fact that she'd been crying. But no matter what she did, it showed in her reddened eyes.

"Maybe I should go out to the car and wait," suggested Brandje. "You can tell them that I'm not feeling well. It's dark outside. Perhaps Nathan won't notice that I've been crying."

Karen agreed. "Go on, then. I'll get the men."

Within moments Brandje was seated on the passenger seat of Nathan's Mercedes Benz, and it was none too soon. Nathan stepped outside and hurried across the parking lot to the car. "Are you all right?" he asked, climbing into the driver's seat.

Brandje turned to face him, grateful for the shadows of the night.

"I'll be fine," she reassured, though she was dismayed to hear her voice tremble. "It's just been more day than I had planned."

Jean-Luc helped Karen into the back seat, then went around and got in on the other side. "Are you feeling a little better now?" asked Karen.

Brandje smiled at her, giving her a wink that no one else noticed.

"A little," she admitted.

Nathan started the engine and drove the car out of the parking lot and onto the busy street. When he'd shifted the gears, he slid his hand across the seat and caressed her fingers. She placed her hand in his, and savored the comfort that it gave her. Somehow it seemed that when he held her hand, a warmth would spread over her, beginning at the point of contact, then permeating her entire body with a sensation of renewed strength and courage that she sadly lacked without him.

When they arrived home, she went quickly upstairs to her bedroom to check the color of her eyes. The redness had dissipated in the cool night drive and she sighed with relief. She slipped into her pajamas and robe, then went back downstairs.

"Shouldn't you be in bed?" Nathan asked the moment she arrived. "I'm feeling a little better," she argued. "I think that fast dance wiped me out."

"I think you should rest," he insisted. "What do you think?" he asked, looking at Karen.

Karen smiled. "Well, she has more color than she did in the powder room. Perhaps she can rest as well on the sofa as she can upstairs.

Nathan stood up and offered her the sofa. She sat down upon it, but he frowned. "I'll be right back," he said. He dashed upstairs and returned moments later with a pillow and blanket from the hall closet. Then he sat at one end of the sofa and placed the pillow on his thigh.

"Come on," he said. "You're going to rest, even if it's not in your own bed."

Brandje smiled and placed her head upon the pillow with her feet at the other end of the sofa.

Nathan covered her with a blanket, then caressed her long golden hair. "Someone's got to watch after you all the time," he teased. "You're like a fragile, porcelain doll."

"Only much more stubborn," hinted Karen.

They laughed and it broke the tension. Within a few minutes Jean-Luc was telling them a story about his father who fought in the second World War.

Brandje listened as long as she could, but it took hardly any time at all before she was fast asleep.

She awakened for only a moment when Nathan lifted her head and slid off the sofa. He picked her up and carried her upstairs to her room where Karen had turned down the bedding.

"Mmm," she whispered. "Sorry."

"Sleep on," he whispered back as he placed her upon the bed and pulled the comforter over her. Then he kissed her forehead and left the bedroom.

Brandje smiled dreamily and went back to sleep, too tired to listen to the faint whisper of voices downstairs.

Later that night, Nathan paced back and forth across the living room floor. Jean-Luc and Karen had already bid goodnight and retired upstairs some time ago. But Nathan doubted he would sleep at all.

It had been five weeks since Brandje's surgery. Five weeks! People usually recover in that length of time. He didn't even know what kind of surgery she'd had. He didn't know how serious it was, he didn't know anything about it. She wouldn't tell him.

He suspected Karen knew, the two women had grown tenaciously close. He'd even approached Karen about Brandje's health one afternoon the past week when Brandje was napping. He remembered the moment with exact clarity.

Karen stood at the kitchen counter, pinning a doily she had tatted onto a fabric covered board, preparing to spray it with starch.

Nathan sauntered in, nonchalant as he could manage, and asked casually, "How do you think Brandje's doing?"

"Good," Karen replied.

"She seems to be healing from her surgery well?"

"She does."

"Sometimes I see something in her eyes, like she's trying to hide some kind of pain she's having."

"Hmm," Karen mused aloud.

"Does she still have that pain, the kind that made her faint that first morning you were here?" he asked.

"You'll have to ask her that question," said Karen.

Her answer irritated him and it took great effort on his part to control his temper. Finally, in a straight forward manner he said, "It seems to me that she's getting worse, not better."

Karen only shrugged.

Nathan persisted. "Karen, I have strong feelings for Brandje. Surely you've noticed that."

"I have."

"Then why won't you tell me what's going on with her?"

"I think that's up to Brandje," Karen stated. "Now, stand back. I'm going to spray this with starch."

Nathan realized it was Karen's way of saying that, as far as she was concerned, the conversation was over.

Now, several days later, he felt that he had reached the end of his endurance level. He couldn't understand why Brandje could go several days without a hint of illness. Then, without any warning, she seemed to succumb to something inside her that was progressively getting worse.

Nathan knelt at the sofa and poured his soul out to God, asking for answers to all the questions that troubled his heart. When he was done, he waited for those answers to come, but he was beyond feeling.

He sighed wearily when he finally stood up. Then he turned out the lights and went up to his bedroom. Once he was in bed, he opened the Bible and began to read. But the scriptures he wanted most were in Brandje's room, and he didn't dare disturb her to get them.

In desperation, he closed his eyes and quoted every Book of Mormon scripture he had ever committed to memory. When the effort had exhausted him, he fell into a restless sleep.

Chapter Twelve

*O*n Sunday Brandje accepted Nathan's and the Rousseaus' invitation to go to church with them in Nantes. Although she had rested most of Saturday, the ride over to Nantes tired her. With grim determination, she mentioned this fact to no one. She didn't want anything to disturb the calm in her stormy relationship with Nathan.

At the meetinghouse, Brandje was introduced to dozens of people who shook her hand, smiled brightly, and welcomed her to the ward. They seemed genuinely happy to meet her, and Brandje was surprised at their efforts to make her feel as though she had finally come home. It was an experience in love that she could neither analyze nor explain.

In Sunday School class, she sat between Nathan and Karen, with Nathan holding her hand. She listened attentively as Jean-Luc gave a lesson from several chapters in the Book of Mormon.

Nathan had suggested earlier that Brandje attend an investigators class with him, but she flatly refused. She didn't consider herself an investigator. Besides, she had been looking forward to hearing Jean-Luc teach his class. The chapters that Jean-Luc presented his lesson on happened to be some that Brandje had read that very week, from the Book of Helaman. Jean-Luc was able to clear up several points about the prophet Samuel, who could not be injured when he preached upon a great wall, even though arrows were shot at him.

It was interesting to Brandje that everyone at Sunday meetings addressed Jean-Luc as Bishop Rousseau. Even Nathan called him

Bishop Rousseau today, as he had on that first day they were together. She recalled that Bishop Rousseau had insisted he was to be called Jean-Luc when he was outside of the gospel setting. Jean-Luc was the only name Brandje had ever used to address him.

Relief Society was an important highlight of her visit. All of the women called one another sister. Karen suddenly became Sister Rousseau, and even Brandje was addressed as Sister Fulton. Brandje learned that the practice was a constant reminder that they were all members of one large family, with God as their First and Eternal Father, who was now separated from them by a thin, yet penetrable veil.

Sacrament meeting kept her interest up as well. Young boys, many of them not much older than twelve or thirteen, passed the sacrament to the members. This surprised Brandje.

The church seemed to have its members come right up out of the congregation to be the speakers. The Bishop of the ward, a man named Buerge, didn't give any sermon at all. He just sat back and let another man conduct the meeting.

Brandje whispered to Nathan, "Don't they pay Bishop Buerge enough to give the sermon?"

Nathan stifled a chuckle, as did Karen and Jean-Luc.

"The church has no paid ministry," Nathan explained.

"That's why he doesn't speak much," Brandje observed.

"No," said Nathan. "When he feels moved upon by the spirit of the Lord, he speaks to us. Or when it's part of an assignment from the stake, or when it's his turn."

"His turn?" asked Brandje.

Karen smiled warmly at both Brandje and Nathan. "She needs to come more often, so she can get a sense of what it is that we do here."

While Nathan nodded, Brandje remained silent. What she really wanted was a straight answer. Why were they deliberately evasive? She closed her eyes and bowed her head for a moment, whispering her concerns silently, asking the Lord to respond.

Halfway through the concluding speaker's talk, Bishop Buerge stood up and whispered to him for a moment. The man concluded his speech shortly thereafter and the bishop, a portly man with dark brown hair and round blue eyes, came to the podium.

"Brothers and sisters," Bishop Buerge began. "Sometimes the spirit moves us when we least expect it, and that has happened here this afternoon. Someone in our congregation has asked the Lord why I'm not giving a sermon today. The spirit has asked me to bear my testimony to that person, and that is what I'm going to do."

Brandje's mouth fell open, as did her companions. She listened carefully to the bishop as he spoke about the duties and obligations that he had, now that he was bishop of the ward. He confessed his love to the congregation, and thanked them for all that they do to make his workload lighter.

Then Bishop Buerge looked straight at Brandje and said, "I testify in the name of the Lord, Jesus Christ, that the Book of Mormon is true. Every word is from God. There is no truer book on the face of the earth. If you will read it and ask God, he will tell you in your heart, and in your mind, and in your soul that it is true. Seven years ago I sat in your place and wondered who the bishop was, and why he didn't preach a sermon every Sunday. Seven years ago I was reading the Book of Mormon and seeking answers, like you are. I read, I prayed, and I received a divine witness that God heard my prayers. My testimony to you is your witness that God hears and answers your prayers. I testify that God loves you and will give you the answers which you seek. Continue to pray to Him, and He will guide you wherever you may go."

He concluded his testimony in the name of Jesus Christ. The congregation sang a hymn, bowed their heads for the benediction, and it was over.

Brandje knew now, like she'd never known before, that God does hear and answer prayers, sometimes instantaneously.

Her companions could speak of little else all the way back to Croix de Vie. Yes, it was a miraculous thing, Brandje agreed. But she didn't feel like shouting it from the rooftops as they did. She felt irritable and uneasy. Her abdomen hurt and she took a pain pill immediately upon returning home.

Without supper, Brandje retired early to rest. By six in the evening she was sound asleep.

Around two in the morning Brandje awakened. She slipped into the bathroom and took another pain pill. It was the first time she'd had to take two in less than twelve hours, but she couldn't bear the pain in the upper right portion of her abdomen any longer.

Back in her bedroom, she closed the door and turned on a lamp beside the bed. She picked up the Book of Mormon and held it in her lap as she positioned the pillows just right. Then she began reading.

She was now in third Nephi. It didn't take her very long to become absorbed in the story of the great destruction that came upon the Lamanites and Nephites at the time of the Savior's crucifixion. Then came the resurrection.

Brandje's spirit was caught up in the miracles that occurred as Jesus showed Himself unto the survivors in the land Bountiful. Her mind and her heart were opened with visions of Christ's visit, and of His dissertations to the remaining people. With great reverence, she spiritually witnessed the repentance and the humility of the Nephites.

When she came to the seventeenth chapter of third Nephi Brandje paused. She heard a still small voice within, telling her that the scriptures she now read were some she had read before, in a dream she'd been given weeks previous. She understood that this chapter was written for her time, for the people who've lived upon the earth since the Book of Mormon was translated, and more particularly, for her. Brandje read the seventeenth chapter of Nephi over and over again, and feasted upon the spirit whispering to her heart and soul that it was true.

Never before had she read such tender scenes in the Savior's life as this. The Savior wept just as all humans weep at some time. This made Jesus seem so real to her, much more human than the one-dimensional personage whom she'd been taught about in her youth. For the first time in her life she had a clear picture of who the Savior was, and she wept, knowing that He, her elder brother, could cry also, just like Martin wept that night when Dr. Graham telephoned.

Her mind was opened up to greater revelations and she saw the Savior weeping specifically for her. *He is real,* Brandje realized. *Jesus is a real person, with deep feelings of love for me and for all His brothers and sisters. The Savior loves me!* Brandje marveled in absolute wonder at the amount of love He felt for her.

With absolute clarity, her heart and mind were filled with images of

Jesus Christ that she'd never imagined before. With love in His heart and tears in His eyes, He testified that everything she'd read in the Book of Mormon was true. The realization filled her with peace and harmony like none other. Further understanding touched her spirit: If this much was true, then the Church of Jesus Christ of Latter-day Saints was, indeed, the only true church upon the earth. Because of the great visions opened up to her, Brandje now had absolute knowledge that Alma, while baptizing in the waters of Mormon, had authority from God to act in His name.

After the vision of Alma, she saw the Savior stretch forth his hand, in which He held a scroll. He revealed to her the names that were written upon it. How thrilled she was to see that her name was upon the scroll that the Savior showed to her. In fact, hers was at the top of the list.

Gratitude filled her soul and spilled over. She could no longer contain all the joy that spread through her. With humility in her heart, she knelt beside the bed and thanked the Lord for everything that she had been given, and expressed her gratefulness for the visions she had received. She thanked her Father in Heaven for her mother and father, for Martin, Karen and Jean-Luc, Marcelle and Henry, and for Elisha. Last, but certainly not least, she thanked God for Nathan.

During her prayer, she asked the Lord for nothing. She felt that she needed nothing He did not already know about. With all the fervor she possessed, she thanked God for all her blessings. As she did so, a thought popped into her mind that she could not dismiss. The list she'd seen in the Savior's hand, the list with her name upon it, was symbolic of something else. With tears of joy, yet also tears of dread, Brandje realized it was the donor list upon which her name belonged, the list for which she had not yet given her consent.

Brandje also realized that, whether Nathan loved her or not, her allegiance belonged to God. Whether Martin needed her or not, God needed her name on that donor list. It was part of His plan for her, although she didn't understand it completely. But she knew, when she arose from her knees early that morning, that she would have to fulfill God's plan for her.

She sat on her bed for a long while afterward, thinking on the miracles that had occurred within her bedroom. Never in her wildest dreams had she ever imagined the Savior could take such a personal interest in her. When finally the first rays of daylight danced upon the bedroom curtain, she prepared herself for a new day.

Within a few moments she washed her face, brushed her hair, slipped into a comfortable summer outfit, and stepped outside the bedroom. Nathan's door was closed and she could hear his gentle snoring behind it. She may have a few minutes before the household awakened, she hoped, to telephone her brother.

Sitting at the desk in the living room, she dialed the number. As she waited for him to answer, she realized he may be outdoors already, feeding the livestock or doing chores. Brandje was delighted when she finally heard Martin's voice answer, "Fulton here."

"Martin," she said cheerfully, "remember me?"

"Brandje!" he exclaimed.

She heard footsteps on the stairs and hesitated. "Can you hold for a minute, Martin?" she asked.

"Of course."

Brandje covered the mouthpiece with her hand and looked up to see Karen coming down the stairs, already dressed for the day.

Brandje sighed in relief. "Oh, it's you. I thought for a minute that it was Nathan."

"I can go back upstairs, if you'd like some privacy dear," said Karen.

"No," Brandje gave her a bright smile. "I think you'll want to hear what I have to say."

Karen sat down on the corner of the desk, eager to listen.

"Just keep an eye open for Nathan," Brandje insisted.

Karen nodded and Brandje returned to her telephone conversation with Martin.

"Are you still there?" she asked into the mouthpiece.

"Yes, but who's there with you?"

"Karen Rousseau," Brandje smiled. "She's the dearest woman I've ever met."

Relief was evident in his voice as Martin asked, "Oh, a woman, then?"

"Yes," replied Brandje. "But listen to what I need to tell you, please Martin. And don't say a word until I've finished."

"All right, you have my undivided attention."

Brandje gulped. "Martin, I know about the cancer."

She heard him gasp. "I–I —" he stammered. Then he asked, "Are you all right? You're not —?"

"Shhh," she reminded. "Listen. I can't take long, I don't want to wake up the others."

"The others?" Martin asked at once.

"Shhh," Brandje insisted. "Martin please!"

He stopped speaking immediately, so she continued. "Thank you. Now this is what I want you to do. Call Dr. Graham and tell him to put me on the donor list. I need to go on it straight away. I won't stay in hospital until they find a donor, though. I have a special nurse who has agreed to stay with me, if need be. Do you understand?"

"Yes," he agreed.

"I may have to sell the villa to help pay for it," she said. "And I still have my share of Father's life insurance."

"Brandje," he said. "I have a confession to make."

"What?" she questioned, wondering what it could be.

"I sold the farm."

"You what?" she asked, her voice louder than she intended.

"I sold the farm. I told Dr. Graham last week to put you on the donor list. I planned to arrive there at the end of the month, when everything here is finalized. I hoped to drag you to the United States, if need be, so you would be available to receive your transplant."

"You sold the farm?" Brandje asked in a sad whisper.

"Brandje, what good is the farm if you're not here?"

"But Martin, that's your livelihood."

"I could live off the interest from my share of Father's life insurance for the rest of my life and be happy," he admitted. "I'd been thinking about it for quite a while, even before I knew about . . ." He hesitated. "Brandje, I'm sorry I didn't tell you about the cancer. Is there any chance you'll forgive me in this century?"

"Of course," she agreed readily. "Martin, I don't know what to say. I hadn't expected you to tell me that you even knew."

"I wasn't going to, not at first. But since you left, I began to feel as though I'd betrayed you."

"You did," she admitted, "because I was in the kitchen when Dr. Graham called that night."

He gasped. His voice trembled as he asked, "You've known all this time?"

"I went to see Dr. Graham that same week."

He sighed. "I should have told you straight away. I should have shared this burden with you."

Suddenly she heard Nathan's door open upstairs.

"Martin, there's a lot that I haven't told you, but I will," she promised. "I'll try to call you later. I've got to go now."

"But Brandje?"

"Later, Martin. Bye for now."

She hung up the receiver before Nathan had a chance to come downstairs. Fortunately he went into the bathroom first.

"Come with me," said Karen, taking Brandje's hand and leading her out through the back door. She led her to the largest of two patio settees and sat her upon it. "What's happened to you?" she asked. "Did you and Nathan talk things over?"

"No," said Brandje. "But God and I did."

Karen inhaled sharply, her eyes brimming with tears.

"Now don't you start," said Brandje. "I just can't do the tears anymore. I'm exhausted from them, aren't you?"

Karen hugged her tightly. "I'm glad to hear it," she admitted.

Nathan watched from the kitchen door as the two women hugged briefly while visiting on the back patio. It annoyed him that Brandje could confide in Karen, but not in him. He didn't know how to earn Brandje's confidence or trust, and he feared he had once again let his anger destroy their relationship by going off with Isabelle, and then spending the rest of the week fuming over her appointment to meet Pierre. Nathan sighed. Would he ever win the heart of the woman who had stolen his? He pushed the back door open and walked outside. "There you are," he said to Brandje and Karen. "I thought I heard someone downstairs."

Brandje stood up and walked straight over to him, "Good morning," she said. She stood on tiptoe and pulled him down close enough to reach his cheek, where she planted a quick kiss. "Isn't it a beautiful morning?"

"You didn't go out to the Point this morning, did you?" he asked, concern for her etched in his voice.

"Don't be silly," she said. "That won't happen for two more weeks. Haven't you looked at the tide tables at all?"

Karen slipped past them and went back into the house, without their being aware of it.

"I looked at them," he said. "That's why I was concerned. The tide's too high to watch sunrise from the Point."

"You know what," she grinned mischievously. "You worry too much."

"Well, " he drawled, "someone has to worry about you."

"Why?" she asked. "I feel wonderful today." To emphasize her point she took his hands and did a very fast polka with him around the patio, singing lightly as she did.

Soon he was caught up in her happy mood. It wasn't long before Karen and Jean-Luc brought out a CD player and turned it on, then danced with them as the sun began to sprinkle streaks of light across the lawn and patio.

When they had danced and laughed so hard their sides ached, they collapsed on the patio furniture and giggled even more.

The sun warmed Brandje's feet and legs as she stretched out on the settee, using Nathan's thigh for a pillow.

"I can't figure you out," he admitted. "In the morning you're vibrant and full of life. By evening you feel miserable, and you're pale."

"I don't do evenings well, do I?" she bantered.

He smiled. "At sunrise, you go through some kind of metamorphosis, and become this beautiful imp who dances about singing silly songs and changing everyone's demeanor for the better."

"Face it, Nathan," she teased. "I'm just a walking miracle."

He stroked her hair. "Can you believe her?" he asked Jean-Luc and Karen.

As they responded affirmatively to his question, a thought occurred to Brandje that she hadn't ever considered. This morning she had been cheerful and bright, and it had lifted everyone's mood. The realization that she had the power to do that, made her feel special somehow.

Silently she made a promise to her Father in Heaven that she would try her best to keep the others' spirits up.

She wondered for a moment at the change that had come over her since the Lord spoke to her a few hours ago. She still had cancer. She was still dying. Without a donor, she would most certainly die by Christmas. But now, her prognosis no longer mattered.

She was a special person, a daughter of God, a sister to the Savior. God had a plan for her, and a special purpose. Perhaps it was nothing more than to help everyone else get through the coming months. Perhaps being on the list would do absolutely no good at all. Perhaps they would not find a donor, and she would die anyway. Maybe God's entire plan was that she learn to give comfort to those around her. Maybe she was supposed to be bright and cheerful for them.

She didn't know all the answers. Delicate as an unopened blossom, Brandje was still gaining knowledge about God like a plant receives nourishment. The only thing she knew for certain regarding what God expected of her, was that her happiness was contagious, and she would try her hardest never to lose sight of that again. It was a special gift God had bestowed upon her. Now that she knew she had it, she would cling to it with all her strength.

Chapter Thirteen

Early Wednesday morning, Brandje and Nathan waved goodbye to Jean-Luc and Karen. Then Nathan headed the Mercedes Benz toward the Loire River, holding Brandje's hand as she sat on the seat beside him. When they arrived at the Loire, they turned East and followed the gentle road leading toward Chinon.

They stopped near Challones for a light, continental breakfast served outdoors on wrought iron tables with red and white table covers. Soon they were on the road again, driving through the stomping grounds of Joan of Arc.

"Look," said Brandje as they passed an estate that appeared as though it had been built as early as the seventeenth century.

The immaculate gardens were trimmed to perfection, with rose trees, camellias, gardenias, jasmine, and all manner of other summer flowers. Two large buildings, separated by a flowering vine tunnel, graced the property. Both roofs, covered with a charcoal-colored thatching, had smooth, rolled edges at all the gables. The smaller of the two buildings had four red-trimmed dormers in the front, with a flurry of vinery growing all over the cream-colored limestone blocks from which the exterior walls were built.

Nathan slowed down so Brandje could view the gardens better. "It's called the Chateau Chenonceaux," he explained, "with the most elegant gardens in the entire Loire Valley. The buildings maintain a style reminiscent of King Henry the Second, the time period in which they were built."

"It's beautiful," she said as they passed by slowly. Then they continued on their journey.

The countryside was dotted with dairy, cattle and sheep farms, as well as vineyards. Atlantic winds penetrated the Loire Basin, giving it a Mediterranean atmosphere. Palms, eucalyptus, cedars, magnolias, camellias and fig trees grew wild along the roadway. The scented fragrance of blossoms mingled with the earthy smell of grape vineyards.

"Chinon is famous for fresh red wine," Nathan told her, "made from the Cabernet Franc grape. Soon you'll smell the heavy fragrance of green peppers and pea pods, but don't be fooled. It's only the aroma of the Cabernet Franc. In this part of the country, they say the earthy fragrance is actually the smell of money."

"I thought Chinon was well known for white wine," said Brandje, surprised at his description.

"Yes," he agreed. "There are more than eleven different varieties of grapes grown here, and that many more wines. Some are nurtured religiously in the white limestone caves that abound in the area. The entire Loire valley is also known as the gentle garden. Nearly all edible plant species are cultivated here. White asparagus, grown between the Loir and Sologne branches of the Loire River, is considered the most delicate vegetable in the world."

"I've tried it," she agreed, "and you are correct. It is beyond delicious."

Driving through Chinon, Brandje noted how the streets were made entirely of brick tiles. These were undoubtedly red to begin with, but time and traffic had changed the color to a brownish red. The tiles were pressed so close together it would be impossible to wedge a credit card between the pieces. She saw no formal sidewalks, the street stretched right up to the shop doors. Fortunately, there were also few vehicles. It seemed as though they had stepped back in time two hundred years. The buildings lining the street were made with cream-colored, limestone bricks of uneven shapes and sizes, mortared together with a pale gray cement. Wrought iron balconies jutted out from the second-story buildings, where shop owners usually resided above their places of business. A man with a gray beret, farmer pants, a plaid shirt and three long fishing poles waited patiently for them to pass before crossing the street to the other side.

When they arrived in Chinon, Nathan turned the Mercedes onto the Avenue Gambetta and parked in front of a stately white brick home the size of a small mansion. Pots of geraniums and begonias hedged the building, the scent of eucalyptus hung heavily in the air, and bright camellias bloomed freely along the sides of the house.

Brandje could feel excitement welling up inside her when Nathan held the car door open.

"Mademoiselle," he bowed, "welcome to the *Château de Richelieu*." Brandje took his hand and stepped out of the car. "Nathan, it's beautiful!" she exclaimed.

Before Brandje could comment further, she heard a gleeful squeal from inside the house.

The front door opened and a petite, older woman rushed forward with arms outstretched. *"Ma petit-fils!"* she exclaimed, reaching up on tiptoe to pat Nathan's cheeks, as only a grandmother would. Her silver white hair was pulled into a bun at the nape of her neck, her dark brown eyes were a reflection of Nathan's. She wore a blue floral house dress with a white bib apron, tied neatly around her tiny waist.

Nathan bent over and planted a big kiss on his grandmother's cheek. "Grandmaman! How I've missed you!"

Noticing Brandje by Nathan's side, she grinned, and in careful English said, "But let us not be rude. This is the young woman of whom Isabelle spoke?"

"Grandmaman Richelieu, meet Brandje Fulton," Nathan introduced his companion with a wink and a smile. "Just what did Isabelle tell you?" he asked seriously.

"It is of no importance," the old woman waved his question away. "Your, how you say, *cheri*, is much lovelier than described."

"She speaks fluent French, Grandmaman," Nathan informed his grandmother.

"Ah! C'est vrai?" the woman asked.

"Yes, it's true," Brandje replied, grateful for the many months she'd spent at the villa with her grandfather, who'd insisted she speak only

French to him.

"We will speak the English," Grandmaman declared with an air of authority. "I need the practice, *non?*"

Brandje smiled. "May I call you by your given name?" she asked.

"Please, call me Grandmaman. After all, you are my grandson's *ami de la fille . . . Cheri?* Sweetheart! *C'est vrai?*"

Brandje opened her mouth to correct the older woman but Nathan nudged her and frowned ominously. She smiled and remained silent.

The Richelieu's spacious home was decorated in typical French Provincial, with marble Parque floors, mahogany furnishings and handmade tapestries. The main floor held a sitting room, a long, formal dining room, a massive, well-implemented kitchen, and maid's quarters. There were five bedrooms and three bathrooms on the second floor. A walk-in attic, and a fruit cellar for storage and wines, completed the impressive chateau.

Brandje accompanied Grandmaman into the kitchen while Nathan carried the suitcases upstairs.

"Tonight," the old woman beamed, "we will travel to Azay le Rideau to see the Image de la Touraine, Symbole de la France. It is a special program, one that is honored this year by Isabelle's performance." A smile of pride swept across Grandmaman's wrinkled face. "You will go with us, will you not?" she asked candidly.

"I can't speak for Nathan, but I would be honored." Brandje agreed.

"I've already said yes," Nathan interrupted as he walked into the kitchen. "I understand Isabelle is an outstanding dancer."

"Ah, and boastful, too!" Grandmaman chuckled.

"That, too," Nathan agreed.

Brandje hadn't been given the opportunity to get to know Isabelle, and now she felt a bit resentful at their praise of her. "Nathan, I'm anxious to see the formal gardens you told me about," she suggested.

"Is that all right with you, Grandmaman?" Nathan asked.

"We shall lunch by one," the old woman answered with a nod.

They exited through the kitchen door. Nathan casually placed his arm around Brandje's shoulder. She was glad for his support. The pain in her stomach had subsided for the most part, and she enjoyed moments when she could melt against him. This was a special time for her.

She tried to ignore what little resentment she still felt toward Isabelle, and Nathan's game of deception at not introducing them.

He led her into a beautiful garden of Hyacinths, narcissi, cyclamens and dahlias. The formal gardens were surrounded by fruit trees of every kind, and beyond the orchards swirled the graceful Loire River. The peaceful setting assuaged some of her resentment as they walked along a paved pathway near the banks of the Loire River. After a long silence, Brandje whispered, "It's lovely here, Nathan."

Nathan sighed. "It's my fault that you don't care much for Isabelle," he admitted.

"It shows that much?" she asked.

Nathan nodded.

Grateful they were out of hearing range of the house, Brandje said, "I would have liked the opportunity to get to know her. It is your fault that I feel a little resentful."

"I'm sorry," he apologized. "The last thing either one of you needs is a wedge that I've driven between you. What can I do to help you get over this?"

Surprised by his apology, she looked up into his dark brown eyes, and concentrated her gaze upon his lips, sensual and inviting. "I'll think of something," she suggested flirtatiously.

Without another word of encouragement, Nathan gathered her into his arms and kissed her thoroughly. Her arms went around his neck and she wound her fingers in his thick, sandy-brown hair.

The clicking of a woman's heels upon the pavement stopped them both. Brandje stared into his brown-black eyes as he arched an eyebrow. She couldn't decide whether he'd enjoyed the kiss or not. It was, after all, her ploy. She had suggested that he kiss her, even though no words had passed her lips, as penitence for his deceitfulness about Isabelle.

"I'm sorry," came the voice of a familiar French girl. "I do not wish to interrupt your little games, but Grandmaman is ready for the lunch." Isabelle waited patiently for a response.

"Bother!" Brandje mumbled beneath her breath.

"What was that?" Nathan whispered in her ear.

"I said, I hope she didn't go to any bother," Brandje replied hastily. Nathan gave her a knowing smile and escorted both women back to the house.

Sitting in the large dining room, Brandje listened with interest as Nathan and Isabelle monopolized the conversation throughout lunch. Isabelle, ecstatic about her role in the Touraine, was still much like a child in her enthusiasm and sense of adventure, a darling teenager, eager to please, one with a loving and generous nature. On their first acquaintance Brandje had been so blinded by jealousy she had not been willing to think anything good about Isabelle. Now she could see that Isabelle was not a threat to Brandje whatsoever.

Nathan took an active interest in his cousin, encouraging Isabelle in a dancing and acting career, since that was her desire. He suggested several techniques that may help her in landing larger parts, and asked for permission to recommend her to a well-known master in the acting arena as a gift for her eighteenth birthday.

Brandje could imagine him counseling his own daughter or son years from now. He would allow no generation gap to separate him from his children. He was far too astute to allow that to happen.

When she finally sensed a break in the flow of conversation, Brandje stood up. "I don't mean to be rude," she said, "but I would like to rest for a while before we go to the performance tonight."

"Please," said Grandmaman Richelieu, "Do as you wish, Brandje. Isabelle told me you were ill, and with my manners, I did not think."

"I'm feeling well enough," said Brandje. "But I know that if I don't nap this afternoon, you will not want me to attend with you tonight."

"Ah, you must have a temper like my *petit-fils*?" she asked, swatting Nathan on the shoulder. "This is not good to hear at all."

"Actually, his temper is improving," Brandje said. She bent over to whisper in Grandmaman's ear, "I've learned how to get even."

Grandmaman smiled. "That is good to hear," she said. "Ah, so like his Grandpapa, is my Nathan." Then she made the sign of the cross and whispered, "May he rest in peace."

Brandje smiled. She gave the tiny woman a kiss on the cheek.

"Thank you for a delicious lunch," she said.

Grandmaman hugged her back and Brandje went quickly upstairs.

On the second floor, Brandje saw a door that opened into a large bedroom with twin beds, pink fluff curtains and matching bedspreads. Floral-stitched quilts were folded neatly at the foot of each bed, and her overnight bag rested on the bed to her left. She removed her shoes and put the bag on the floor, then stretched out lazily on the bed to rest. Before long she began to shiver. She pulled the quilt up over her and tried to sleep, but thoughts of Nathan kept her awake.

Nathan's interest in his extended family made Brandje realize that he would become a sterling father some day. She wondered if the Lord intended her to become the mother of Nathan's future children. Why wouldn't Nathan tell her how he felt about her? For all that she knew, she was just a summer fling.

Why? she asked herself. *Why is he so irresistible? Why couldn't he be short or fat or bald?* Then she smiled to herself. Martin was already getting bald on top, with a few silver streaks on the sides of his auburn hair, yet she'd always considered Martin a handsome man. Her grandfather had been short, stout and jolly, yet Brandje still loved him, regardless of his outward appearance.

Was it just Nathan's handsome, rugged exterior that she loved, or was it the man inside? If he were disfigured today in a horrible accident, would she still love him? Her heart sang out a resounding *YES!*

Her thoughts turned next to the miracle of her conversion, as it always did just before she fell asleep. Nathan didn't know about it yet. The only one with the slightest glimpse of what had happened to Brandje's spiritual inclinations was Karen.

Yet Brandje's faith, even at that very moment, had not faded one iota since that morning in her bedroom. She had a strong desire to be baptized, and soon. Now that she'd read the Book of Mormon, and received the witness that Moroni had spoken of, she must learn what comes next. Would she be able to find someone who could baptize her?

Since Monday, she'd finished reading the Book of Mormon, and had started on another book in Nathan's binder called the Doctrine and Covenants. She didn't understand the complete story regarding Joseph Smith, or what his calling in the Church of Jesus Christ of Latter-day

Saints was. She had many questions that remained unanswered and she could hardly restrain herself from asking Nathan about them.

Even with her name on the donor list, she could still be going home soon, for death doesn't wait for donors. Her fragile life was imminently shortened with the passing of each hour. Her baptism would have to be performed soon, or all would be lost.

With these troubled thoughts on her mind, Brandje fell asleep.

Late that afternoon Brandje sat beside Nathan, while his grandmother and Isabelle rode in the back seat, as they drove toward Azay le Rideau for the annual Son et Lumiere.

The air was warm against her body, filling her with a sense of relief that she had rested well and was now refreshed. She wanted this evening to be an especially memorable one, to recall with fondness in the months ahead.

The performance was magnificent from beginning to end: The actors wore costumes dating back to the thirteenth century, and the presentation gave a brief sketch of the Touraine History in song and dance through each generation to the present. Isabelle's choreography was skillfully executed as she portrayed Maria Jazelle, who befriended Joan of Arc in 1429.

At the conclusion, the crowd grew wild with applause. The curtains reopened four times for additional cheering. After the massive theater was vacated, they visited Isabelle backstage.

"Was it not splendid, the performance?" Isabelle gushed. Her enthusiasm was ecstatic, like a child at Christmas. "You have invited Brandje to come to the festival?" she asked Nathan.

"Festival?" Brandje queried.

Nathan shrugged. "Just a little family gathering that is celebrated every year after the performance."

"Oh, please, Nathan," Brandje entreated. "May we go?"

"You might be sorry once you've met all my relatives," he

suggested, "and their relatives, and their —"

"Please?" Brandje interrupted him.

"I'm a pushover," he admitted, grinning at his grandmother.

Isabelle squealed with delight and hugged Brandje ferociously. "You will love it!" she exclaimed. "We have an enormous family, and many, many handsome cousins!"

Nathan pouted, but Isabelle punched him in the arm playfully.

It was obvious to Brandje that Isabelle was little more than a child, teasing her cousin mercilessly, living her life for each moment that came to her. It was rather refreshing to Brandje, and she finally felt herself warming to Isabelle.

The festival was held in the courtyard of what was once the Richelieu Castle, near Chinon. This rather obtrusive building, no less than four hundred years old, had been held in the family name for nearly two centuries before it was sold. Out of respect, the current owners permitted the courtyard to be utilized by the Richelieu clan each summer, following the *Son et Lumiere*. Illuminated by lanterns strung from lamp pole to lamp pole, and trees decorated with thousands of tiny white lights, the courtyard was the perfect gathering place for Nathan's kinsmen.

Several tables were set up all around the area, some for holding buffet items so numerous they would never be eaten, even by a thousand guests. Other tables were prepared for guests to sit and enjoy the conversation, the food, and the ambiance. Musicians played in a corner on the piazza. Several varieties of local wines in goblets were carried around on trays by waiters dressed in white shirts, black pants and burgundy colored aprons.

By the time Brandje had been introduced to the twentieth relative, she began to lose track of names. She'd met cousins and second cousins, nieces and nephews thrice removed and scores of aunts and uncles, both grand and great.

After two hours of introductions, there still seemed to be no end in sight, nor end in numbers of new arrivals. Brandje put on a happy smile, and tried to endure cheerfully. But even her feet were beginning to complain as they walked up and down the spacious courtyard visiting with, what seemed to her, total strangers.

One particularly beautiful woman with blonde hair done up in a twist, and quite a remarkable figure, approached them on the arm of an older man, whom Brandje recognized as Isabelle's father, Nathan's Uncle Charles, who collected and sold antique automobiles.

"Nathan, darling," the woman gushed.

"Anneva?" asked Nathan. "What's it been, four years?"

"Five," she teased, taking hold of his tie and bringing his face nearer hers.

He straightened and gradually worked his tie out of her grip.

"You must come with me," Anneva said, "Tante Madeline is in a positive stew! She will only rest if you settle a disagreement."

"He's not too good at things like that," Brandje suggested with a giggle. "But he's all yours, if you think you can handle him."

Nathan looked at her as though she'd run him through with a sword. "But —" he protested.

"Oh, go on, Nathan," encouraged Uncle Charles. "I'll keep an eye on Brandje for you."

"That's what I'm worried about," said Nathan as Anneva grabbed him once more by the tie and led him away under duress.

"Don't worry," teased Charles. "I only collect antiques."

Brandje laughed as Charles held out his arm and escorted her toward the opposite end of the courtyard where he offered her delicious petit choux from a refreshment table.

"What I really need," she confided, "is a drink —"

Before she could finish, Charles raised a hand and snapped his fingers together. Within seconds a waiter materialized almost out of nowhere with a tray of wine glasses filled to the brim.

"— of water," she suggested.

Charles apologized and patted her hand patronly. He handed the waiter a generous gratuity and said, "Bring Miss Brandje a bottle of artesian water." The waiter pocketed the money, nodded, and departed immediately.

Meanwhile, Charles escorted her along a floral pathway until they reached a stone and mortar summerhouse. He offered her a seat on a nearby settee next to the door of the summerhouse and glanced around to see whether the waiter was coming back with her water.

"You are tired," Charles guessed, sitting beside her. His voice held just enough tenderness to be convincing.

"I am," she agreed. She swept her honey blonde hair off one shoulder to let it cascade down her back.

"Your hair," Charles said with a smile, "is the talk of the family tonight. No one has ever seen this color, like pure, golden honey, and so long and beautiful. Isabelle is green with envy, as are her cousins."

Brandje blushed with delight at receiving such a sweet compliment. "I'm told my mother's hair was this color," she offered.

"You should always wear it long and flowing down your back like you do," he suggested. "Very few women can wear it this way with any success. But you," he sighed. "Ah, Nathan is a very lucky man!"

"Thank you." She gave him a tender smile.

The waiter arrived and presented them with a bottle of pure sparkling water and a goblet on a small silver tray. "Thank you," Charles said, taking the tray in one hand. Then he sent the man away with a wave of the other.

While Charles poured the water, Brandje opened her handbag and removed a pain pill from within. After taking her medication, she said, "Thank you so much. You're very kind."

"So, what do you think of our family?" asked Charles, setting the tray aside. He made no inquiry as to her medical condition, for which Brandje was grateful.

"It's big," she said with a definite nod. Then added, "But I've had a lovely time."

"And Isabelle?" he questioned, unable to keep the fatherly pride from his voice.

Brandje smiled. "She is absolutely delightful."

"We have missed her this summer," he confessed. "She has been with her Grandmaman for six weeks now."

"That must be difficult," Brandje suggested. "Isabelle is such a charmer."

"Thank goodness the performance only runs another week, then she can come back home."

They were interrupted when the summerhouse door opened and two young men exited, paying no attention to Brandje or Charles, who sat near the open door, on the settee. Brandje recognized them as Lamonde and Bertrand, two of Nathan's cousins she'd been introduced to earlier in the evening.

Bertrand spoke first. "I noticed Anneva wasted no time in capturing our cousin from America."

"For tonight only," replied Lamonde. "I understand that Nathan is fond of the blonde he brought with him. He'll probably marry her."

"Too bad," Bertrand responded.

"Why?" asked Lamonde.

"I was thinking of marrying her myself!" Bertrand laughed.

Uncle Charles stood and clicked his heel against the ground to attract their attention.

The boys were stricken with surprise. "Forgive us, Miss Fulton," Lamonde implored her, his face taught with anxiety. "The last thing the Richelieu family needs is another upset with our cousin from America."

Brandje smiled, recalling Nathan's description of his family's opinion of him. The ogre, he'd said.

"I'm flattered," she responded. "But I'm afraid you both have the wrong idea. Nathan and I are not engaged."

"Rumors," Charles told her quickly. "Think nothing of their foolish remarks."

"If you have an interest in him," Bertrand warned, "I wouldn't leave Anneva alone with him."

"Silence!" Charles scolded, giving the boys a frown. "You may get away with talk like that now, but here comes Nathan, and Anneva is no longer with him."

The two young men paled, turned away, and made a hasty retreat, leaving them alone.

"Youth," Charles grumbled. "Anyone with maturity has long ago forgiven Nathaniel his harsh words to his cousins."

Brandje smiled as she stood up beside him, relieved to know the Richelieu clan still held Nathan in high esteem.

"Did Uncle Charles bring you to the garden for fresh air and a resting place, or did he have an ulterior motive?" Nathan asked when he arrived.

"Perhaps a little of both," Uncle Charles agreed. "At my age, to be seen in the company of such a beautiful woman is quite a feather in my cap."

"You scoundrel," Nathan teased. "I knew you couldn't be trusted."

"Your uncle has been a perfect gentleman," Brandje intervened. "He recognized when I'd had enough and took me out of the competition."

"He's got you fooled," Nathan replied. "Are you ready to go back?"

"Yes," she agreed, taking his offered hand.

As Charles accompanied them to the car, he said, "I told Isabelle I would bring her and Grandmaman home later on."

"Thank you," said Nathan. "I expect Brandje is getting tired."

Brandje nodded. "Thank you again, Uncle Charles. I enjoyed our little visit."

They bid farewell and soon Nathan had the Mercedes Benz parked back in front of the *Château de Richelieu*. He held the door open for her as she got out. "I had a lovely time, Nathan."

"Did you?" he asked. "I was beginning to think you wanted to get rid of me, the way you pawned me off on Anneva."

"You were having fun," she accused with a laugh. "I wasn't going to spoil it for you."

"Tante Madeline, Anneva's aunt, by the way, wanted to settle a dispute about us," he confessed. "Rumors have been circulating around the family."

"I heard them," she admitted. "Whoever started them?"

"Probably Isabelle," he laughed. "She adores you, and thinks you'll make a fine catch."

"Then I have her seal of approval?"

"And Grandmaman's," he admitted cautiously.

Brandje wanted to ask him if she had his approval as well, but she refused to give in to the temptation. She'd already given him several veiled suggestions, revealing her desire to know how he felt about her, as had many of his Richelieu cousins this evening—even in her presence! So far he'd evaded all their hints. She was unconvinced that Nathan loved her at all. Was Brandje just another woman who happened to cross his path? Would he have fun with her, tease her, romance her, without really caring about her the way that she wanted him to? Because of his evasiveness, she had serious doubts that he would ever return her love.

Regardless, Brandje was determined to keep her daily focus on remaining cheerful. She gave him a quiet smile.

Nathan took her by the hand, then led her into the house where they were greeted by two of Nathan's cousins who were staying at Grandmaman's during the vineyard season to work. Nathan quickly made an apology to them and led her up to the bedroom she would share with Isabelle.

After brushing his lips lightly against her forehead, he sighed, "Goodnight, Brandje."

"Goodnight," she whispered. As she entered the bedroom and closed the door behind her, she smiled to herself. She may not have Nathan's undying devotion, but she'd won the hearts of both his cousin and his grandmother. That should account for something!

For a few moments she wondered why she had not been jealous of Anneva tonight. Perhaps this lack of emotion came from the serenity she now felt knowing that God was mindful of her. She dropped to her knees and asked the Lord to help her understand Nathan more completely. She confessed that there was one thing she knew for certain . . . she could not go home to God without regrets unless she knew that Nathan would find some happiness in his life. If that happiness could not come from her, she genuinely wanted him to find someone from whom it could. It was probably the first unselfish thought she'd ever had in regards to Nathan, she realized. And it only confirmed the depth of love she had for him.

Changing the topic, she then asked God to help her find a way to talk to Nathan about getting baptized. She had to be baptized as soon as possible. Waiting for the right moment was not a luxury available to her. She didn't have enough time to play a waiting game where her eternal salvation was concerned.

Chapter Fourteen

Before noon the next morning, Nathan and Brandje bid farewell to his cousins and Grandmother, and were back on the road, driving through the quaint little town of Chinon.

"Would you like to go directly out to the Bay," Nathan suggested, "and drive up along the coast to the villa?"

"That depends," Brandje hesitated, having resolved one issue in her prayers earlier that morning.

"On what?" he asked.

"Well, you might want to stop the car first, perhaps somewhere quiet, so we can talk for a few minutes."

"Why?" questioned Nathan. "You think I can't talk and drive at the same time?" He gave her a little smirk.

She laughed. "Oh, I know you can talk and drive at the same time," she said. "And if that's how you want me to ask this question, then I'll proceed."

"Go ahead," he responded. "I think I can handle one question and the road at the same time."

She cleared her throat and gave him a beguiling expression. "Okay," she warned. "Are you ready?"

He smiled, obviously amused at her antics.

Brandje took a big breath. "Who would I have to talk to about getting baptized?"

Nathan's chin dropped, his eyes widened and his feet hit the brakes. He looked at her as though she'd kicked him in the shin! Then his eyebrows crinkled in a frown.

She gave him a saucy grin in response.

He quickly returned a grimace.

"What?" she asked in a lighthearted manner. "Is that such a tough question?"

"You're right," he grimly admitted. "Let's find a quiet spot where we can talk."

Now Brandje was worried. Was Nathan angry with her again? She hoped the topic of her baptism could be discussed joyfully. She'd promised the Lord that she would approach life in a cheerful way, and Nathan was spoiling it for her.

Within minutes he parked the car near a quiet little park that was, for the most part, abandoned, then he turned to face her. "Okay," he said, "Now, I'm ready."

Refusing to let his attitude defeat her resolve, she smiled brightly and tried a second time. "Nathan, I want to be baptized. I wonder if you know whom I would have to see to make the arrangements."

He blinked, but he didn't answer her.

Brandje tried a third time. "I'd like to get baptized as soon as possible. But I don't know who I should see about it. Nathan, surely you have some idea."

He stumbled over his words, his voice a mixture of confusion and distress. "Brandje, are . . . are you sure you understand what you're asking? "

Since she'd already made three attempts to get a straight answer, her resolve to keep the situation cheerful melted. Perhaps he didn't want her to get baptized. Irritated, Brandje's temper flared. "What is it with you, Nathan? Are you no longer a member of the Church of Jesus Christ of Latter-day Saints?"

"Of course, I'm a member!" he barked. "I'm still a Stake Missionary. Whatever gave you the idea that I wasn't a member?"

"Well, let's see!" she snapped smartly, counting the reasons on her fingers. "You refuse to talk religion with me. You refuse to discuss the Book of Mormon with me. You have no interest in teaching me anything about the church. You haven't asked me any Golden Questions. Am I getting close?"

"What?"

His voice seemed strained and she could tell her questions had made him uneasy. "If you can't answer one basic question about baptism," she pressured him, "what kind of Stake Missionary are you?"

He shook his head as he answered, "The kind who knows when to leave well enough alone. You're the one who said you always say no when someone asks if you want to know more about the church. I felt that when you were ready to know more, you'd ask."

"Don't get me wrong," she argued, "but it seems to me that I just asked, and look at the response I'm getting."

"You caught me off guard!" He sighed. "Try again." This time he swallowed and held his breath.

"Very well," she said, gathering courage once again. "Nathan, I need to get baptized right away. How do I go about it?"

He nodded as though he understood her question completely. "We can stop over in Nantes and make an appointment with the bishop. Would that suit you?"

"Can we do it today?" she asked. "I don't want to wait any longer."

"What's your hurry? You haven't had any of the discussions yet."

"There are discussions?" Brandje sighed in dismay.

"Yes, there are discussions." He ran his fingers through his hair. "After the discussions, you meet with the bishop for an interview. Then you need to decide who will baptize you, who will confirm you and give you the gift of the Holy Ghost."

"I have to choose?" she pouted. "But Nathan, I don't know anyone who can baptize me. Do you?"

He laughed so hard she felt relieved that he had parked the car and wasn't driving it at that moment.

"Let's see," he said when he finally stopped laughing. "There's

Nathaniel Duncan, for one —"

"You can?" she interrupted, unable to keep the surprise out of her voice. Then, hesitantly, she asked, "Do you want to baptize me?"

"Not until I'm convinced you know what you're doing!"

"How long will that take?"

"Brandje, you've given no logical reason why you want to be baptized. You've taken no discussions."

"Can't I take those after I'm baptized? I know they won't make any difference in how I feel."

"Getting baptized is not something that you enter into lightly. In this church, they don't baptize anyone who doesn't fully understand the significance of what the baptismal covenant means."

Brandje glared at him for a moment. Then her heart softened unexpectedly as she recalled the special vision she'd been given, and all that she'd read these past two weeks. "It means," she began calmly as her heart filled with the spirit of the Lord, "that I will no longer wander in darkness as did the people before Alma started baptizing in the waters of Mormon. I will be able to come out of the darkness and into the light. It means that all my sins will be washed away and I will become clean, like a newborn baby. It means that I will be able to receive the Holy Ghost as my constant companion, that I will become a pure and delightful daughter unto the Lord. It means that I'll be able to face Him when I . . ." She couldn't hold back the tears any longer and they spilled from her eyes. "I'll be able to face Him when I die, and He'll be able to look at me and welcome me into His arms." She sniffed, wiped at her eyes with a handkerchief from her purse, then continued. "I won't have to be afraid anymore because I know that God is my father. And Jesus Christ is my brother. They're my family and I belong to them. Can you possibly imagine what that means to me? To know that I actually belong to God! Have you been entrenched in the church so long that you've lost the vision of what the gospel is really all about? Or why God restored the church for people like me?"

Nathan's eyes spilled over as he faced her. "Let's take you to Nantes," he whispered. "Perhaps you should teach me the discussions."

His words startled her. "Nathan," she said, "Why are we quarreling?

Isn't it the most wonderful thing in the world right now that I want to get baptized?" Her eyes were no less moist than his.

"Of course it is," he responded with a sigh. "I just wish that I had some part in helping you want baptism. I feel that I've let you down."

"You loaned me your Book of Mormon," she reminded. "And you encouraged me to attend church with you last Sunday."

"But you had no one to answer your questions." His tone expressed the disappointment he felt.

"I could have asked you, or I could have asked Karen."

"Are we going to argue about this, too?" questioned Nathan. "Because I'm not going to fight with you anymore."

"Good!" She exclaimed happily. "Can we go to Nantes now?"

"Yes." He started the engine once again.

"Will you teach me along the way?"

"Anything that I can answer," he nodded, "I will answer."

As Nathan drove out of the park and headed the car toward Nantes, Brandje reached across the seat and squeezed his hand. "First," she said, "I want you to teach me about the new and everlasting covenant. I don't understand that at all."

"You're going to start at the top and work your way down?" He arched an eyebrow in surprise.

"Am I?"

"You are!" It wasn't an observation, it was a statement of fact. "But if I don't know enough about that particular gospel topic, I never will."

"Then tell me," she insisted. "I want to know everything."

By the time they reached Nantes, Brandje learned more about temple ordinances, including baptisms for the dead, and sealing to parents and spouses. She was keenly disappointed to learn that new members had to wait a year before they could go to the temple.

When they arrived in Nantes, Nathan looked up Bishop Emil Buerge's number and made the telephone call. Within thirty minutes, the portly bishop was shaking their hands at the front door of his home. "I have a private office," he explained as they were invited inside. "But this afternoon my wife has taken our two teenagers to the beach. We have the house to ourselves. Perhaps you would be more comfortable in the living room."

"Thank you," Nathan said. "We appreciate your staying home to visit with us."

Nathan and Brandje sat on the sofa, and Bishop sat opposite them in an overstuffed chair.

"On the contrary," said Bishop Buerge, "I was expecting Sister Brandje to show up at any moment."

Nathan smiled. "You knew she was coming?"

"Yes, ever since last Sunday at church."

Brandje nodded. "Your testimony was meant for me," she stated.

"Yes, I felt that it was," said the Bishop.

"That is still so strange to me," she confided. "But I'm getting used to what the spirit of the Lord feels like."

"You have been given a great gift," said the Bishop. "When the Lord has spoken to you as clearly as He has, it also comes with a grave responsibility."

Brandje's eyes widened. This man knew far more about her than she had ever imagined. Suddenly she felt uncomfortable. Surely he wouldn't say something to Nathan about what he already knew.

"You are here because you would like to be baptized," suggested Bishop Buerge.

"Yes," said Brandje, remembering that Nathan had told Bishop Buerge this on the telephone earlier.

"Then I think it would be wise if I interviewed you, to determine whether or not you are ready for such a big step." He nodded at Nathan.

As if on cue, Nathan stood and said, "I'll wait outside." He squeezed Brandje's hand. "You'll be all right," he encouraged, then he went outside to wait on the front steps.

Brandje turned and watched him go, grateful that she could speak with the bishop in private.

"That makes you a little more comfortable?" inquired Bishop Buerge.

"Yes." Brandje smiled. "Thank you."

"Let us begin," said the Bishop. "I understand that you have much to tell me."

"How much do you know?" she asked. "Maybe you should tell me what's going on in my life."

He laughed. "No. I am privileged to receive some inspiration along the way, occasionally. Fortunately for you, the spirit speaks with fervor. Otherwise, I may not have heard Him last Sunday when He pointed you out and told me to answer your question."

"Where do I start?" she asked.

"At the beginning," said Bishop Buerge. "But first, remember that as the designated Priesthood leader in this district, I am also assigned by the Lord to act as your father. I hope I am the kind of father who listens to everything that his children have to say, and that I am kind to them and respect their privacy above all else."

"Thank you," said Brandje.

For the next three hours, Brandje poured her heart and soul out to Bishop Buerge. She held nothing back, not her feelings for Nathan, her concerns regarding whether or not he really cared about her, nor the reality of her cancer. She shared the remarkable experience she'd had in her bedroom when the Savior showed her the scroll with her name on it, and the clear message she'd received regarding the donor list. When she had finished, they both shared many tears.

Bishop Buerge, true to his word, listened carefully to everything Brandje told him. When she was finally finished, he asked her if she would kneel in prayer with him. She did so, and as he pleaded in her behalf, Brandje was touched by his genuine concern for her, and his willingness to take her case to the Lord. When he was finished, he remained on his knees for several minutes. Then he offered another prayer, thanking the Lord for his guidance and wisdom.

When they stood up, he gave her an affectionate handshake. "Don't worry about Nathan. The situation between the two of you will soon be resolved. The Lord would like you to be baptized right away. Would Saturday be too long for you to wait?"

"That's only two days. I think I can make it that long."

He smiled. "You must share with Bishop Rousseau the extent of your illness, Brandje. His wife is carrying a terrible burden by herself. You must do this as soon as you get home. He is a discreet man, and he can be helpful to you, if you'll let him."

Brandje gulped. "You won't tell anyone else, will you?" she asked. "I told you why I can't tell Nathan."

"You are wise to wait until you know for certain that you have captured Brother Duncan's heart," said Bishop Buerge. "As for myself, I will tell no one the details of our discussion. Your secrets are safe with me."

"Thank you," Brandje said.

"There is just one thing I would like to say to Brother Duncan. I wonder if I may have your permission?"

"What is it?" she asked, worried.

"I feel that I should say to him: Please, Brother Duncan, watch over Brandje carefully, for she is of great worth to the Lord."

Brandje smiled. "He already does that," she admitted. "Is that really what the Lord would have you say?"

"Yes," he replied in earnest. "That is what I believe."

By the time Nathan and Brandje arrived back at the villa, it was dark. They had talked all the way home from Nantes, with Brandje asking one question after another. As they came through the front doorway, they were both laughing.

"Karen!" Brandje called out as Nathan nudged her to make her bold confession.

"What is it?" asked Karen from the kitchen.

"Come in here, please," Brandje pleaded. "I have something important to tell you.

Jean-Luc looked up from the evening paper. "Do you want me to give you some privacy?"

"You'd better stay," said Nathan. "And don't stand up. You'll need to remain seated to hear what Brandje's going to spring on you."

"Sounds serious," said Jean-Luc. "I guess I'm ready."

Karen came in drying her hands. "Did you two have supper?"

"We've been feasting on something else all day," hinted Nathan.

"Sit down, please," Brandje asked the older woman. "I have an announcement to make."

Karen sat beside her husband and placed her hand on his knee.

Nathan led Brandje to the other sofa and sat down beside her. Tenderly he placed her hand in his, and said, "She's so giddy, she's liable to pass right out before she tells her secret."

"What?" asked Jean-Luc. "Brandje, don't keep us in suspense."

Brandje gave him a warm smile, but when she spoke, her eyes were fixed on Karen's. "This Saturday, at two o'clock in the afternoon, I'm getting baptized."

Jean-Luc was dumbfounded. Karen smiled serenely. Jean-Luc eyed his wife suspiciously. "You knew?" he questioned.

"No," Karen admitted, "but I suspected as much."

Jean-Luc stood and walked swiftly over to Brandje. He pulled her to her feet and gave her a firm handshake. "That's the best news I've heard all month!"

Karen came forward and hugged Brandje. Then they sat down to talk about what had happened in Brandje's life to convert her to the gospel. She shared with all of them the miracle that had occurred in her bedroom that Monday morning, being careful to leave out the experience regarding the scroll and putting her name on the donor list. Then she read all of third Nephi, chapter seventeen to them.

When she came to the part about the Savior healing the sick, Karen looked up at Brandje. Perhaps she wondered whether or not the miracle of Brandje's vision included a special healing. Brandje shook her head slightly, in response. Fortunately, Karen was the only one who noticed.

After two hours of sharing testimonies and feelings with one another, Brandje announced, "I'm starving."

"I have some leftover stew," said Karen. "Does that sound good?"

"No," admitted Brandje. "I have my heart set on a root beer float. Do we have any root beer?"

"No," said Karen. "I wish I'd known. We drove into town today and could have picked some up."

"Nathan," hinted Brandje, "they have a mini-market at that little petrol station at the south end of town. Do you know where it is?"

"Yes," he said, "And I'll be right back with some root beer."

"Thank you," she squeezed his hand.

He gave her a quick kiss on the cheek, and slipped out the door. Not until she heard the Mercedes descend the steep hill did she turn to Jean-Luc and Karen.

"He'll only be gone for ten minutes," said Brandje. "Bishop told me I should have given you permission to share privileged information with your husband, Karen. I'm sorry. I didn't even think about the strain it would put on you, keeping such a terrible secret. Will you forgive me?"

Karen looked almost startled. "Does this mean what I'm thinking?" she asked.

"Yes," said Brandje. "Bishop gave me strict instructions to tell Jean-Luc the truth."

"The truth?" he asked.

Gathering courage, Brandje explained. "I'm sorry, Jean-Luc. But Karen needs you to be there for her, and without knowing everything, you can't possibly comfort her. She can explain it all to you later on."

To Karen, Brandje said, "Karen, I give you my permission to share with your husband everything that I've told you, everything that I tell you, in private, at times when you know Nathan will not hear you."

To Jean-Luc, she continued, "I must have your word of honor that you will not say a word to Nathan."

"I never share confidences," said Jean-Luc. "Apparently it's contagious. I have no idea what you two have been keeping from me."

Satisfied with his answer, Brandje took a deep breath and said, "When I first came to the villa by myself, I had just learned that I have cancer. At that time, the doctors said I had less than six months. I've already used up six weeks of that time."

"That's why you've been sick all the time?" Jean-Luc asked as tears unexpectedly filled his eyes. Without warning, he broke down and sobbed openly. "I'm sorry," he finally managed to say. "I had no idea." Then another wave of crying hit him.

"This will never do," said Karen. "Nathan can't come home to find you blubbering, dear."

"I know," he said. "Give me a few minutes, I'll be okay." He squeezed Karen's hand and stood up. Brandje stood up as well. There would be no handshake this time. He embraced her in a big bear hug and whispered, "I will keep you in my prayers, more fervently than ever."

"Thank you," she said. "I'm sorry to have upset you."

"I'd rather know than not," he said with a nod. "Why won't you tell Nathan? The poor man is half out of his mind worrying about you!"

"Karen will explain all that later on," Brandje said.

"Yes," she agreed, "maybe we'll go on one of our moonlit walks tonight."

He nodded. "I'll go upstairs and freshen up a bit. Otherwise, I won't be able to explain these tears to his satisfaction."

"You could tell him that you're so happy to see me baptized you can't help but cry," Brandje suggested.

"That would be true enough," said Jean-Luc. "But there's a big difference between tears of joy and tears of sorrow. And at the moment, sorrow seems to be winning over joy."

After Jean-Luc went upstairs, Karen wrapped Brandje up in a warm embrace. "Nathan hasn't said anything yet, regarding his feelings toward you?" she asked.

"No," said Brandje. "Although I prodded him often enough. Sometimes I think that he doesn't really love me at all."

"Are you sure, Brandje? Because I've seen so many signs," said Karen.

"So have I," admitted Brandje. "Sometimes I think that he really does love me. Other times I worry that our relationship is just a flirtatious, let's-have-a-fun-summer-together sort of thing. I've given him several opportunities to jump right in and tell me how he feels. For that matter, so has his family. But Nathan won't."

"Don't give up on him," Karen suggested. "Some men just take a little longer than others, that's all."

"I won't give up" Brandje confided. "I'll always love him, even though it's the most stressful feeling I've ever had to face. It's even worse than thinking about no Christmas. I wish Nathan would say something about how he feels, but to be truthful, I don't see that happening."

"Oh, Brandje," Karen complained. "I'd like to give that man a piece of my mind!"

"You can't. He has to have his agency to choose, just like I have. And it's time for me to face that fact. This is just another sad chapter in my fairy tale. Unfortunately for me, where Nathan's concerned, *Sleeping Beauty* bit the dust."

Chapter Fifteen

*N*athan studied his reflection in the dresser mirror. His sandy brown hair was combed as orderly as possible, regardless of the one straggler that always stood straight up. Even Brandje's suggestion that he use raw egg white had failed him. However, he looked like a missionary, and that was all that mattered today. His shirt and tie with dress slacks may seem a bit much to her, but he'd never taught the missionary lessons in casual clothing, and he wasn't about to start now.

He hoped he was ready to teach her the discussions. He'd been on his knees half the night, praying about Brandje. He still had a sinking feeling about her. She was too private, too fragile, too secretive, too difficult to read. And he was too hopelessly in love with her to do anything about it. Whoever said *Love Is Bliss* had apparently never met Brandje. *Such Sweet Agony* would be closer to the truth.

Part of the agony he had to blame on himself, he realized. He hadn't been open with her, and because of that, he had missed out on many aspects of her conversion. He chided himself over and over again for his misconduct.

Another part of the agony he felt within had to do with the commitment he'd made to the Lord, that he would only marry in the temple. Brandje would be baptized tomorrow. The standard waiting period for a new member to go to the temple to be sealed for time and all eternity was one year. They lived on separate continents. He could see a very big problem with waiting one year.

What if she met someone else while they were apart? Just contemplating the word *apart* sent agony creeping into his soul, making him feel weak, almost faint. How could he ever live apart from her after all the time they'd spent together?

Should he tell her now, before the end of August, that he loves her? Should he propose to her now, or should he wait until just before he leaves the villa? He opened the dresser drawer and removed a burgundy velvet box. As he lifted the lid, he smiled. *It's really quite an extraordinary ring!* he thought to himself, admiring it.

A lump formed in his throat as he tried to come to terms with his worst fear, that he had somehow misinterpreted her feelings for him.

He recalled the kiss she'd given him two days earlier, at his grandmother's formal garden in Chinon. He trembled with emotion as he thought on that moment. He was just as irritated as she was when Isabelle had interrupted them. Remembering Brandje's expletive, *"Bother!"* and the cover-up remark she'd added to it, thinking he hadn't heard, made him smile wistfully.

He prayed he hadn't mistaken the feelings Brandje had for him two days ago. She'd hinted a few times on their trip to Chinon that she was looking for some kind of commitment from him. Of course, that was before he knew she'd been converted to the gospel.

Had he intended to break the covenant he'd made with the Lord, that he would not marry outside the temple? No matter how much he loved her, could he have told her his true feelings when he had no hope, before they left Chinon, that he could ever take her to the temple? Somehow he doubted it. Yet, on the other hand, if that were really the case, why had he ordered the ring weeks ago? He returned the velvet box to its hiding place and closed the dresser drawer.

Had he known of her conversion, and her commitment to the Lord prior to their going to Chinon, what would he have said when she'd given him her little hints?

He would still have to face this terrible separation that loomed ahead of them, which was now only a few short weeks away. What on earth was he supposed to do about Brandje?

There was also the appointment for her baptism tomorrow. She'd been touched by the Spirit perhaps stronger than he ever had! How had he been so blind to all of that? He didn't understand how he could have missed the signs. But thinking about it now, he realized, she hadn't given any indication, at least not to him. He hadn't even known whether or not she'd been reading the Book of Mormon. Yet in two weeks, she'd also read most of the Doctrine and Covenants.

Her interview with Bishop Buerge had taken three hours! Nathan had never known a baptismal interview to take that long! She apparently had a lot to say to the good bishop. How many sins could she have had to repent from that would take three hours?

Nathan recalled how relieved he felt when he was finally invited back into the bishop's home. Bishop Buerge shook his hand, gave him a simple smile, and said, "We'll have her baptism on Saturday. She'd like you to perform the ordinance. She's asked that you also confirm her, with Bishop Rousseau and myself standing in. Will that be agreeable?"

"Yes," said Nathan. "I'd be honored."

"She's a very special woman," said Bishop. "She and I have prayed together and the Lord has blessed us both with many promptings from the Spirit. I have felt in my heart that the Lord has a word to say to you regarding Brandje Fulton."

"What is it?" Nathan had asked.

Slowly, deliberately, Bishop Buerge had placed his hand upon Nathan's shoulder and said, "Please, Brother Duncan, watch over Brandje carefully, for she is of great worth to the Lord."

Bishop Buerge's message troubled him. Nathan still shivered when he considered the words. They seemed to take possession of him somehow, as though he wasn't doing all that the Lord required of him.

The words tumbled around in his head and in his heart, over and over again. He doubted he would ever forget them. Having learned that Bishop Buerge was a divinely inspired messenger of the Lord, Nathan had committed his words to memory: "Watch over Brandje carefully, for she is of great worth to the Lord."

The message filled Nathan with fear. He'd hardly slept because of it. Half the night he'd prayed, asking the Lord to show him how to watch over Brandje, asking where he'd been lacking. The rest of the night he'd prayed that the Lord would help him understand how to teach Brandje the gospel when she seemed to know it almost better than he did.

Totally bewildered, Nathan left the bedroom and went downstairs, where he was greeted by Jean-Luc, Karen and Brandje, who were gathered around the dining room table.

When he first looked at Brandje, she gave him a smile that made his heart skip several beats. "I think before we begin the discussions, we should have a word of prayer," he suggested.

By the time Saturday arrived Brandje felt well-prepared to accept the Lord's calling that she be baptized. The Rousseaus and Nathan spent hours teaching her the things she needed to know to take the plunge. She'd learned more about God in those few hours than she had in the first twenty-three years of her life.

A healing spirit came over her as well. She felt better than she had in weeks. She did not doubt that the Spirit of the Lord was with her, helping her each and every moment.

Friday night, Jean-Luc loaned her a booklet on the restoration, and she spent several hours reading it. She had no trouble whatsoever believing that Joseph Smith was a prophet of God. Since she'd gained her testimony on the truthfulness of the Book of Mormon, she accepted readily all of the many prophets who had written, preserved, and translated it.

As they traveled to Nantes, Nathan and Jean-Luc did most of the talking, which was fine with Brandje. She was content to let the wind whisk her hair back behind her and feel the sun beat down on her face.

Karen fidgeted in the back seat, searching for something in her purse. When at last she'd found it, she exclaimed, "Aha!"

"What were you looking for?" Brandje turned around to ask.

"Something to hold your hair down," suggested Karen.

"Oh, I'm sorry. I didn't think."

"Not for in the car, dear," Karen explained. "But I happened to think that when you're put under the water today, with all that beautiful hair, it's quite likely it will float on the surface, in which case you'd have to be baptized all over again." She handed Brandje a rubber band.

"I want to get it right the first time," said Brandje. "Thank you."

By the time they arrived, Bishop Buerge, his two counselors, and several families from the ward were waiting for them. The baptismal font had been filled and Relief Society sisters were on hand to secure the proper clothing for Brandje. Karen attended her in the dressing room, helping secure her hair so that it still looked lovely, but would not be the cause of a second baptism.

Then they went into a room that overlooked the baptismal font and participated in the opening exercises. After a song and prayer, Bishop Buerge gave a short discussion on the purpose of baptism. Then he announced that it was time for Brandje to step into the baptismal font.

They waited a few moments in silence for Nathan to enter the font from the other side. Just as he did, Karen embraced Brandje. "You've made the right decision," said Karen. "This is the only way you'll be able to enter into the Kingdom of Heaven."

"I know," said Brandje. "I know."

Nathan had tears in his eyes as Brandje stepped down into the font beside him. She noticed that he could hardly keep his emotions under control to offer the ordinance prayer. When she came up out of the water, he gave her a smile and a quick handshake.

"Thank you," she whispered.

After Brandje changed into dry clothing, she used a hair pick to untangle her long golden hair. Then she joined the others for the concluding ceremony. Bishop Jean-Luc Rousseau spoke this time about the gift of the Holy Ghost and the important role it would now play in Brandje's life.

When Nathan and the two bishops laid their hands upon Brandje's head, she was given the gift of the Holy Ghost, which descended upon her immediately, filling her spirit with the light that was promised in the Book of Mormon, to all those who accept that sacred ordinance. She had stepped out of the darkness and into the light of God.

She was also given the gift of comfort and peace in the troubled times that loomed ahead of her. Since Nathan was voice, this statement surprised her, for he had no idea what she'd needed to hear just then. Nevertheless, the Lord worked in His mysterious way, the blessing was pronounced, and Brandje finally felt that she could go home to God, her father and finest friend, without fear.

Afterward, Bishop Buerge invited those who wanted to participate in a brief testimony meeting, to stand in place and share. One by one the members stood up and testified to Brandje, and one another, how they felt about the gospel of Jesus Christ.

Bishop Jean-Luc Rousseau shared his feelings toward Brandje, breaking down several times to wipe his eyes. Fortunately, today his tears were joyful ones, and he was able to express his love to Brandje and to Nathan, for the wonderful friends they'd become.

Karen stood briefly and thanked the Lord for sending Brandje into her life, then expressed her love for the gospel before sitting down.

Nathan stood last. He looked down at Brandje and smiled. His eyes were filled with tears, and his words were directed toward her, and her alone. "Brandje," he began, "I'd like to tell you how pleased your Father in Heaven is today, for the choices that you've made and the sacrifices you've accepted, to become a member of the one and only true church of Jesus Christ upon the earth.

"I, too, am pleased with your progress, and I thank God every day for the closeness we've shared. I also ask you to forgive me for not recognizing the struggle you faced alone as you came to realize the power of prayer, through the testimony of Bishop Buerge last Sunday, and through your own prayers as you studied and read the Book of Mormon. I, too, know the Book of Mormon is true. I once told you it was my favorite book in all the world. But even I did not begin to comprehend its divine power to convert the sons and daughters of God, not like you understand. Brandje, I ask your forgiveness, as well as the Lord's, and I do it humbly, in the name of Jesus Christ, Amen."

Bishop waited for only a moment to see whether or not anyone else wanted to share their testimony.

Brandje remained silent. Her heart was so full of the spirit of God that she doubted her mouth would work, had she taken the opportunity to share her feelings as these good people had.

Just before she left, Bishop Buerge took her aside to say, "Brandje, you have a strong testimony of the gospel. Will you be offended if I ask you to share it with us tomorrow, during Sacrament Meeting?"

She hesitated. "What could I say that would add any more to what these beautiful people have shared this afternoon?"

"Pray about it," he encouraged. "I won't put you on the program. But if, between now and then, you decide there is something you want to share, will you nod to me at the beginning of tomorrow's meeting?"

"Yes," she said, as a sudden determination came upon her, reminding her that she must do all that she could to help anyone else's progress.

"If you get frightened," said Bishop Buerge, "or you feel uncomfortable in any way about doing this, just shake your head. No one but you and I will know."

And God, she thought to herself.

Later that evening, Karen barbecued marinated pork medallions, while Brandje made a salad and the men set the patio table with blue ironstone tableware. After a light supper, they put the dishes in the kitchen sink to soak, then went back out on the patio to visit.

Jean-Luc shared his father's conversion story during the Second World War.

"I thought he was raised in a Mormon family," Brandje interrupted.

"He was," Jean-Luc explained. "But everyone has their own conversion story. For some, their conversion comes while they are in their youth, learning bit by bit to love the gospel."

"That's my story," Nathan interrupted momentarily.

"For others," continued Jean-Luc, "they grow up in the gospel, but are truly converted later on."

"I'd never considered that," said Brandje. "How could you ever doubt the gospel if you were raised in it?"

Jean-Luc and Karen both smiled, while Nathan squeezed her hand.

"Take my own story," Karen explained. "I was raised in a big family, my fourth great-grandfather lived in Nauvoo and knew the prophet, Joseph Smith, as a dear friend. He slept on the floor near the prophet's bed with a rifle at his side, as one of the prophet's many bodyguards. But I had no interest in that when I was young. I was a rebellious teenager and left the church when I was seventeen."

"You never shared this story," said Brandje. "Why?"

"We get a little gun shy when dealing with non-members, I suppose," Karen explained.

"Gun shy?" Brandje asked with a giggle.

"An old expression," Jean-Luc explained, "having to do with getting shot down fairly often when asking non-members the Golden Question."

"I understand," Brandje said quietly as Nathan winked at her. Then she looked back at Karen. "Go on, please," she pleaded.

"Well, it was nothing miraculous such as you experienced. After my high school years, I moved from Utah to Iowa, where I trained at the University of Iowa Medical Center, in Iowa City. This area is mostly Protestant. After graduating from nursing school, I stayed in Iowa City, and worked full-time. I thought I'd left the gospel far behind me. At the ICU where I worked, one of the other nurses invited me to study her religion. Since I considered her a friend, I agreed. But as we began our study, I realized that her interpretation of the Bible was totally inaccurate. I questioned some of her faith's doctrines, which turned out to be a big mistake in terms of our friendship. She dropped me like a hot potato and never spoke to me again. Because of her behavior, I decided that it was time I discovered just what I believed. After some exam-ination of other faiths in my area, I recalled that my father had borne a fervent testimony when I was younger. I finally went to him for answers. He invited me to move home, he even arranged for my employment at LDS Hospital in Salt Lake. He welcomed the opportunity to bring one of his own children back into the gospel. I began attending my meetings and then, one day in Relief Society, the sisters had a testimony service right after the lesson. To my utter surprise, I stood and shared mine. It wasn't until that very moment that I realized I had one."

"After that it was all rather simple," interjected Jean-Luc. "She met me at a Missionary fireside that I, and a few of my fellow missionaries, had planned. Afterward, she introduced herself, and we kept in touch by letters. She was twenty-five, and I was twenty-one. But that made no difference to me. When I returned to Nantes after my mission, I soon realized she was the woman for me. I flew back to Utah, married her in the Salt Lake Temple, and brought her home to France."

"What a wonderful story," said Brandje. "Thank you for sharing it with me."

"Not all of us receive the miraculous conversion you did," suggested Nathan.

Jean-Luc agreed. "Nathan's right. You are the exception to the rule. Be grateful for what you've been given."

"I am," Brandje murmured. "Believe me, I am."

Karen stood up, taking Jean-Luc's hand in the process. "Come along dear," she said. "Let's do the dishes."

"We'll help," said Brandje.

"No," Karen suggested. "You two probably need some time without chaperones tonight."

Brandje wasn't going to argue with her. "Thank you," she said.

After the Rousseaus went into the house, Brandje snuggled up to Nathan as he put his arm around her shoulders.

"How does it feel?" he asked, his voice husky, yet exquisitely tender.

"It's been one of the happiest days of my life," she said. "Even the sunset tonight looks different to me. Do you know that God made all these beautiful creations for us to enjoy, but few of us scarcely appreciate them?"

"You seem to be feeling a lot better, physically," he suggested.

"I am," she said. "Remarkably so."

"I'm glad to hear it," he admitted. "You were beautiful as you came up out of the baptismal waters. I don't know that I've ever seen you look more beautiful."

"Thank you." Graciously she accepted his compliment.

"I still feel guilty for not helping you learn about the gospel sooner," he confessed. "We have to work on our communication skills, don't you think?"

She laughed. "We're fairly good at yelling at one another," she said. "I wanted to throttle you in the car Thursday."

"When you told me you wanted to get baptized?" He smiled. "You do have a temper, almost as bad as mine!"

"You deserved it," she teased. "The most important event in my life and you had to twist it around and practically accuse me of not comprehending what my baptism would mean."

"Hmm," he sighed. "It's a good thing you forgave me, again!"

"You seem to have a forgiving spirit as well," Brandje admitted.

"Do you suppose this means we could spend one entire day without getting angry at each other?"

"You mean like today?" She leaned her head back and gazed up into his dark eyes.

"Exactly like today," Nathan agreed.

His lips gently caressed hers until she ached for him almost beyond all reason. She pulled away and looked at him with all the love she had for him. Certainly the longing in her eyes was every bit as evident to him, as the desire in his eyes was for her. He continued to gaze at her with such passion it unsettled her, yet his voice remained silent. Finally, she whispered, "We can't. You're not the only one with sacred covenants."

She stood up and pulled him to his feet.

"You're right," he said, as if in a daze.

"Absolutely," she agreed.

Together they sought the companionship of Jean-Luc and Karen for the rest of the evening.

When Brandje went to her Father in Heaven for counsel later that night, in the privacy of her bedroom, she was not disappointed. The

Spirit of the Holy Ghost whispered to her in such a profound and tender way that she knew she had chosen perfect actions for one whole day. It was the first day in her entire life when she felt that there was hope for her, and a place for her, in the Kingdom of Heaven. This knowledge gave her the comfort she needed to sleep peacefully, even with the special questions that still lingered in her heart where Nathan was concerned.

Chapter Sixteen

At Sacrament Meeting on Sunday, Brandje gave Bishop Buerge her nod of consent. She was then asked to stand and share her feelings regarding her baptism the day before.

She worried that the entire baptismal experience was still too new, and the testimonies she was given by others, touched her so profoundly that she didn't have the strength or the courage to say anything. As she walked forward to stand at the podium, she felt her whole body tremble with fear. *Help me, Lord*, she prayed silently. *I want to say what is in my heart, so if you can find a way to get my heart out of my throat, perhaps that would help. . .*

Looking out over the congregation, Brandje found her eyes went straight to Nathan. Just seeing his smile gave her the courage she needed to begin. "I've never done this before, so I hope you'll be patient with me. I have so many feelings coursing through me that I hardly know how to categorize them. First, I'd like to thank Bishop Buerge for interviewing me, for listening, and for the inspiration he had last week when he stood and told you that someone in the congregation had a question. I was that someone. Because God answered my prayer that day in such a personal way, I was able to understand that He cared about me and would answer all my prayers, if I would just ask.

"There comes a turning point in everyone's life when they must decide what they believe, and why. I thought that turning point came last Monday morning, in the wee hours before daybreak, when I received a personal witness that the Book of Mormon is true.

"But now I realize that the turning point came a few weeks earlier when a noble Elder had the courage to ask me if he could offer a blessing on our food. I knew from the moment he first started to pray that his prayer would change my life forever."

Tears filled her eyes, but she disregarded them and continued, "You see, his prayer was different from any other prayer I'd ever heard. He knew God personally. He knew that God is his very own father. When he spoke to Him, it wasn't a conditioned prayer or a prayer that would be memorized by a child. It was, quite simply, a polite discussion between a father and his son. That noble Elder knew God on an individual, very personal basis, and spoke to Him as though they stood face to face. He thanked Him for everything that he could possibly think about. He asked God for guidance and blessings, for things completely out of the ordinary. He asked God to watch over a couple whom he'd never even met before, who were at that moment, traveling from Nantes to be with us in Croix de Vie. I learned from him that God is our personal confidante, our Father in Heaven, our best and finest friend.

"Because of Brother Duncan's courage, I learned that God is the one person to whom I can turn for any problem, no matter how big, or how small. Brother Duncan had the courage to ask for my permission to pray, and his prayer touched my heart.

"He thinks he had nothing to do with my conversion. Well, he's wrong. He taught me that God is there for me, that I can pray to Him as though I had known Him all my life. He set an example for me, and I soon started to pray the way I'd heard him pray.

"Then last Sunday, in his testimony, Bishop Buerge taught me that, not only can I talk to God on a more personal level, God will answer my prayers, sometimes rather quickly.

"There is no way to express what these two gifts have given me, how grateful I am to have learned that God is my father, that He hears and answers my prayers. If God will do this for me, He will do it for anyone. I say these things in the name of Jesus Christ, Amen."

After church more than half the congregation thanked Brandje for sharing her testimony with them, and welcomed her into the church of Jesus Christ.

On the way home, Nathan sat in the back seat with Brandje cradled against him, while Jean-Luc drove the Mercedes Benz back to Croix de Vie. Karen, in the front with her husband, fidgeted with the radio until she found a channel suitable for listening.

Brandje leaned against Nathan, closed her eyes, and prayed that this moment, with Nathan holding her, with her hair blowing away from her face by the wind, with the sun warming her skin, would never pass away.

She thought about the prayer she'd offered that morning, just before leaving for church. The Holy Ghost had given her an answer to the question she'd been asking for weeks: Yes, Nathan loved her. The answer came so strongly she'd felt fairly giddy ever since. Now she just wanted to savor every moment she could have with him, regardless whether he ever gathered enough courage to tell her himself.

As the Mercedes Benz rounded the last corner and headed up the driveway, Brandje opened her eyes and gave Nathan a delicious smile.

"Tired?" Nathan asked, stroking her cheek tenderly.

"No," she insisted. "I'm savoring the moment."

"Why didn't you ever tell me how you felt about my prayer?"

"Why didn't you ever tell me about the gospel?" A teasing grin swept onto her face as she bantered his question back to him.

"We have a terrible time communicating, don't we?" he asked.

"We certainly do."

Jean-Luc parked the car and got out. "You two coming in?"

Nathan agreed. "We'd probably better."

After lunch, Karen went upstairs to take a nap. Nathan stretched out on one sofa to rest while Brandje sat on the opposite sofa, next to Jean-Luc, to crochet the last remaining rows on Martin's afghan. Jean-Luc began to read the scriptures he would need to reflect on during the week for next Sunday's lesson.

"Why don't you read those to us?" Brandje suggested.

"I'd be delighted," said Jean-Luc. "We're beginning third Nephi next Sunday."

"Oh, it's absolutely my favorite book," she said.

"I know that." Jean-Luc smiled.

"I like the Book of Ether," teased Nathan. "Lots of answers are found in Ether."

"Go ahead and read," said Brandje. "We'll listen."

Jean-Luc began to read, and Brandje soon found herself caught up in the miraculous stories. But within ten minutes, Nathan was fast asleep.

"Didn't take him long, did it?" Jean-Luc asked with a smile as he looked up from his reading.

"Don't worry," said Brandje, "I won't fall asleep."

While Jean-Luc read, and Brandje crocheted, they feasted upon the spirit and power of third Nephi. She never ceased to be amazed at all that had happened on the American continent during the reign of the Indian Nations at the time of Christ's ministry on her side of the world. She looked at the Navajo afghan she was making and realized it would be perfectly symbolic to present to Martin with a copy of the Book of Mormon, along with her testimony, written in her own handwriting.

Around six that evening, Nathan was still asleep, Jean-Luc had dozed off as well, and Karen was napping upstairs.

After tying the last knot in the afghan and clipping the yarn, Brandje stood up and held the afghan out for inspection. It was, beyond any doubt, her best work. Pride filled her as she thought of her brother using the afghan, with it's various shades of autumn, for his legs on cold winter nights. He would be forever reminded of his little sister and the love they shared.

She looked at Nathan sleeping peacefully upon the sofa. Tomorrow she would go into town and buy some more yarn. It was time to start an afghan for Nathan. He, too, would treasure such a gift in years to come.

Lovingly she recalled that very morning, when the spirit whispered to her, telling her that Nathan didn't have to confess that he loved her anymore. Through the promptings of the spirit, she already knew that Nathan loved her with all his heart. With that realization came responsibility. Somehow she must find a way to tell him about the cancer.

How he would react to this news she had no idea.

Silently she slipped upstairs and knelt beside the bed. "Dear Father in Heaven," she prayed, her voice a soft whisper. "I love him so much, and I know he loves me, too. The spirit has spoken it to me. Please, give me the courage I need to tell him the truth about me. Will he be angry with me for keeping it secret for so long? Will he still love me after I tell him? Please guide me, Father. I can't do this without you. Please give me the strength I need."

When she had closed her prayer, she waited for the sweetness of the spirit to pour out upon her, as she had in times past. She was not disappointed.

She remained on her knees even after she heard footsteps on the stairs, and realized it was Nathan when she heard his bedroom door open. Silently she thanked the Lord for the courage and the comfort He had given her. Then, remembering that she hadn't closed her bedroom door, she quickly ended her prayer with the Savior's name.

"Amen," said Nathan as Brandje stood up. He was leaning against the door frame, watching her with tender emotions building up within his chest.

Brandje wiped the tears quickly from her eyes and stood up. "Hi there, sleepyhead."

As she smiled, he marveled how she always seemed to find something to say that would cheer him.

Nathan shook his head, walked over to her and took her hand in his. "Come along," he said with a sigh of commitment. "It's time we have a little talk."

He led her out across the bluff, behind the hydrangea, and down the gardenia surrounded pathway. When they reached the steps, he said, "Look! The tide's coming in." He checked his watch for the time, calculated quickly in his head when the next low tide would arrive. "In about six more days we'll come out and watch the sunrise together from Timbal's Point."

"It's a date," she agreed.

They sat down together a few steps from the top. Nathan slid back, put her on the same step in front of him, between his legs, so she could use his chest as a back rest and still look at the sea she loved so well. He wrapped his arms around her, with his hands resting gently at her waist. He kissed the sides of her face, her neck, her ears. She shivered.

"I love you," he whispered, his voice husky, yet sweet and tender.

"I know," she said simply.

"You do?" he asked in surprise. "I thought I'd caught you praying that I would tell you how I felt about you."

She smiled as she leaned her head back and looked at him. "I already know you love me," she confessed, "because God told me so this morning."

Although he could see love reflected in her azure blue eyes for him, Nathan wanted to hear her speak the words, as well. "And you?" he asked. "Do you feel the same way about me?"

She lifted an arm and bent his head down to reach his lips with hers. The kiss she gave left him with no doubt as to her real feelings. Then she withdrew and tilted her head back. She gazed up into his dark eyes and said, "You know I do. You know that I've loved you from the moment I first saw you averting your eyes to protect my privacy while handing me my bathrobe."

"That long?" he asked.

"I'm afraid so," she admitted. "My father always told me that when I met the man of my dreams, I would recognize him immediately."

"Hmm," he mused. "You never mentioned it before."

"What was the point?" She gave him a mischievous grin. Then her expression took on a seriousness that left no doubt in his mind regarding her love for him.

His eyes caressed her face with their gentle searching. His lips sought hers, and he found her willing to return his kisses, as though with a passion she had saved only for him.

Remembering their covenants, he withdrew after a few minutes. He pulled her onto his lap, which allowed him to have eye contact straight on. She smiled as though this position pleased her. He moved his mouth nearer hers, wanting to kiss her once again, but she stopped him.

"I have something else to tell you," she said, putting a hand against his lips.

Straightening, he accepted her gesture reluctantly. "I have something else to tell you," he repeated.

"You first," she suggested.

He opened his hand in front of her and revealed an engagement ring and wedding band. Made of fine gold, together the two rings formed the shape of a gardenia, with petals surrounding a large central diamond. "Will you marry me?" His question came tenderly, without fear of rejection, and it pleased him to know he no longer had reason to fear.

Brandje gasped in surprise. "Where did you get this?" she asked. "I've never seen anything so lovely."

"A jeweler in town," he answered. "I had it designed especially for you."

"When?" asked Brandje.

"I ordered it that day we ate at DeMerite, before Pierre interrupted our lunch."

"No wonder you were so angry."

He nodded, gave her a brief smile, then brought her back to the question at hand. "Well?"

Brandje gave him a bright smile. "I would like nothing more than to be your wife," she admitted.

Nathan smiled as he slipped the gardenia shaped ring on her slender finger. It fit perfectly, and he sighed in relief.

She wrapped her arms around his neck and pulled him close. It was all that he needed to encourage him. He caressed her back and held her fiercely to him, as though satisfying a deep and awful hunger he'd felt the past few weeks while worrying if she would ever love him in return. Tears sprang to his eyes and he could hardly utter the words. "Oh, Brandje, Brandje! I never knew love could be this tangible. I never realized that two people could share what we share. I feel like you're a part of me that's been missing for thirty-one years. I wish I'd told you weeks ago. I've ached to tell you."

She responded with kisses across his forehead, his cheeks, his chin, his neck. She looked straight into his eyes and he felt her love radiate through him.

"I've ached, too," she confessed. "Nathan, I —"

"Brandje! Nathan!" came a familiar voice across the hydrangea bushes.

"Don't tell Karen and Jean-Luc yet," Brandje whispered.

"Why?" he asked, puzzled by her request.

"Please, we have to wait until —"

"Brandje!" came Karen's voice once again.

Brandje stood up quickly. "We're here," she said.

"Oh my," said Karen from across the hydrangea. "I suspect you've got quite a view from over there."

"We do," Brandje agreed. "Come join us, if you'd like."

"Bother!" Nathan muttered to himself, wishing their time together had not been interrupted so quickly.

Brandje nudged him with the toe of her shoe. When she slid the ring around her finger, so the bright diamond wouldn't be noticed, he felt betrayed.

"Why don't you want to tell them?" Nathan whispered to her while Karen came around the hydrangea.

"Not yet," Brandje insisted. "Not until I tell you —"

"What a beautiful spot!" Karen exclaimed as she walked between the gardenia plants and over to the steps. "And don't the gardenias smell heavenly!" She pointed to a massive rock below them that appeared as though it were wandering out to sea. Wild waves were beginning to swirl around it, climbing higher with each one. Soon the rock would be completely submerged. "Oh my!" she enthused. "Is that Timbal's Point?"

"Yes," said Brandje. "Scoot down a couple steps, Nathan. We can all watch the sunset together."

Reluctantly he complied.

Karen looked back at the villa, across the hydrangea and the yard. She motioned for Jean-Luc to join them. Within a few moments all four of them were watching the sunset together as they sat on the granite steps. It was a moment to savor and treasure forever.

"The sunset really is beautiful," said Karen. "I'd like to come out here every evening."

"You can see both sunset and sunrise from here," Jean-Luc offered. "With the cliff facing south as it does here, looking out onto the Bay of Biscay, this is probably one of the few areas of France where both times of day can be viewed without encumbrances."

"Sunrise is my favorite," Brandje confessed. "To watch the sea change as dawn breaks upon it is almost like being reborn. It reminds me that God has given me one more day to get my life straightened out."

Nathan smiled to himself as he recalled how dearly Brandje loved sunrise. He prayed with all his heart that they would soon share all their sunrises together. He had to admit he was disappointed she didn't want Karen and Jean-Luc to know about their engagement. Hopefully, he would find a way to convince her otherwise.

Before long, Timbal's Point was completely submerged. Waves pounded over it with a ferociousness unequaled anywhere that they had ever seen.

They left the ridge just before all light faded from the sky, so they could see to get back to the villa without a flashlight.

As the two couples approached the house, Jean-Luc and Karen in the lead, Nathan held Brandje's hand the entire way. Before they reached the patio, Nathan waited a moment, giving Brandje no choice but to wait with him. When the Rousseaus were out of hearing range, he whispered in Brandje's ear, "Wait! Wasn't there something else you wanted to tell me?"

To his dismay, Brandje only shrugged the question off with, "I'll tell you tomorrow. Let's do sunrise together."

"You're at least five days early," he reminded. "You'll be lucky to see any sunrise from Timbal's Point before the tide rolls in."

"Then we'll resume our conversation on the steps, where we left off when Karen arrived," she whispered. "It'll be enough. I promise."

His eyes glistened and he felt tears stinging them. "I can't wait," he insisted. "I want to share our happiness with everyone. Why can't you tell me now, so we can share our engagement news with Karen and

Jean-Luc?"

"Please, Nathan," Brandje pleaded. "I want to share with them as much as you do, but I also want to wait until after we've talked."

"Just tell me," he begged. "Whatever it is, just tell me."

"No," she said. "Not yet. I promise I'll tell you in the morning."

Nathan sighed wearily, but he acquiesced to Brandje's wishes, at least for the moment.

After a late supper of salad, french bread and melon, they played an enduring game of scripture chase on the patio. The entire time Brandje tried to keep her left hand from being noticed by the Rousseaus. They hunted through the Book of Mormon with their flashlights in the dark, challenging each other. To everyone's amazement, Brandje won more times than she lost. Her familiarity with the Book of Mormon astounded them all.

Nathan was in high spirits that evening. Jean-Luc and Karen both remarked about it. To Brandje's relief, Nathan blamed it all on her conversion. She didn't want to share the other reasons with them, not yet, not until she told Nathan everything.

By midnight they had shared so much fun together, laughing at and with each other, that Brandje rejoiced at having kept the secret safe.

Before they shared their engagement news with the Rousseaus, she wanted Nathan to know about the cancer. She was still uncertain he would want to marry her after he knew the truth.

As Brandje finally went upstairs to her bedroom, Nathan followed, whispering, "Why can't we share our engagement plans with Jean-Luc and Karen?"

"Tomorrow," she said. "I'm selfish."

"Aw," he groaned. "I'm dying to tell them."

"No," she insisted with a grin.

"Please," he persisted. "I'm never going to sleep. I've got to share this with someone."

"No," she said, nudging him in the stomach.

"Please, please, please," he begged.

"No, No, No, No, No," she laughed.

Jean-Luc rounded the corner and bantered, "I don't know what you're begging for, Nathan, but I think Brandje said no."

Nathan turned around and joked, "Aw, you two spoil all my fun!"

They bid goodnight and went to their separate bedrooms.

Brandje felt comforted after prayer and snuggled back into the bed, fluffing up the pillows as she did. Her heart was filled with gratitude for the glorious day she'd spent at church, in prayer, with Nathan and the Rousseaus. Before long, she felt herself drifting off to sleep.

A knock came at the bedroom door that startled her.

"Who is it?" she asked.

"Please, Please, Please!" Nathan begged from the other side of the door, loud enough to wake the house.

"Go away," she said.

"Please, Brandje!" Nathan teased once again, louder this time.

"No!" she insisted, a smile tugging at the corners of her mouth.

"Then I'm coming in there!"

"Not without the Rousseaus!" She tried to stifle a chuckle.

"We're coming," said Jean-Luc from down the hall.

Brandje laughed joyously as Nathan pushed the door open and turned on the light. He was dressed in his pajamas and robe, his hair tousled, and his face teasingly handsome.

"Please, Brandje," he begged, kneeling next to the bed.

She threw a pillow at him. "Go away," she moaned in a playful tone. "I'm tired."

"So are we," said Jean-Luc as he and Karen entered Brandje's bedroom dressed in their pajamas and robes.

"I see," Nathan said with a ridiculous grin. "It's not that you don't want to, it's just that you'd rather have a pillow fight!" He picked up the pillow she'd thrown at him and issued the challenge. "Okay, I'll fight you. Come on," he said, tossing the pillow directly at her.

She rolled off the other side of the bed to miss it.

As Nathan dashed into his bedroom to grab more pillows, Brandje quickly slipped on a robe and knotted it at her waist. Moments later Nathan returned and clobbered her with his pillows.

She fought back with pillows of her own as Karen and Jean-Luc tried to keep out of their way. It was obvious they were on Brandje's side, as they cheered her on and helped her escape Nathan's grasp.

Finally Jean-Luc complained like a weary parent, "Do you two children realize that it's two in the morning?"

"You know what?" asked Nathan. "It could be five in the morning and it wouldn't matter. You know why?"

"Why?" Karen inquired.

"Nathan!" Brandje warned menacingly, still in a teasing manner. Nathan raced after her and she jumped up quickly onto the bed, bouncing on it with her feet, much like a young child. "Don't you dare!" she insisted, trying to keep a serious tone, and failing miserably.

Nathan raised an eyebrow and said, "I just can't help it, Brandje. I have to tell them."

"Tell us what?" asked Jean-Luc. "You two are up to something with all the energy you're burning."

Nathan turned around to face the Rousseaus, and with the antics of a young boy he blurted out, "We're getting married!"

Brandje threw a pillow and caught him square in the back of the head. He fell backwards onto her bed, but she jumped off it and ran behind Jean-Luc.

"He's crazy," she said, holding Jean-Luc by the arms to keep Nathan from reaching her.

"I am!" Nathan admitted. "I'm crazy about her! And you know what else? She's just as nuts about me!" The wide grin on his face spoke volumes more than his simple words could.

Karen laughed aloud as she exclaimed, "He told you he loved you!"

"Yes," Brandje admitted, holding up her left hand to reveal the gardenia shaped engagement ring. She did this while still using Jean-Luc as her personal barrier.

"She loves me, too!" grinned Nathan, trying to swat her with the pillow, but catching Jean-Luc in between them.

Jean-Luc turned sideways, obviously on Nathan's side now. "In that case," he said, "I believe we men should stick together."

His movement gave Nathan an advantage. Nathan lunged for Brandje, narrowly missing her as she shrieked and jumped back on the bed again.

"Aren't you going to stop him?" Brandje demanded playfully. "He's turned into a madman."

"Nope. Now I'm on his side," said Jean-Luc. "You accepted his proposal. That would put his energy level at least six miles in the sky! Then you expect him to toddle off to bed without telling anyone. You should be ashamed of yourself," he bantered. To his wife, he said, "You get the first watch. I'll relieve you in two hours." And with that, Jean-Luc turned around and went unceremoniously to his bedroom.

"Hey," said Nathan as he stuck his head out the doorway. "I thought you were on my side."

"I already raised four sons," said Jean-Luc. "I know when the ship is sinking! Sorry, pal. You're on your own."

Nathan laughed and threw himself across Brandje's bed once again. She jumped off it, then turned back around and slammed a pillow against his chest. In doing so, she inadvertently gave Nathan the opportunity to grab her arm and flip her onto the bed beside him.

Then he proceeded to tickle her foot mercilessly. "She's ticklish, too!" he exclaimed, giving Karen a wink. "And she's beautiful! Don't you think she's beautiful?"

The older woman sank wearily onto the window seat, "She is lovely," she admitted. "But how long do you two intend to play these games?"

Brandje laughed until her sides ached.

"All night!" Nathan declared. "How can anyone sleep on a night like this?"

"Easily," said Brandje. She stretched back on the bed and closed her eyes.

Nathan took a tissue from the night stand and tickled Brandje's face with it until she burst out laughing again.

She looked over at Karen and realized the older woman was doing all that she could to prevent herself from openly laughing at them.

"You had all sons," she said to Karen while trying to keep Nathan from tickling her ears. "Were they like this the night they returned home from proposing and their sweethearts said yes?"

"You have no idea what you're in for," nodded Karen. "They were insufferable for weeks before their weddings."

Brandje sat up and grabbed Nathan by the pajama collar with both hands. "Do you want me to call Bishop Buerge and have him come get you?"

"Only if I can bring you with me," he teased, sliding onto his knees on the floor. "Brandje, I can't sleep. I love you. How on earth can you expect me to sleep when all I can think about is how much I love you?"

"He has no shame," she giggled as she glanced at Karen.

"And no pride and no manners and no will to resist you," he said, burying his head in his hands. "What have you done to me woman? I'm not even the same man I was yesterday!"

"I think you'll recover," Karen told him. "But not if you keep the entire household awake tonight. One of us is liable to strangle you."

"And it'll probably be me!" they heard Jean-Luc exclaim from the other bedroom.

With his remark, Karen could stifle her laughter no longer. Her giggling inspired more and soon all three of them were at it again.

A few moments later Jean-Luc came back into the room, wearily waving a white handkerchief tied to a pencil. "I surrender," he said. "Let's go downstairs and feed these two something warm. Maybe that will help them sleep."

By three in the morning they were still sitting at the kitchen table, telling stories from their childhood, holding hands, eating cream of potato soup. Finally Nathan began to wind down, Brandje noticed. His eyelids were puffy and he had a definite laziness to his New England accent.

By four in the morning, the household had settled down. The

Rousseaus were in bed, and Nathan was finally asleep.

Brandje stretched out on her bed and waited for slumber to capture her. She didn't feel tired anymore as she smiled to herself, remembering Nathan's behavior just a few hours earlier. She rarely saw this happy, playful side of him and she loved it! Could they share more such gleeful moments together?

If Brandje had told him last night about the cancer, as she had intended, he would have been too distraught to let such playfulness overcome him, and she would not have the special memory of their pillow fight now. For those joyful moments alone, she was grateful she had waited.

Regretfully, today she would have to tell Nathan about the cancer. Afterward, would he ever laugh again? Somehow she would have to find a way to help him laugh.

randje tossed and turned, but sleep escaped her. She slipped from the bed and put on her robe and slippers.

The sun hadn't risen yet. Had Nathan remembered their date to meet at Timbal's Point? She doubted it.

The Rousseaus were finally sleeping. She and Nathan had kept them awake until four this morning. *The dear old souls. They'll probably sleep until noon,* she thought.

Stepping across the hall to Nathan's bedroom, she opened the door and smiled as she watched him sleeping peacefully.

She sighed and wondered if she should wake him. Stepping on her toes, she crossed the space between them and stroked his forehead with her fingers. He didn't stir. Reluctantly, Brandje decided to let him sleep.

Stepping to his dresser, she snatched a piece of paper, then wrote a short note upon it. She put the note on the night stand, in front of Nathan's alarm clock, so he would have to move it before he could see what time it was. Then she slipped quietly down the stairs and out the back door, closing it carefully so she wouldn't awaken anyone.

As she walked across the back yard to the hydrangea, the sky had not yet begun to change from black to charcoal.

Brandje sighed as she passed behind the hydrangea and out to the granite steps. The scent of gardenias filled her with a sense of comfort and content. Although the sky was still dark, a half-moon brightened the pale gardenia blossoms against the green foliage, enabling her to see the flowers. She picked a single gardenia and tucked it into her hair, enjoying the sweet fragrance. Holding carefully to the bronze chain, she quickly descended the steps, leaving her slippers a few steps down from the top, and walked across the sandbar to Timbal's point, where she climbed the massive rock with ease. The tide would be coming in soon, but she hoped she could see a few glimpses of sunrise before she had to retreat to higher ground.

Sitting in her favorite spot, a smooth, flat surface almost dead center at the top of Timbal's Point, she crossed her legs Indian style and savored the fresh salt air as it filled her lungs with each inhalation.

How many times had she and Martin played *King Arthur* on this massive rock? How many times had he let her run him through with a rubber sword, and fallen to the ground like a valiant knight dying in the heat of battle?

As she recalled all the glorious memories she'd shared with her family, she longed to travel back in time at least fifteen years. She wanted to hear her grandfather calling her name as she hid on the eastern side of Timbal's Point during a game of hide-and-seek. How many sunrises had she shared with her grandfather, as well as with her brother, Martin, at this place? How many sunsets?

Her thoughts switched from Martin to the other man in her life. She ached with all the love she had for Nathan. She felt physically ill as she resolved that today was the day she would tell him the entire truth, the first moment they were alone together, before she lost her courage. At last Brandje knew that he loved her beyond all reason. In the moonlight, she admired the gardenia shaped ring on her finger with a lingering smile of nostalgia. Knowing that Nathan loved her in return made her task seem more difficult. How do you tell the man you love that you're dying?

Concerns tumbled through her mind like disjointed fragments of time, always leaving her with questions for which there were no answers.

"I haven't died yet," she said firmly to the vast horizon in front of her "Do you hear me? As long as there's a breath inside me, I'll fight to stay alive. I want to spend every minute, every second of the time I have left with Nathan."

She wanted to marry Nathan! But would that be in his best interest? Would he still want to marry her after today? She couldn't give him a temple marriage, not yet. The disappointment she felt at learning, only three days ago, that new members must wait a year before they can go to the temple had nearly crushed her. She would never survive a year, not without a transplant. Her chance of receiving a liver in time were slim to none. She doubted Nathan would even consider marrying her outside the temple. Could he bring himself to break the covenant he'd made to the Lord regarding how he would marry? Did she have the right to ask him to break that vow?

At least they would be together, she reasoned. He could have her sealed to him in a year past her death. Would that be too terrible for him to consider?

Would it really be fair of her to marry Nathan at all? Her part in the situation was fairly clear cut. She could marry him today, go home to God tomorrow.

Nathan's role would be much less desirable. He could marry her today, bury her sometime before Christmas, have her sealed to him a year later, then join her on the other side in . . . say fifty or sixty years.

Would he ever find another woman to love? Would he be sealed to her also? Would Brandje be able to accept such a sealing?

She had far too many questions, and not enough answers.

She didn't know why she was told to put her name on the donor list. She only knew that she had. But what did it all mean? Did God intend to provide a suitable donor for her? Or in the final result, would this just be a way of helping Nathan and Martin deal with her death? They would then be able to console themselves with those ill-fated words: *At least we tried everything!*

Would a donor be found in time? She was taking her pain pills and delirium medication with some regularity now, though Nathan knew nothing of that. Sometimes when the pain came, it was so severe it doubled her over. Fortunately, she'd been extra careful, napping every afternoon, retiring early, drinking lots of liquids, getting some exercise each day. It seemed to her that ever since she'd received her answers from God about the Book of Mormon, and about placing her name on the waiting list, she'd felt much better. At least, her spirits had been much lighter. Why should today be any different?

Of course, she knew the answer to that. Today she would tell Nathan the truth.

The sun lightened the dark sky behind the villa and the hills surrounding Croix de Vie, but Brandje had not noticed. Nor had she paid attention to the rising tide, now almost to the top of Timbal's Point.

She was lost in thought, worry etched in the azure blue of her eyes, which, with each passing moment, came closer to matching the color of the sea.

Her wake-up call came suddenly as an unexpected wave drenched her in one fell swoop, knocking her over, nearly sweeping her off Timbal's Point into a foaming, watery grave. Clinging to a jutting rock, horror etched upon her face, she realized that the tide had rushed in while she was deep in thought. With angry, white-tongued waves, the incoming surge licked a deadly path towards her. She recalled with vivid clarity the fate of the seal that had been thrown off the Point and against the cliff by enormous waves such as these.

Without realizing she had done so, Brandje screamed.

Nathan sat bolt upright in bed! At the same time, the telephone rang noisily in the living room. "Will someone answer the phone?" He moaned, then fell back onto the bed and rolled over sleepily.

He heard the patter of footsteps on the stairs, then the phone stopped ringing.

Within a short time, Karen tapped on Nathan's door. It wasn't closed all the way and she pushed it open. "Nathan," she said, "it's Brandje's brother, Martin. I tried to find her, but she's not in the villa."

Nathan looked at the clock to see what time it was. Immediately he noticed Brandje's note. He picked it up and read it aloud,

> *"Darling, If you wake up in time for our date, you know where I'll be. Love, Brandje."*

He yawned as Karen raised a questioning eyebrow. "It's not what you're thinking," he said, holding his hand up to prevent any protest. "Right after I proposed last night, Brandje was going to tell me something important. When you arrived, she postponed it until this morning." Nathan pulled on his bathrobe. "I'll go down and talk to Martin, then I'll go find her."

"Oh, dear," sighed Karen, obviously disturbed at this information. "I suppose I shouldn't have interrupted you last night."

"Believe me," he said, "you came at precisely the right moment."

Karen smiled, apparently relieved. "That makes me feel better," she admitted, before she returned to her bedroom.

Nathan put on his robe and slippers, then hurried down the stairs. Picking up the telephone receiver from the desk, he said, "Hello, Martin? Martin?" He thought for a moment that he heard an intake of breath. "Listen, she'll have to return your call. She's out watching the sunrise."

No one answered, but he heard a distinct click as the line went dead. He placed the receiver back in the cradle, then stepped out through the back doorway. He wondered if Brandje would be angry that he'd stood her up. Somehow he doubted it. Truthfully, he was surprised she hadn't slept later. They'd all had quite a night.

Nathan rounded the last hydrangea bush and walked across the path to the stairs, but Brandje wasn't there. When he looked down, he saw her slippers resting a few steps below him. His heart sank in his chest. He felt like someone had knocked the wind out of him. His eyes searched the roiling surf below him, first to the east, then to the west. The sandbar was completely submerged with foaming, churning water. With horror, he realized that she could be drowned by now. The tide was at the top of flood, and the water was well over twelve feet deep.

His eyes followed the water-buried pathway out to Timbal's Point. When he looked atop the massive boulder, what he saw made his hair stand on end. Huge waves were breaking across Brandje as she clung to Timbal's Point. "Brandje!" he yelled, running down the stairs three at a time. Within seconds he was up to his chest in white, foaming seawater.

Nathan dove into the breakers and swam beneath the turmoil,

holding his breath as long as he could. When he surfaced, he was only a fourth of the distance to Timbal's Point.

He dove again, deep, out of the churning foam. But the current was unbelievably wild and he was pushed against the ocean bottom, the air crushed from his lungs, his chest bruised against the sandpaper earth.

Nathan resurfaced. The incoming tide had nearly buried Timbal's Point, and Brandje with it.

"Brandje!" he yelled in futility.

She couldn't hear him above the roaring surf, and her gaze seemed transfixed upon the incoming waters.

Swimming to his left he came in directly behind the point where the water was slightly calmer. His strong arms stroked along the surface until he struck solid ground. He stood about two thirds of the distance up Timbal's Point, yet his head was barely above water.

"Brandje!" he yelled again.

Brandje turned. She saw Nathan struggling toward her, within a few feet of the Point. She cried out in terror, "Go back! Nathan, go back!"

But Nathan continued forward. "Brandje!" he yelled again, banging a knee into solid rock, ripping his pajamas and leaving a wide gash below his kneecap.

Suddenly an enormous wave broke over Brandje. She lost her grip and was washed back across the rock. Another wave followed the first, immediately sweeping her into Nathan's waiting arms.

She spit saltwater from her mouth and clung desperately to him.

"Why? Brandje, why?" he yelled, still not comprehending how she'd been caught out on Timbal's Point at high tide. With one arm holding onto her, he used the other to power stroke toward the stairs.

Brandje did not help their progress. In her panic to breathe, she sucked in seawater and began to choke and cough violently. Nathan turned her around to face him. Holding her shoulders with his hands to keep her head above water, he used his knee to perform a variation on the Heimlich maneuver. Suddenly she went limp in his arms.

Nathan shuddered. Had she fainted, or had she stopped breathing altogether? He pulled her face near his to discern if she was breathing, but in the churning, roiling foam he couldn't tell.

With renewed strength, he put his arm across her chest, his hand gripping her robe tightly.

He would have to pull her out into the worst breakers if they were to survive at all. If he couldn't make it, they would both be crushed against the cliff.

As the waves pushed them toward solid granite, he continued to swim sideways with his free arm, counting the seconds since he'd last seen her take a breath of air, knowing that he was in a desperate race to save her life.

A monstrous wave approached. If he could get a little more distance along the wall, it could lift them both right to the stairs.

He wrapped his arm tighter around Brandje's limp form and struck out with his other arm, swimming with all his strength.

Suddenly the wave broke over them, curling them around, rinsing them down to the ocean floor. Nathan wrapped both arms around Brandje's waist and held onto her with all his strength. When they finally resurfaced, he realized they were within a few feet of the stairs. He reached out and grabbed onto one of the bronze posts, pulling Brandje along with him.

A sense of relief washed over him, almost more tangibly than the water surrounding them. But he knew she was not safe yet. He swung his legs over the chain, and with renewed effort, he felt his feet touch solid granite.

Lifting Brandje over the chain, he carried her up the stairs and out of the water's reach. She was not breathing as he placed her limp form on the steps and used the Heimlich maneuver, and mouth to mouth resuscitation to revive her, praying every instant for divine intervention.

What seemed like hours of struggling to help her breathe was actually only a few moments.

Brandje coughed violently. He rolled her over, onto her side, until she had expelled the salt water from her lungs. When she finally stopped coughing, he watched with trepidation until she opened her blue eyes, now almost gray-blue in the early morning light.

Relief permeated every fiber of his being. Never had he felt so strongly the guidance of the Lord in rescuing her. If Martin hadn't called, if Nathan hadn't heard the phone, if he'd been one second later, he wouldn't have been in position to catch Brandje when she was washed across the top of Timbal's Point.

He held her close to him, studied her face, and tried to find the sparkle that he loved in her eyes.

She coughed violently once again. Nathan rolled her over one more time. When she was finished, she started to shiver, but her color began to improve. Within moments she looked up and gave him a weak smile.

"Th–thank you," she stammered.

Realizing that she was going to pull through, he felt a rush of anger and, without thinking clearly, he yelled, "What on earth were you trying to do? Have you no common sense at all?"

Tears formed in her eyes as a hint of the azure he loved returned to them. "Sorry," she managed to say. "Didn't mean to —"

"You didn't mean to stay out there?" he asked, hoping he had understood correctly.

Brandje stammered. "I was lost —" she coughed, "—lost in thought," she amended. "I lost track of time."

Nathan held her close for a moment, thinking over what she'd said to him before she was swept into his waiting arms. "Why did you tell me to go back?" he asked, his temper easing as she tried to explain.

"I love you," she said. "I was afraid you would die while trying to rescue me."

He gave her a knowing smile and responded. "I would have died willingly in order to save you." After he kissed her tenderly, he scolded her. "You should have realized that the moment you saw me out there."

Brandje shivered once again.

"Let's get you back to the villa," he suggested.

"No," she whispered. "Not yet. I have to tell you," she said.

"Later," he insisted. "You're freezing."

"I don't care about that," she said. "Please, Nathan. Just hold me. Let me talk to you. Please."

Against his better judgement, he relented. He lifted her carefully and carried her several steps closer to the top, so there would be no danger of their being washed out to sea. Then he sat down and held her on his lap. He circled his arms around her in an effort to keep her warm while she talked to him.

"Don't say anything," she pleaded. "Wait until I'm through. Nathan, you have to listen now, and try to understand."

"As you wish," he whispered hoarsely as a strange weariness settled upon him.

"I didn't know how to tell you everything," she said. "I tried to awaken you this morning, but you were sleeping too soundly. I just stroked your forehead, then wrote a note for you, then I came out here. It was still dark, and the tide hadn't made much progress yet. I had so many things to think about."

"I'm sure there's a point to all this somewhere," he teased, hoping to lighten her mood, but she put her hands on his lips to silence him.

"Shhh," she said, "let me finish."

He watched Brandje tremble as she stared into his dark eyes. Tears slipped down her salt-watered cheeks. "Oh, Nathan," she said, turning her head from side to side. "There is just no easy way to say this."

She buried her face against his wet robe and cried with great, wracking sobs of anguish.

A lump formed in his throat and a feeling of overwhelming compassion came over him. He wanted to know all the secrets she had been keeping from him. Her heart-wrenching sobs nearly broke his heart. "Tell me," he said, wanting to protect her, to comfort her. He kissed her forehead. "Together we can handle anything, Brandje. I promise."

She waited only a moment, then she inhaled sharply, as though driven by some inner courage. With grave finality, Brandje said, "I have cancer, Nathan. I truly am dying. I won't be here to give you children. I won't be able to marry you in the temple because I won't live another year. By Christmas I'll just be a memory in your heart."

Every muscle in Nathan's body tensed. He tilted her chin with his strong hand, forcing her to look at him, then stared in disbelief into her azure blue eyes. The torment he witnessed in them was indescribable.

A sick feeling, unlike anything he'd ever felt before, came over him, and he gasped, "No! It can't be true!" Tears wrenched from his eyes, stinging, blinding him. "It can't be!"

He pulled her tightly against his chest, as if he could squeeze away the terrible aching pain that seemed to consume his entire body.

Though his mind insisted such a thing was impossible, deep inside himself, he knew, and this knowledge ripped him apart. He wanted to tear down the Heavens piece by piece and ask God why! Why?

"Nathan, I'm so sorry," Brandje cried. "I wanted to tell you sooner. But I didn't know how you felt about me. If I was just a summer fling for you, I didn't want you to know. As you started to mellow out, I realized that you might be falling in love with me. Still, I just couldn't tell you until I knew for sure."

"That's why all the praying and the tears yesterday?" he asked.

She nodded. "I'm so sorry," she said again. "I can't imagine how you must feel. I've tried to put myself in your shoes, but it's impossible. I'd rather die myself than see you —"

"I won't let you die, Brandje!" he vowed, his lips brushing against her wet hair. "Have you explored all your options? Chemotherapy —"

She lifted her head and kissed his words into silence. Then she pulled back so that her face was inches from his. She stared straight into his dark eyes. "Chemotherapy doesn't work with this particular kind of cancer. It's called primary neuroendocrine carcinoma, and it's confined to my liver. It's a rare cancer that doesn't metastasize to other organs. My only option is to have a liver transplant."

"That's —"

She kissed him again, silencing him once more. Then she placed a finger against his lips, and said, "I'm on a donor list in the United States. The big problem is that my blood type is very rare. The odds are not in my favor, darling."

"Oh, Merciful Father," he choked as he crushed her against him. "Why? Why?"

"Don't," she said, pulling away. "Nathan, please. You need to let me finish."

"There's more?" he asked, fearful of what else she could say.

She gave him a hopeful smile. "Eight days ago I had no intention of going on the donor list. Karen was furious with me for that and begged me to reconsider."

"Then she knows?" he asked.

"Will you listen?" she insisted. After he nodded, she continued, "That morning when the Lord gave me my answer about the Book of Mormon, he also told me that I must go on the donor list."

"He did?" Nathan asked, a whisper of hope replacing a portion of the anguish in his heart.

She nodded and gave him an encouraging smile.

"Then there's hope," said Nathan as tears spilled from his eyes.

He stood and carried her up the steps. When they reached the top he refused to put her down. He swung back around and looked at the wide horizon, the gray-blue sky, the foaming sea. "There's hope!" he yelled at the top of his lungs. "There's still hope!"

He carried her across the ridge and around the hydrangea. "Nathan, please, let me walk," she said. "Don't treat me like I'm an invalid, not yet."

Suddenly realizing that her independence must be granted, he gently put her down and let her stand beside him. Then he held her hand in his. "You've been through a lot this morning," he said. "Are you sure you're all right?"

"I'm never without pain now," she admitted, "but I'm learning to endure some of it." They took a step forward and she winced. Then she smiled and said, "My best pace is often slower than yours."

Nathan began a slow, agonizing stroll across the expansive lawn toward the villa, holding her hand. As they walked, he asked, "How many other people know?"

"Karen and Jean-Luc," she answered. "Martin and Bishop Buerge."

"That's all?" he asked.

"Well," she teased, "Pierre knows."

He stopped and gazed at her for a moment, remembering her tears when they'd left the restaurant that day. He'd been consumed with anger! Angry that she'd gone to meet Pierre at all, angry that she'd cried. If he'd known the truth, he would never have teased her about what he'd considered a ruse to get rid of Pierre. A ball of fire arose from the pit of his stomach, a new, scalding anger aimed at himself. Crispness in his voice made him realize he was very near to losing his temper once again. "You should have told me sooner!" he snapped. "We've wasted time sitting here at the villa!"

"I couldn't tell you," she insisted. "I explained all that."

"How could I have been so blind?" he asked aloud, his voice bitter. But the regret was aimed at himself, not at her. Frustration made his voice harsh. "The terrible pain, the fainting, that look in your eyes of such horrible sadness and fear all mixed together. Six weeks recovery time from an operation and you're getting worse, not better. And then, with Karen hovering over you as though you were on the brink of death, why didn't I put it all together?"

"Nathan!" she complained. "You had no way of knowing unless someone told you."

"That's a laugh!" he hissed, stopping in mid-stride. "You know what I thought it was?" His voice raised in pitch as anger ignited emotions that should have been contained. "I thought your condition was due to some female problem, something too personal to discuss. I even wondered if you couldn't have children anymore, that would certainly have explained all those signs! But I was prepared to deal with that! We could adopt children, I thought, if it came to that. It wouldn't matter."

"Your temper is showing, Nathan. Does it anger you that I'm dying?" she questioned. Her lower lip trembled.

"You're not dying!" he growled. "Don't ever say that!"

He turned her toward him and looked down at her, a mixture of fear and remorse on his face.

"All right," she challenged. "Does it anger you that I have cancer?"

"No!" he denied. "I'm angry that you didn't tell me sooner!"

"Oh!" she snapped. "I suppose the moment you walked into my bedroom with my robe in your hands I should have said, 'Hi. My name's Brandje and I have cancer!' Is that what I should have done?"

"No!" he yelled. "But it would have been nice if halfway into our relationship you'd have told me! That first time on the beach would have been more appropriate! You could have said that you had cancer then!"

"What would that have accomplished?" she demanded, yelling at him in return. "Would it have made you less likely to have fallen in love with me? Would that make you feel better now?"

"No!" he denied vehemently. Then, forcing himself to soften as he realized he'd angered her again, he said, "Brandje —"

She cut him off. "What you're really trying to say is that when I told you there were extenuating circumstances, I should have stated immediately what those circumstances were. If I'd done that, you would have fled back to New York where there would not be the remotest possibility of your falling in love with someone who's making funeral arrangements for December!"

Brandje whirled around, putting her back to him. Then she stiffened and moaned in agony.

Nathan scooped her up into his arms. He looked into her eyes for only a moment and was dismayed to see a look of pure anguish within them, as though she was suffering from terrible pain.

He watched helplessly as she tried to control this new bout of pain by taking deep, agonizing breaths. Although he'd had no intention of causing her additional suffering, he feared that he had done exactly that. Tenderly, she reached her hand up and placed it against his cheek. "Oh, Nathan," she whispered. "Why do we always have to quarrel?"

Immediately following her question, she clutched at her abdomen as if trying to ease her pain. "This is the worst it has ever been!" she gasped raggedly. Then she fainted in his arms.

Chapter Eighteen

Maneuvering the door knob with his hand, Nathan used his leg to bump the door completely open. He carried Brandje up the stairs, yelling as he did so, "Jean-Luc! Karen!"

Within moments the elderly couple appeared from their bedroom. Nathan placed Brandje carefully on her bed and started to remove her wet robe.

"Gracious!" said Karen as she and Jean-Luc entered. "You're both soaking wet!"

Nathan made an attempt to control his fear and anguish, but his efforts were futile. The first thing he said to the elderly couple was much harsher than he intended. "It was irresponsible of all of you not to tell me sooner!"

"Blame Brandje for that one," said Jean-Luc, unwilling to let the younger man belittle them. "You know how stubborn she is. She absolutely forbid it."

"That's no excuse!" Nathan barked as he ran his fingers anxiously through his hair while Karen sat beside Brandje on the bed and began to assess her condition.

"I'm trying," Nathan said, "I'm really trying to stay calm, so please, forgive me if I'm unable to, but when she passed out I suddenly realized that if I'd known she had a problem with her liver I may have taken greater precautions when performing the Heimlich Maneuver. It's only by the grace of God that she's alive at all."

He paced back and forth while Karen took charge of the situation. "I'll need some smelling salts," she said. "Jean-Luc, where did you put the first aid kit?"

"In our bedroom," said Jean-Luc. He quickly retrieved a heavy bag and brought it to her.

"Oh, Nathan, please stop pacing," said Karen. "Go take a shower and get the salt washed off you. Once I've got Brandje settled, the three of us will sit down calmly and talk."

"No!" he snapped. "She was half-drowned at the top of Timbal's Point by the time I reached her! She couldn't breathe! She was choking on sea water. Without knowing about her liver problem, I kneed her in the stomach to open her airway. When I finally got her out of the water she still couldn't breathe. I may have performed the Heimlich Maneuver completely wrong. I may have punctured her lungs, or done something horrible to her liver. We need to take her to the hospital."

Karen stood up and gathered herself as tall and rigid as she could. "She is absolutely not to be taken to any hospital without her prior consent. I gave her my word of honor that I wouldn't allow anyone to do that, not even you!"

"Your word of honor has no bearing here. She's my fiancé!"

Karen held her ground. "Until she's your wife, I am bound by moral, ethical and legal jurisdiction to protect her right of agency."

"Fine," he growled, "I'll go get a marriage license and a preacher!"

He turned and stormed out of the bedroom.

"Nathan, wait!" Jean-Luc pleaded, following him down the stairs. "You're still in your pajamas! Nathan, before you cause any more damage, let's sit down and talk this over like two adults!"

Nathan turned back to face him. "Any more damage?" he accused. "You're the ones who withheld information from me, so that I had no way of knowing I could possibly inflict any damage to her in the first place!"

"I'm not talking about your saving her life, I'm talking about your quarreling with her out in the yard." Jean-Luc pleaded.

His words stopped Nathan cold.

Then Jean-Luc asked, "Do you think we couldn't hear you? Your bedroom window isn't the only one that's open around here."

Nathan exhaled and sank wearily onto the sofa. "I'm coming apart!" His voice was ragged with fear and raw emotion. "I can't believe what's happening to her! Why didn't you tell me sooner?"

"Because she had hope in her heart before today, before you ripped into her like a hungry shark," Jean-Luc said. "Nathan, that's all she's got now is hope. Take that away from her and she'll have nothing."

Nathan, realizing that Jean-Luc had his finger on the pulse of the problem, placed his head in his hands and wept bitterly.

An hour later Karen came downstairs. It was obvious that she was exhausted, but at least she had a faint smile on her face.

"She's resting comfortably," said the older woman. "I scrubbed her from top to bottom, and washed the sand and salt from her hair, during which time, I examined her thoroughly. She has a few bruises on her legs and arm, but none on her abdomen. Her lungs are fine, her ribs are all intact. You did no damage to her liver, Nathan."

Nathan sighed in relief.

"She revived easily with the smelling salts. It was the pain in her liver that caused this episode, and I gave her some medication to control that. I expect this was more likely brought on from her not resting properly. She didn't nap yesterday at all, like she usually does. And then she was up all night." Karen continued, "Furthermore, you are absolutely right, Nathan. We should have told you sooner. But let's not quarrel over spilled milk. The only way Brandje is going to get through this ordeal is if she feels love and hope, from all of us."

"He's calmed down now," said Jean-Luc. "We've had a long talk and I've explained to him everything that we know about her condition."

Nathan lifted his head and nodded. "I apologize," he said to Karen. "I didn't mean to offend you."

Karen gave him a nod as she walked over to the sofa, sat beside him and gave his hand a gentle squeeze. "I accept your apology," she said, softening.

"When a man's been kicked in the stomach by a mule," said Jean-Luc, "sometimes the only way he can recover is to fight back."

"How long before I can see her?" Nathan asked.

"I should think you'd want to clean yourself up a bit first," smiled Karen. "Otherwise, you might frighten her again. "

Nathan looked down at his torn pajama bottoms. Blood had soaked through one pant leg from the knee down, a sleeve was completely ripped off his robe, and his slippers were gone, most likely lost at sea. In his anxiety to protect Brandje, he hadn't realized the episode at Timbal's Point had left him with any physical damage.

"Will you need me to look at that knee?" asked Karen.

"No, I'll do it." He headed for the stairs, then turned back with a forlorn glance. "Thanks," he said, "for everything."

At the top of the stairs Nathan stopped at Brandje's bedroom door and looked inside. She was sleeping in almost the same position as that very first morning he saw her, with her beautiful hair covering the pillow like spun gold. As it had before, his heart raced inside his chest and he felt an overwhelming sensation to protect her. She was almost too sweet, too beautiful to look upon.

An hour later he emerged from the bathroom, bandaged, dressed in Levis and a denim shirt, and well-groomed, except for a stubborn lock of hair that, even now, defied the laws of gravity.

Brandje was still sound asleep as he stepped downstairs and found the Rousseaus in the kitchen. "Did you get in touch with Bishop Buerge?" asked Nathan.

Jean-Luc held up a piece of paper. "He called the stake president. You can meet with them both tomorrow, if Brandje's up to it. In the meantime, the stake president is going to contact someone at church headquarters for final authorization."

"Thank you," said Nathan. "I don't know how I can thank you enough."

Tears threatened to fill his eyes again, but he forced them away.

"I made a sandwich for you," said Karen, taking it from the refrigerator. "You'll need to eat something. You've burned up a lot of energy these past few hours."

Nathan nodded. He felt numb inside, like something was no longer connected and he couldn't function. "I'd like to have a blessing," he told Jean-Luc. "Would you arrange for someone to assist you? And then, if Brandje will permit, I'd like her to have a blessing as well."

"You could act as voice for her," suggested Jean-Luc.

"No," he shook his head. "I'm too close to the situation. I'm afraid I'd say something not in keeping with the Lord's wishes."

"I see your point," said Jean-Luc. "I'll arrange these blessings for tomorrow, when we visit the stake president."

For the next several hours, Nathan, Jean-Luc and Karen, sat in the living room, making plans and telephone calls so that Brandje could begin the next phase of her life. There was so much to arrange for, and Nathan was grateful for the Rousseaus' companionship, as well as their forgiveness.

Finally, around three in the afternoon, the Rousseaus went back upstairs to take a nap, while Nathan sat in a chair beside Brandje's bed. He watched quietly as she slept. Not wanting to disturb her, he just wanted to be near her. For several hours he sat beside her, gazing upon her lovely face, committing to memory every feature, every eyelash, every lock of her golden hair.

When the telephone rang, it startled him. Quickly he dashed downstairs to answer it, before it awakened the others.

"Hello," he said, speaking into the mouthpiece. "Fulton residence."

"Martin Fulton here," came a deep male voice. "Is Brandje available?"

"Not at the moment," said Nathan. "But I'm glad you've called, Martin. My name is Nathaniel Duncan. I met your sister a few weeks ago."

"Oh?" asked Martin cautiously.

"Yes," said Nathan. "And I'm going to tell you straight out. I'm in love with Brandje, and I'm planning to marry her right away."

Nathan heard a surprised gasp, then Martin asked, "When will I be able to speak to her?"

"She had a bad spell with her liver problem this morning, and Karen has sedated her. She'll likely be up and around by tomorrow. Shall I have her call you then?"

"Karen Rousseau?" Martin asked, fear evident in his voice. "Is she a nurse?"

"Yes," Nathan responded quickly. "Karen is also a dear friend. She's agreed to help care for Brandje until she's feeling better."

"I see," said Martin. "And how did you meet my sister?"

"It's a long story," Nathan admitted. "But I'm sure she'll share it with you when she telephones tomorrow. Would that be all right?"

"Very well, then. Thank you for telling me." He hesitated a moment, then he asked, "Do you truly love Brandje?"

"I love her with every ounce of strength that I've got," Nathan admitted.

"And she's told you about —?"

"The cancer in her liver?" Nathan interrupted.

"Precisely," Martin said.

"Of course. That's why we're marrying so soon. I want to make these next few months as happy as I can for her, until the liver transplant is over. Then I plan to spend the next fifty or more years keeping her happy and healthy."

"Amazing! Simply amazing," came Martin's response.

"Isn't it!" Nathan agreed.

"I'll look forward to hearing from her then. Please remind her to ring me."

"I will," said Nathan. "Nice meeting you, even if it is by telephone. Brandje's told me all about you."

After Nathan replaced the receiver, he went back up to Brandje's bedroom. She rolled over when he came in and gave him a tender smile that melted his knees entirely. He sat beside her on the edge of the bed, where he studied her face, her eyes, trying to decide whether or not she was still angry with him.

"Well?" she asked timidly, as though wondering the same thing.

Her simple question gave him hope. He leaned over and gave her a tender kiss, delighted when she kissed him back eagerly. Then he sat up, surprised at the depth of love he had sensed from her, and said, "Well, I guess your last theory won't hold water, either."

"What?"

He grinned. "No, I see all sizes of holes in that theory."

"Remind me," she smiled back. "What theory are you talking about?"

Nathan stated sincerely, "If you'd told me that first day what the extenuating circumstances were, I would have stayed and married you."

"Why?" she asked, puzzled.

"Because I fell in love with you the moment I first saw you sleeping right here in this bed, with your hair shining and curled all over your pillow, and that perfect little nose that I love to kiss."

"You're just saying that," she teased, "to make me feel better."

"I'm not," he confessed. "But do you feel better?"

"No," she answered with a sigh. "My liver hurts so bad! You have no idea . . ."

"I think I do," he disagreed. "But I'm not going to fight with you over that. Now, tell me where your pain pills are and I'll get them for you."

"In the top drawer of my dresser."

Nathan stood up and opened it. "Oh, you mean in here along with the bras and the panties?

"That's my stocking drawer," she smiled.

"Hmm, that's why I didn't recognize these things. They're never on your feet."

"My pills, sir," she insisted, holding out her hand.

"You have three different kinds."

"Bring them all."

He removed the bottles and brought them over to her. She quickly swallowed two pills with a glass of water from the night stand.

"I think we can keep these out here now," Nathan said, putting the medicine bottles on the night stand next to a pitcher, "where you can reach them easily if you need them. No reason to hide them from me anymore," he teased.

Brandje sighed. "I really made a mess of things, didn't I?" she asked.

"That's right," he said, kissing the tip of her nose, teasing and hoping to make her smile again. "Because if you'd told me that very first morning while you nibbled the toast and ignored the omelette, what the extenuating circumstances were, I would have taken you out that very same day, found a preacher, and married you. Then, instead of fighting each other all these weeks, we could have been kissing, and making love, and hugging, and making love." He winked. "We would really know one another now, and we wouldn't be fighting."

She laughed, "We'd still be fighting, and you know it."

"Yes," he said, stretching his lean body out upon the bed next to her, but on top of the quilt. "But after we finished fighting we'd be kissing, and making up, and hugging, and making love. And we wouldn't have this quilt separating us anymore. Don't you think that would have been better than the way it's been all these weeks?"

"I couldn't have married you the very first day."

"Why not?" he asked, kissing her forehead, her cheeks, and stopping short of her lips.

"Because you didn't have a car to go find a preacher."

"Details," he whispered huskily. "All you can remember are the details."

"Like this one?" she asked as she reached up and put her arms around his neck, then pulled him closer and brushed his lips with hers. He responded by kissing her soundly. Afterward, he said, "I'm going to be one desperate man by the end of the week."

"Meaning you're not already?"

"Meaning," he smiled deliciously, "I won't be desperate anymore after the end of the week!"

"Why not?"

"Because we're getting married at the end of the week," he stated with a wide smile and a wink.

"We are?" She blinked, as though uncertain she had heard correctly.

"If all goes well," he admitted with a nod and a big grin. "Now, where were we?" he asked, studying her lips sensuously.

"Nathan," she complained. "We can't. What about our covenants?"

"We'll just have to make some new ones," he suggested.

"But Nathan —"

"Details, details," he grinned. "Hmm, can I remember some of those details you're so interested in? Let's see, there's the day detail, that's Friday morning. Then there's the place detail, somewhere in London."

"Why London?"

"Because," he said, kissing her tenderly, lingering, until she finally pushed against his shoulders, releasing her lips from his.

"Why?" she demanded.

"Well," he drawled seductively, "that's where the London Temple is located."

"What? But you said I had to be a member for a year."

He grinned. How he loved her reactions of surprise and astonishment when he teased her! "That was before I knew about the extenuating circumstances," he admitted. "You see, Brandje, the Lord has a contingency program for extenuating circumstances, and it just so happens that we are sharing the villa with a man who knows exactly how to arrange everything. If you're up to it, we can go for our temple recommend interviews tomorrow."

"Not if you don't get off that bed," said Jean-Luc in a teasing, yet firm manner, as he looked at them from the doorway. "I'm still the chaperone here, and I intend to get you two to the temple while you're still worthy!"

Nathan shrugged. "Bother!" he whispered to Brandje.

"What was that?" Jean-Luc asked.

"Maybe he's glad you still . . . bother to care," Brandje suggested with a grin.

Nathan slid off the bed and sat back in the chair beside it. Properly holding her hand in his, he gave Jean-Luc an arched eyebrow.

Jean-Luc nodded his approval, then went downstairs to the kitchen.

The following morning Jean-Luc drove Karen, Nathan and Brandje to Nantes. He dropped Karen off at their son's home so she could visit the grandchildren. Then he took Nathan and Brandje to see Bishop Buerge, who interviewed them both separately, and signed temple recommends for them. Afterward, Bishop Buerge accompanied them as Jean-Luc drove from Nantes to Chateaubriant, where they met with the stake president.

After detailed interviews with Brandje and Nathan, President Mikhail spoke to both of them together, counseling them to cherish whatever time the Lord intended to give them, to refrain from quarreling, to leave no scarred moments in their marriage, so that they would never have any regrets regarding their relationship. He asked Brandje to begin right away in gathering names of her parents and ancestors, so that their ordinance work could be properly attended to, and recommended that she may want to consider having her parents, in particular, sealed to each other, and she to them, while they were in London for their own sealing.

"Can I do that?" Brandje questioned.

"You can," President Mikhail assured her.

Tears sprang to Brandje's eyes. "I would love that," she said. "I've prayed that the Lord would open the way for me to be sealed to them."

President Mikhail smiled kindly. "The laws of Great Britain require that you marry civilly prior to being sealed in the temple," he explained. "Normally I advise young people to marry civilly in the morning, then be sealed in the temple later that same day. Where rest seems to be a premium commodity in determining how you feel, Sister Fulton, I would advise that you marry civilly and take out your endowments that same day, if you're feeling up to it. The endowment session can be quite taxing the first time through. There is much to learn, and you may find yourself exhausted afterward. Your health may dictate that you wait until the following day for your sealing to Brother Duncan. Since he has expressed his desire that the two of you wait to consummate your marriage vows until after you are sealed, you may want to consider my advice. The day after you take out your endowments, after you've recuperated, you would only have to return to the temple for a short time, long enough to participate in your marriage sealing, thus saving your strength and energy for the other festivities involved on your wedding day."

Brandje nodded and gave Nathan a demure smile as he squeezed her hand. Ever mindful of her needs, she felt grateful for his consideration, regardless of his own personal desires.

President Mikhail then explained that he had copies of two letters, faxed to him earlier in the day from church headquarters in Salt Lake. Both were required for Brandje's temple recommend. The first was originally from William Graham, M.D., describing Brandje's medical condition and the prognosis inherent to it, which had been faxed to Salt Lake the previous day for immediate consideration. The second was signed by Apostle Russell M. Nelson, the apostle best qualified to understand her medical disorder, authorizing the temple to permit Brandje the opportunity of temple ordinances, taking into account the seriousness of her illness. President Mikhail gave them two copies of each letter, along with copies of his own, addressed to the temple president. They were to present one copy of each page to the temple president, who was also a personal friend of President Mikhail. They could retain the second copies for their own records.

Then President Mikhail invited both bishops back into the room, asking them to assist in the special blessings that had been earlier requested. Jean-Luc anointed Nathan. With both Bishops assisting, President Mikhail gave him a blessing of comfort and strength, and a word of caution regarding not allowing bitterness or anger to creep into his relationship with the woman the Lord had provided for him.

Afterward, Nathan anointed Brandje. Then, with Nathan and both Bishops assisting, President Mikhail blessed her by first expressing how much the Lord loved Brandje, and what a priceless jewel she was to Him, who held her life in His hand. Although the blessing did not promise that a donor would be found, nor that she would live a long and healthy life, she was promised that she would be able to endure the trials ahead of her. The Lord was mindful of her special needs, and He stood 'ever at the door,' ready to assist her in whatever way He felt would be best for her. She was asked to accept the Lord's will, regardless of her own wishes and desires, and if she did this, she would be richly blessed. President Mikhail concluded by asking the Lord to bestow upon Brandje all other blessings she may be in need of, that had not been mentioned, recognizing the Lord's will in all things.

Through her tears, as Brandje hugged each priesthood bearer after the blessing, she thought hopefully, *Now all I have to do is wait and see what the Lord has in mind.*

Chapter Nineteen

Wednesday morning Nathan and Brandje walked hand in hand down the long corridor to the main terminal at Heathrow London Airport where Martin waited for them. Jean-Luc and Karen followed alongside, having consented to accompany them to the temple.

Brandje could easily see Martin, but he hadn't spotted her yet. The few silver streaks in his auburn hair seemed more abundant than when she'd left England. And the top of his head appeared a slight bit balder, if that were possible.

His contagious smile was still evident, she decided, as his face lit up for joy when he finally located her. She left Nathan's side and ran forward to embrace him. He wrapped his arms around her petite waist and whirled her about.

The family resemblance was strong between brother and sister. Martin was only two inches taller than Brandje, and almost as thin. Yet he was strong and well-muscled from years of hard labor on the farm.

"I'm so glad you came!" Brandje exclaimed, when Martin finally put her down.

"You're looking well," Martin offered, but Brandje noticed a quiver in his voice. After a short hesitation, he asked, "Are you going to introduce us?"

"Oh!" she exclaimed with a blush. "I've forgotten my manners!

Martin, this is Jean-Luc and Karen Rousseau, the couple I told you about on the phone."

"Pleased to meet you," Martin said, shaking each of their hands. "Thank you kindly for taking such good care of her. She looks absolutely marvelous!"

"I feel marvelous!" she agreed. "And this," she took Nathan's hand in hers and squeezed it encouragingly, "is Nathaniel Duncan, the Third, my fiancé."

Nathan held his hand out, "Glad to —"

But Martin did not accept Nathan's offered hand shake straight away. Instead, he looked at his sister and said, "Brandje, I know you believe you're doing the right thing, but could we talk about this? Seven weeks ago you ran off to France to recuperate from an appendectomy and today I welcome you back with a fiancé in tow, and a different set of religious convictions, knowing that you've but little time to —"

She placed her fingers against his lips and said, "Shhh, it's all right, Martin. I understand how you're feeling, but it's all right now. I love Nathan with all my heart." She hugged Martin once again, gave him a kiss on the cheek and said, "Even if a donor can't be found, even if I die and leave you here, you're going to be all right. We can get through this thing if we share one another's burdens. Just wait, you'll soon find Nathan is the perfect match for me. I can't go through this without both of you. You are my comfort and Nathan is my strength. Together, we can conquer this thing."

"You're comforting *me*?" he asked, taking a wisp of her golden hair and holding it affectionately in his hand. Then his eyes traveled past her to Nathan. "I owe you an apology, Mr. Duncan," said Martin. He extended his hand as a token of friendship.

"No need to apologize," said Nathan, shaking Martin's hand firmly. "I understand your concerns."

Tears welled up in Martin's eyes. "I had feared the worst from you. But now I see that you've wrought a delightful change in my little sister. In years past, I've had to be the strong one. Today she is *my* comforter."

That same evening Martin dined with Brandje and Nathan at the *Landmark London*, a luxurious hotel where they would also be staying. He felt as though he were an intruder remaining with them, but he wanted to witness for himself that his sister truly loved Nathaniel Duncan. He observed them both quietly, offering little to their conversation. Although he'd noticed remarkable changes in Brandje, he still had misgivings about whether or not such a whirlwind courtship could ever work out. And with the cancer facing her, he wasn't completely convinced that marriage right now could possibly be in her best interest.

"It's all happening so fast," said Brandje, cutting up a piece of chicken cordon bleu.

Nathan smiled across the table at her. "Not fast enough," he corrected.

Martin glanced up from his plate long enough to see Brandje blush. Then he studied his sister's fiancé quietly. The two seemed to banter conversation about playfully, and it was clearly obvious the love she felt for this man.

Nathan looked over at Martin. "Before I leave you with your sister this evening, I'd like to speak with you in private, if I may," he said to Martin. "I have a particular wedding gift in mind for her, and I will need your help arranging it."

Martin nodded, while Brandje gave her fiancé a disappointed look. "But I've not had time to get anything for you," she protested.

"You're giving me the rest of your life," Nathan reminded, his eyes searching her face, as though marveling at how much he loved her. "That's worth more to me than any other gift you could ever give me."

Her eyes locked with his across the table. An almost tangible feeling of love and joy was shared between the two of them, and for a brief moment, Martin caught a glimpse of it. Before his own eyes could fill with fluid, an event that had already happened more than once, he said, "Excuse me for a moment."

He went straight to the men's room where he stood behind the closed door of a stall and forced his tender emotions to settle. Using a tissue, Martin wiped his eyes and blew his nose.

When he finally felt that he was back in control, he stepped to the sink and washed his hands. He reflected time and again about the changes that had come over his sister. Before Brandje left the farm she'd been willful, defiant, sometimes cold and unreachable. Except with Elisha, he remembered. That little girl brought out the best in his sister.

Now he could see that Brandje had qualities and tenderness that he hadn't realized before, and Nathan had kindled those attributes in her. It was the greatest blessing in his life to witness his sister's love for her fiancé reflected in her eyes. But tonight he had witnessed a similar reflection in Nathan's eyes as he'd looked at Brandje.

Except for the love his parents had shared, Martin had never seen a love so strong! He was humbled by the experience. Suddenly tears rolled down his cheeks again and he sought the closed restroom stall once more. It took him quite a while to recover.

When Martin finally returned to the dining room, the waiter had rolled out a cart filled with pastries under a glass display. He had missed the entire main course. It really didn't matter, he decided. He wasn't the least bit hungry.

"Martin, are you all right?" asked Brandje, when he rejoined them at the dining table.

"My allergies," he said with a sniffle. "What's keeping the Rousseaus?" he asked, hoping to draw her attention to something else.

"They just said not to wait for them if we got hungry," said Brandje.

"I expected them to be late," Nathan confided, but he didn't comment any further.

If either Nathan or Brandje were unconvinced that his red eyes were due to anything other than his professed allergies, they were kind enough not to mention it, and for this, Martin was grateful.

More especially, he was grateful to have learned for himself that Brandje's love for Nathan, and vice versa, was exactly what she needed.

After dinner the two men left Brandje in her suite, and went across the hall to the room Nathan had reserved for himself. She wondered what Nathan was up to now. He'd been secretive ever since they left the villa near St. Gilles Croix de Vie.

The central living area of her suite overlooked Regent Park in the heart of Marylebone. She went out on the balcony and enjoyed the lovely view from above. She had so much for which to be grateful. She was a member of the church of Jesus Christ. Tomorrow she would take out her endowments and be sealed to her parents. Those two gifts alone would have been enough to console her in the coming months. Since receiving the Holy Ghost she had noticed a genuine difference in the way she perceived her life. She'd already felt the gentle whisperings given her by the Holy Ghost, and she treasured every single one of them.

If she had never met Nathan, but had somehow found the gospel, she would have felt completely satisfied with God's will in allowing her body to grow a cancerous tumor. Because she had met Nathan and fallen in love with him, she wanted to live for him, and if possible, to have his children.

She still wanted to adopt Elisha and wondered if she and Nathan could, but with Brandje's medical condition, British law would likely not allow it. Martin had mentioned earlier in the day that the Witherlys had decided to adopt another little girl, one a few years younger than Elisha. Brandje didn't know whether to be relieved, or disappointed. How her heart ached for Elisha.

When she had asked Nathan about visiting Elisha before they left England, he said he felt it more important to get Brandje to the United States first, so that her medical needs could be expeditiously assessed. To her great sorrow, it meant that she may not get an opportunity to see Elisha again.

Brandje heard a knock at the door. She left the balcony and stepped across the central living area to the door. To her relief, Jean-Luc and Karen arrived, bearing gifts wrapped in silvers, golds and whites, with beautiful bows and streamers.

"Surprise!" Jean-Luc exclaimed as Brandje opened the door all the way to let them come in.

The Rousseaus stacked their gifts on the coffee table. "Where's Nathan and Martin?" Jean-Luc asked.

"Across the hall," said Brandje. "More secrets, I suppose." She walked over to Karen and gave her a hug. "What is all this?" she asked.

"It was mostly Nathan's idea," Karen explained. "We just pinched in a little bit."

"I'll go across and get them," said Jean-Luc. "We can't have a party without the groom."

"Before the men arrive, will you come with me for a minute?" she asked Karen.

"Of course, dear," said the older woman.

Brandje led Karen to the bedroom. After she closed the door, she turned and whispered, "Did you find one?"

"Yes," said Karen. "There were three of them in his size. Which one do you like best?" She opened her handbag and held out three small ring cases covered with black velvet.

Brandje opened each one and set them on the dresser. Then she turned the lamp on and studied each ring carefully, discerning how they looked in all areas of light and dark. Finally she chose a man's wedding band that was gold with a silver channel in the center that contained seven tiny diamonds. She counted the diamonds carefully to make sure there were seven of them. The ring wasn't nearly as big or bulky looking as the other two. "This one is perfect," she said, putting the ring in her pocket. "Thank you so much!"

"That's the one Jean-Luc and I thought you'd pick," said Karen. "But here, let's put these other two in my purse. Jean-Luc can take them back later."

"I can't thank you enough," said Brandje. "You've both been so good to me. Tomorrow, Nathan and I would like you and Jean-Luc to take my parents names through with us. Then when I'm sealed to them, we'd like the two of you to act as proxy. Will you do it?"

"Of course," Karen said. "We'd be honored."

"Karen, I don't know how I can thank you enough for everything. You've become such a good friend. I've even thought that, had my mother lived, she would have been just like you."

"Thank you, dear," said Karen. "And I've often thought you are exactly the kind of daughter I would have asked God to send me, had He sent me a daughter at all."

"Where are the women now?" asked Jean-Luc, as all three men entered the living room.

Brandje opened the bedroom door quickly. "We haven't skipped out on you," she teased, "but you've taken my pretend mother away from me long enough today."

"If she's your pretend mother, that would make me your pretend father, Brandje," Jean-Luc bantered back. "And if that were really true, all I can say is . . ."

Quickly Brandje looked at Nathan. He seemed to understand her unspoken message. As Jean-Luc threw his hands in the air, Nathan and Brandje chimed in with him as he exclaimed, "Oh, bother!"

Later that night, after Brandje folded the fabric of a floor length white slip carefully and tucked the knee high stockings into the quilted slippers, she ran her fingers down the lovely white dress, with it's delicate, almost silvery pattern etched into the fabric.

She especially admired her own set of scriptures, engraved with the name, *Brandje Rebecca Fulton-Duncan. S*he planned to spend some time reading them later on that evening.

The gifts that her friends and Nathan had given to her were not only a surprise, but a source of great joy.

After putting the special clothing away, Brandje knelt beside the bed and spoke to her Father in Heaven regarding her brother, Martin, asking Him to give her the courage she needed to face her brother alone.

Jean-Luc, Karen and Nathan had retired to their respective hotel rooms across the hall. Now, for the first time in almost two months, she and Martin would have time alone to visit and share their feelings.

When Brandje came out of the bedroom, Martin was standing on the balcony. Below him at Regent Park, a myriad of tiny white lights in the tree branches around the perimeter sent a soft glow upward, creating a luminescent, ethereal feeling. She went outside to be with Martin, bringing a special package with her. When she settled upon a lounge chair, Martin turned around and smiled at her. He seemed glad to have some time alone with his sister.

"Feeling all right?" he asked.

"Yes. I took a pain pill at dinner, and I'm feeling much better now."

"You were a little pale earlier," he observed. "Are you having a lot of pain?"

"Sometimes," she admitted. "But the medication helps. Nathan says there are more liver transplants done in the United States than anywhere else in the world."

Martin positioned another chair so that he could face her, and sat down upon it. "I hardly know what to say," he confessed. "I'm still so sorry I didn't tell you about the cancer. I should have gone with you to France. I think I'm rather a coward when it comes to dealing with death, especially since Mum died, and then Father, as well."

"If you had gone with me, you would very likely have shot Nathan before he got into the living room that first night."

He smiled. "Yes, that's right. I would have heard him long before he got to the stairs. I never was a heavy sleeper, like you."

"You may have liked him, even then," she coaxed. "You probably would have told him to stay in the third bedroom, since he'd paid his reservation fees in full."

"Likely," said Martin. "I do like the bloke," he added. "It's not too difficult to see where his heart is."

"I'm glad," she smiled. "I was worried you wouldn't like him at all, with him taking me away from you."

"He won't be," said Martin. "I told him about the farm, and my selling it. He says he won't need the money from the farm, he wants to take care of your operation and medical expenses on his own. He has some sort of health insurance policy that insures you the moment you marry him, with pre-existing conditions excluded only the first thirty days, but after that, everything is covered. He said he's had the policy for years, never expected he'd ever need to use it, but felt that a mite of caution was worth a pound of cure."

"He hadn't told me that," she said. "Now about him not taking me away from you."

"Oh, that!" said Martin, "Sort of rambled on there, didn't I? He's got a gentleman's ranch somewhere near Rochester, New York. Says he needs a foreman to manage it, and offered me the job."

"Oh?" she asked, her curiosity piqued.

"I told him I didn't need charity and I could likely lease the villa from you, and live there the rest of my life without having to work, if I cared to."

"You did?" she laughed. "You are a stubborn one, Martin."

He grinned. "But I relented. He invited me to stay with you at his home, until after you get your donor. He likely wants me nearby for when your temper flares, so he'll have an ally to help him get back in the castle." He laughed now, evidently loosening up a little.

She giggled with him. "What did you say to that?"

"I told the bloke it sounded like a decent plan."

"Good," she agreed. "That has been one of the main things I've worried about." As long as Martin was calling Nathan a bloke, she knew they would soon become good friends. Martin only used the term for someone that he liked.

Timidly, Brandje picked up the package and gave it to her brother. "I have a few gifts for you," she said with all the courage she could muster. "Three gifts, actually."

"You shouldn't have," he insisted as he took the package and tore the wrapping off immediately. Brandje sensed the excitement in his voice that he tried to hide from her, and this pleased her.

Inside the wrapping paper Martin found the afghan that Brandje made. It had all the autumn colors that he enjoyed, crocheted into a Navajo pattern, reminiscent of his passion for the Native American culture. Upon the afghan sat a copy of the Book of Mormon, with his name etched in the corner. He frowned momentarily, as though unsure how to proceed. Then he asked, "What's this?"

"Martin," she began. "It is the path I was given to find God in all the trials that we face. Without that book and it's message, there would be no hope for me, for you, or for our parents, to ever be together again."

"Brandje, you know I'm not the religious sort," he offered lamely.

"Martin, don't turn it down without reading it first," she insisted. "It means more to me than anything else I could give you, except for the third gift . . . my testimony, which is written inside for you."

Martin nodded. He opened the first page and read Brandje's inscription aloud:

"Dear Martin,

I testify to you, in the name of Jesus Christ, that the Book of Mormon is the word of God. It does not take away from the Bible, but enhances it and clarifies many points upon which our father pondered when he read to us. The Book of Mormon is not only an experience into the spiritual things of God, it is a history of the ancestors of the native Americans, whom you've admired. I have learned for myself that God hears and answers prayers, through my study of this book, and I pray with all my heart that you will do likewise.

Without the Book of Mormon, and the Lord's infinite communication with me, I would never have gone on the donor list. You owe it to yourself, and to our parents, to read this book and pray about it's truthfulness. If you do, and you really desire in your heart to know, God will tell you it is true, just as He has told me. Martin, God has a plan for all of us! His plan is that we become an eternal family unit. Our family can be together forever! This I have learned through Christ's personal communications to me, one of His least likely followers. Please, Martin, read, pray, and learn for yourself. I love you with all my heart, and I will do so forever.

Your sister,
Brandje."

Brandje sensed that he wasn't pleased by the expression on his face.

She noticed that it took great effort on his part to accept her testimony.

After a long hesitation, Martin finally said, "I won't make any promises that I'll convert, Brandje. But I will promise to read the Book of Mormon."

"That's all I ask," she told him. "Thank you."

"And thank you for the thoughtful gifts. The afghan will look good on my old rocker, don't you think?" he asked with a kind and brotherly smile, changing the subject.

"Yes," she said with graciousness and hope.

"Now," he said, changing the subject further. "Is there anything I can do for you, Brandje? Is there something that Nathan hasn't thought about, or anything else that you need or want, that I can give to you?"

Brandje gave his question serious reflection. Finally she smiled. "Yes," she answered. "Do you remember when Father was here, how every night he'd tell me about our mother?"

He nodded, yet he hesitated. She knew the subject of their mother was still a tender one for him, regardless of the many years since her passing.

"I haven't had that in a really long time, Martin," she persuaded. "Would you please tell me some things you remember about our mother?"

"She was exactly like you," he finally smiled in response. "Come, look at yourself." He led her into the central living area where a large mirror hung above the marble mantle.

Standing behind her and a little to her side, he said tenderly, "Look in the mirror and you will see a portrait of our mother. Study the way you love Elisha, or discipline her, and you will have a clear picture of Mum and her child. Wander through blossom-filled meadows, and you will see Mum gathering wild flowers. Walk along the bluff at Croix de Vie and you will inhale the same fragrant gardenias that she savored. Run along the beach behind Timbal's Point and you will feel her hair, golden as the sun, whipping in the wind about your face."

"Are we that alike?" Brandje asked.

"How could I ever get over losing her, with you as a constant reminder?" he questioned. "You're the image of our mother. Is it any wonder then, that I would rather die myself than watch this cancer take you away from me?"

She turned to face him. Big tears formed in his eyes and slipped down his cheeks. "I always was the blubbering one in our family," he sniffed. "I just can't help it!" He wrapped his arms about her and sobbed against her shoulder unmercifully.

Taken aback, Brandje tried to comfort him. "Martin, I'm going to be fine. You'll see. My word, I've never seen you cry like this, only that night when Dr. Graham called, and when Father died."

"I hide it pretty good, do I?" he asked, wiping his face with a handkerchief from his shirt pocket.

"Evidently," she agreed, pushing her own tears into submission.

"I cry all the time," he admitted with a forced smile, drying his tears with his hands. "I just do it when you're not around. Men are supposed to be strong, you know. Comforters. Towers of strength. Me? When I miss Mum or Father, I cry. When I miss you, I cry. When I miss Elisha, what do I do about it? I cry." He grinned broadly, which took away some of her concern for him.

"Why didn't you tell me?" she asked. "I would have at least cried with you and shared some of your pain."

Suddenly Martin tilted his head back and laughed vigorously. "It's going to take a while to get used to you being *my* comforter," he said, when he caught his breath again. "It's refreshing, but it's definitely going to take some time."

Chapter Twenty

*A*t nine in the morning, dressed in a soft white, knee-length, short-sleeved dress with a simple lace trim at the modest neckline, Brandje stood ready. Martin held out his arm and escorted her into an intimate conference room at the *Landmark London*, where Nathan stood waiting for her, right next to an English Magistrate. An audio cassette played a soft rendition of the Wedding March in the background. In her hand she held a bouquet of gardenias and pink baby roses. When she and Martin arrived in front of the Magistrate, Martin took her right hand and placed it in Nathan's. He gave her a quick kiss on the cheek, then stepped back and sat down next to Jean-Luc and Karen.

The ceremony went smoothly until after Nathan slipped the wedding band on her left finger, followed by the engagement ring.

Brandje looked in dismay at her brother, who had tears streaming down his face. "Martin," she whispered.

He looked at her as though he had no idea what she wanted. When Martin finally remembered, he stood up quickly and walked over to her. "I'm sorry, love," he whispered. He pulled from his pocket the ring she intended for Nathan, and gave it to her. "Sorry," he said again.

After he returned to his chair, Brandje placed the ring on Nathan's finger, enjoying the surprise evident on his face as she did so. He admired it for a moment, then gave her a big smile.

The Marriage Magistrate continued, "Inasmuch as you have both exchanged rings, as a token of your love and the promises you've made, I now pronounce you husband and wife. You —"

But the last portion of his words they did not hear as Nathan swept Brandje into his arms and kissed her soundly, giving her a hint of what was yet to come.

After their kiss, Karen, Jean-Luc and Martin came forward to congratulate them, and the Marriage Magistrate slipped out of the room to allow them time to celebrate without his assistance.

The rest of the day passed by so quickly, Brandje scarcely had time to catch her breath. After an intimate, yet simple breakfast served in the Rose Room with Martin, Jean-Luc and Karen as their special guests, they left the hotel for the remaining activities.

Martin planned to remain in London only until later that afternoon. He needed to get back to the farm before dark, in order to finish a livestock transition with the stockyard, then he had the final contract to sign on the sale of the farm first thing in the morning.

Brandje kissed Martin goodbye at the hotel lobby. Nathan had given her brother a secret assignment for the day, so that he wouldn't feel left out, she suspected. However, she knew that, in Martin's eyes, she was now legally and lawfully married.

They had not shared with him the fact that, in their own eyes, tomorrow's ceremony, the one in which they exchanged eternal marriage vows, would be the only time they would truly consider themselves husband and wife.

After Martin left to run errands, they went to the London Temple, where they walked hand in hand through the doorway, with Jean-Luc and Karen coming close behind them.

While Brandje went through for her own endowment, Nathan went through for her grandfather, and the Rousseaus went through for Brandje's parents. Since Brandje had little information on any others in her family she realized, during the sacred ceremony, that she had much to do in the way of genealogy.

At the appropriate times, Brandje's parents were sealed to each other, and Brandje was then sealed to them, with Jean-Luc and Karen still acting as proxies.

They didn't get back to the Hotel until late in the afternoon.

When they arrived, Martin had completed his "secret mission," and slipped across the hall to Nathan's room to give his report.

Since Martin was planning to leave within the next hour or so, Jean-Luc and Karen agreed, once again, to act as chaperones for Brandje. They would stay in the second bedroom in Brandje's suite that night. While they moved their luggage into the suite, Brandje quickly changed into a pair of cotton slacks and a pink blouse, took her medication, then stretched out on the bed to rest for a few minutes. She felt totally drained from the day's activities.

It was dark when she awakened. She heard Nathan and the Rousseaus visiting in the central living area.

Quickly she rolled off the bed, relieved to find that she had recuperated fully. Glancing at the clock, she was dismayed to see that it was already ten at night. Martin would have left without her saying goodbye to him.

She hurried out of the bedroom and looked around. Nathan, Jean-Luc and Karen were visiting in the central living area. "I missed him," she moaned as she realized Martin was not with them.

"Martin gave you a kiss on the cheek before he left," said Nathan. "But you were sleeping, and like us, he didn't want to awaken you."

Brandje sank down on Nathan's lap and rested her head against his shoulder. "I can't believe I slept so long!" she complained. "I wanted Martin to take the doll with him, to give to Elisha for me."

"Now, dear," said Karen, nodding at Nathan in encouragement. "Your brother left something with Nathan that should cheer you up."

"Yes," Jean-Luc agreed. "You'll never believe what those two have been doing now."

Nathan nodded as she looked into his eyes. "One more surprise," she warned, "and you're in big trouble, Mr. Duncan!"

"Sorry," he admitted with a grin. "Actually, I'm not sorry, but since you're not really interested in this, then . . ." He tossed a small white box to Jean-Luc. "I guess I'll have to give it to Jean-Luc . . ."

"What?" she complained immediately.

". . . so I can tickle you," he continued with a mischievous grin. Brandje jumped off his lap. Nathan chased after her as though anxious to lighten her mood. She ran behind the sofa, around the end table and the second sofa, trying not to knock anything over, while Nathan followed, lunging at her, and narrowly missing every time.

"Oh, bother!" said Jean-Luc. "Here we go again."

Hearing his remark, Brandje squealed in delight and grabbed Jean-Luc by the hand, dragging him to his feet.

"Stop!" he pleaded, holding out the white box. "If I give this back to you, will you promise to sit down?" he asked.

Brandje snatched the box away and kept her eye on Nathan, anxious to see what his next move would be.

Nathan jumped over the back of the second sofa and landed on the soft cushions. "Good idea!" he exclaimed. "I think you've had enough exercise for one night."

"You promise not to tickle me, Mr. Duncan?" she asked before she would sit beside him again.

"Do I have to promise, Mrs. Duncan?" he responded.

She turned to Jean-Luc, "You sit by him," she insisted.

"Okay, okay, I promise," Nathan finally agreed..

Brandje sat back on Nathan's lap and eagerly opened the box. Inside was a white jewelry case and a little note. She opened the jewelry case to find a gold, heart shaped locket. When she opened it, she found a picture of Elisha, dressed in the green sweater Brandje crocheted for her last Christmas. She recognized the picture as one that Martin had taken of Elisha during the holidays. At first she was puzzled. Why would Nathan give her such a sacred reminder of the little child whom she loved so dearly?

Seeing the question in her eyes, he said, "Read the note, Mrs. Duncan."

Brandje picked up the slip of paper and unfolded it. In Nathan's neat penmanship she found these words:

> *"To my darling wife,*
> *Brandje Rebecca Fulton-Duncan;*

You once expressed a desire to adopt a special child, one you love with all your heart. I believe I can love her equally as much as you do. Will you welcome into our family the little girl whose photo is found within this locket? I have made arrangements for Martin to bring her home to New York in a few weeks, when the legalities are completed.

Your loving husband,
Nathaniel Duncan III."

Brandje looked up at him in absolute surprise. "Oh, Nathan," she cried. "Can this really be happening?"

"With God, all things are possible," he answered.

Brandje threw her arms around his shoulders and wept for joy. After a few minutes, she straightened. "What did I ever do to receive so many special blessings?

"I was about to ask a similar question," he said, kissing the tip of her nose.

She rested her head against his broad shoulder. "Sometimes I wish we weren't waiting until tomorrow," she whispered against his ear, hoping the Rousseaus wouldn't hear.

Nathan smiled. "I think we'll live," he encouraged. "I've waited thirty one years. One more day isn't going to kill me."

"Don't worry about him," Jean-Luc offered. "I promised to keep him company tonight, after you and Karen go to bed."

"Thank you," said Brandje, grateful for Jean-Luc's empathy.

"Besides," Nathan said, holding up his hand, openly admiring the seven diamonds channeled into the gold ring on his finger. "I have a suspicion that this ring you gave me has some special significance to it. Perhaps if you told me, it would give me the strength I need to get through one more lonely night without you."

Brandje smiled. She had hoped he would at least be curious why she chose that particular ring for him. With her fingers she gently rubbed the diamonds in the ring. "These seven diamonds mean something I don't ever want you to forget," she said.

"Then tell me what it is, and I won't forget," he promised.

"I think you'll laugh," she hedged, a sliver of worry in her voice.

"Tell me." When she hesitated another moment, he teased, "Please, please, please!"

She smiled. "Do you remember what I told you the first morning Karen and Jean-Luc were at the villa? I was standing near the hydrangea, and you came up behind me and whispered in my ear."

Nathan nodded. "You told me how much you love to watch the sunrise, and about your grandfather watching it with you from Timbal's Point."

She smiled. "I also told you why I love sunrise. Do you remember?"

He thought carefully on that morning before he answered, "You said that you watch sunrise to prove you're still here. You're still alive."

She smiled, pleased that he had remembered almost word for word. "After tomorrow," Brandje explained, "all that will change. After we are sealed to each other, every morning I'll be waking up to you. With our eternal marriage, you will become my . . ." Brandje touched each of the seven diamonds with the tip of her fingernail, as she spelled the word aloud, ". . . S-u-n-r-i-s-e."

She enjoyed the look of surprise in his eyes as they radiated his love for her. Then, solemnly, he promised, "I'll never forget."

Early Friday morning, Brandje heard a knock on the bedroom door. She rolled over lazily and said, "Come in."

Nathan nudged the door open with his foot. He was dressed in his best Sunday suit, and he carried a tray of croissants, fresh fruit and milk. Behind him came Jean-Luc and Karen, still in their pajamas and robes.

"What's this?" she mumbled sleepily.

"Did you sleep?" he asked, ignoring her question.

"Yes, did you?" Brandje sat up, stretched and yawned.

"Not a wink," confessed Nathan.

"Believe him," grumbled Jean-Luc in jest. "After you and Karen went to bed, he and I walked half the streets of London."

The Rousseaus sat down on the settee across from the bed. She giggled. "Oh, Nathan, I'm so sorry."

"How could you sleep?" he asked incredulously. "Four hours yesterday and," he looked at his watch, "seven hours last night!"

"I guess I'm finally content," she admitted. "I rarely sleep through sunrise."

"I was thinking about what you said," he told her as he placed the tray on the night stand, then sat on the edge of the bed. "All night long, as I lay in that lonely room across the hall, staring at this handsome ring in the moonlight as it filtered through the window."

"It was probably sunlight," interjected Jean-Luc. "There wasn't any moonlight left by the time we got back."

"Would you let me do this?" Nathan asked in a scolding, yet playful tone.

"It's your party," bantered Jean-Luc.

"Thank you," said Nathan. He turned back to Brandje. "As I was saying, I studied this ring most of the night —"

"You were with me *HALF* of the night," Jean-Luc objected playfully. "You couldn't possibly have looked at that thing *MOST* of the night!"

"Please," growled Nathan, "Let me do this."

"All right!" teased Jean-Luc. "I'm going to be quiet now."

"You don't know how to be quiet," Nathan pointed out. "You talked my ear off half the night."

Jean-Luc grinned. "Gotcha!"

While Brandje and Karen giggled, Jean-Luc nearly rolled on the floor with laughter.

"Doesn't anyone around here know how to be serious?" asked Nathan.

"Come here," Brandje told him. "I know how to make Jean-Luc serious." She grabbed Nathan by the tie and pulled his face to within an inch of hers.

"You think this will do it?" asked Nathan. Then he planted his lips on hers and kissed her sensually.

After a few moments, Jean-Luc asked, "What time are we supposed to arrive at the Temple?"

Nathan pulled back and nodded, laughing. "That did it. Now, as I was saying earlier: When I studied this ring last night, I realized I don't ever want you to wake up again without me. I know that last night was difficult." Then he reconsidered. "Well, it was difficult for me, if not for you." He paused for a moment. "Hmm, that is a very disconcerting thought."

"What?" she asked playfully.

"I couldn't sleep on our first night of marriage, while you slept the whole night through. We're not getting off to a very good start, are we?"

She pulled him close once more and kissed him soundly. "I promise you," she said, when she finally released him, "I won't sleep all night long tonight."

Nathan arched an eyebrow in eager anticipation. "Neither will I!"

They arrived at the temple sealing room precisely on time. As they entered, Brandje was surprised to find Bishop and Sister Buerge, as well as Henry and Marcelle Fayard, seated around the perimeter.

Jean-Luc and Karen sat beside the others as the officiator began a short greeting, and expressed his appreciation for the privilege of conducting their special sealing. Then he spoke to them about their Father in Heaven, and how happy He was that bright August morning to watch His son and His daughter be united for all eternity.

Then, with tears streaming down their faces, Nathan and Brandje created an eternal family unit by that man who was authorized of God to do so.

Afterward, their guests were asked to briefly congratulate the happy couple.

"Thank you so much for coming," Brandje whispered happily,

giving Bishop Buerge and his wife a quick hug.

"We wouldn't have missed it for anything," they agreed.

"And you two!" Brandje whispered excitedly when she hugged Nathan's aunt and uncle. "Never in my wildest dreams did I expect to see you two here!"

Marcelle gave her a kiss on the cheek and repeated the greeting, "Never in our wildest dreams did we expect to see *you* here!"

"It's been a whirlwind romance," Nathan agreed. "But we wouldn't have done it any other way."

After they left the temple they met back at the *Landmark London* once again, where a small dining room, suitable for eight guests awaited them. Bishop Buerge offered an invocation and blessing on the food, while Bishop Rousseau offered a benediction.

It was a joyous time for Nathan and Brandje, a time to express to those three special couples, their love and appreciation for all that each one had done in helping to convert Brandje to the gospel by their examples, their faith and their testimonies.

When they said goodbye, especially to the Rousseaus, Brandje could scarcely bear parting. Karen and Jean-Luc had become the parents she'd lost. Fortunately, they agreed to stay at the villa until their home renovation was complete. They promised, through their tears, to keep in touch via phone and letters, and encouragingly gave Brandje hope that she would soon receive a new liver. They even set a date to meet again the following summer at Croix de Vie.

When they were finally alone, Nathan took Brandje to the top floor of the hotel, and carried her over the threshold of the honeymoon suite. When he put her down, her eyes widened in astonishment at the gold-leafed furniture and thick, creamy carpet. The entire room was immaculate and tastefully decorated in antique provincial, all embellished with gold etchings.

"Do you like it?" he asked.

Speechless, Brandje could only smile and nod her head.

He placed his hands on her slim waist. "Would you like to share the tub with me?" he asked seductively.

Brandje gave him an alluring smile.

Nathan led her past a wide, ornately carved door into a spacious bathroom complete with a heart shaped, sunken tub, trimmed with gold faucets. Bending over, he turned on the water, adjusted the temperature and poured in gardenia scented bubble bath.

"It'll take a while to fill," he said. "Why don't you get ready, and then tell me when to come in."

Brandje nodded and watched him walk into the bedroom, closing the door behind him.

She removed her dress, then stood before a full-length mirror in her slip and underclothing. Her golden tan of a few days ago was already fading, her skin had a faint, sallow tinge that made her thin face seem even more frail. She studied her slender hands, but did not notice any deep yellowing around the fingernails yet. It was a good sign, she supposed.

Brandje brushed her hair, freshened her makeup, and took her medication. She wanted no complications that afternoon.

Slipping out of her clothing, she placed them neatly on a cushioned stool and stepped into the tub. The bubbles were nearly overflowing, and she was grateful that they covered her body almost up to her neck.

"I'm ready," she called out.

Nathan returned with a bright smile on his handsome face. He had a towel wrapped around his waist and Brandje turned her head away from him to give him privacy, until he, too, was wrapped up in bubbles.

"Our flight is scheduled for eight tomorrow morning," he said.

"I wish we had more time," she responded wistfully.

"Brandje," he coaxed, reaching out to stroke her shoulders with his strong hands. "I've spoken with Dr. Rizner, the specialist from Chicago Research Hospital. He wants us back in the States as soon as possible so they can run some preliminary tests to prepare for the eventuality that a liver becomes available sooner than expected."

"I know," she said. "It's just that —" she hesitated. "I don't want to stay in the hospital until they're ready to operate. Nathan, promise me I won't have to stay overnight until then."

"Brandje, I don't know what kind of tests they will do. How can I make that promise to you?"

"My father died in the hospital connected to every kind of device imaginable. It was horrible. Martin said his final wish was that he wanted to die at home. Martin refused because he thought it would be too hard for me. He felt I was too young, too weak." She started to cry, even though she knew this was not the time nor the place.

Nathan turned her around to face him. "Brandje, I —"

"Promise!" she insisted. "Don't make me stay in the hospital, not until they're ready to operate."

"What if —?" he began.

But she didn't let him finish. "Then hire a nurse, or bring Karen over from France. I don't care what you do as long as I can be at home, with you. I didn't get to be with Father when he died and I missed out on a sacred experience."

When Nathan did not promise immediately, she persisted. "Promise me that you'll let me die at home, if it comes to that."

Finally he caved in. "All right," he said. "I promise."

"Thank you," she whispered, trying to wipe her tears away with her bubble covered fingers.

He laughed at her attempt. "Here," he said, taking a washcloth from the rim of the tub. He wiped the bubbles off her face and kissed away the tears she'd missed.

When she finally calmed down and smiled again, he said, "I've ordered our dinner. Room service will deliver it at seven. In the meantime . . ." He left the sentence unfinished and eased her into his arms.

Chapter Twenty - One

A tall, lean gentleman dressed in a gray business suit approached them when they arrived at the airport in Rochester, New York, the next day. In his sixties, Nate Duncan had thinning silver hair and bushy eyebrows. Except for his height and broad shoulders, he bore little resemblance to the son who shook his hand.

"And this is our little bride," he said, giving Brandje an affectionate hug. "I understand you and Nathan want to go to Chicago for some surgery. I hope you'll spend a few days in Rochester first."

"We'll try," Brandje promised. She would have an easy time warming to Nate Duncan. His jovial, take charge manner was arresting.

"Where's Mother?" Nathan asked.

"She came down with a headache," his father winked. "You know your mother."

Nathan frowned but didn't comment. "Did you contact Dr. Finsen?"

"He's scheduled to see your little bride at the hospital early this afternoon." He hesitated, as though wondering if he should continue. "I've arranged for Gabe Rizner to fly in from Chicago sometime this evening. You spoke with him also, I believe," said Nate.

Nathan nodded. "Thank you," he said. "Dr. Rizner says more of these transplants are being done all the time, with reasonably good success."

"It turns out that Gabe and I served in the same part of France on our missions, ten years apart. I was relieved to learn he's a High Priest, just like me," Nate told them.

"What? Dad, did you just come right out and ask him?" Nathan questioned, teasing.

"I have my sources, son," said Nate with a twinkle in his eyes. "And my secrets."

When they located their luggage, Nathan made certain that Nate didn't attempt to lift any of the heavy bags, due to an old back injury he was still nursing. Brandje could easily see why Nathan was so attentive to her medical condition, having learned to care for the physical needs of his father. It gave her greater insight into Nathan's empathic heart.

Soon they left the airport in Nate's sleek Buick. Since they'd left London at eight in the morning and arrived in Rochester seven hours later, it should have been three in the afternoon. But after crossing six time zones, in New York it was only nine in the morning.

Traffic was sparse as Nate and Nathan conversed freely about the real estate business while Brandje listened. She learned that Nate was successful in his chosen field, and she could easily tell from which side of the family Nathan inherited his drive and dedication. She couldn't recall many days at the villa that Nathan allowed to slip by without writing on his novel.

They headed out of the city and into the countryside for only a short distance when Nate turned the car onto a newly paved, narrow driveway, bordered by two rows of century-old oak trees. The driveway ended in a circle that went right up to the sidewalk of a lovely, red brick, colonial style home. The second story windows were framed by bricks that formed a decorative arch. All the glass panes were separated by white painted frames for contrast.

Massive white pillars supported a newly shingled roof, that formed an appropriate awning for the wrap around porch. Crisply painted, white double doors welcomed them home.

Nathan held the car door open for Brandje. She got out of the Buick eagerly. "It's beautiful," she murmured, taking in every feature of the lovely country estate. White fences in the distance crossed two green pastures, one with a big red barn.

"Aren't you coming in, Nate?" Brandje asked when she finally realized he had not left the car. Nathan closed the door and Brandje leaned against the window well. "You don't need to rush off on my account."

"Your new mother-in-law is expecting me," he explained. "She's throwing a little family gathering, to celebrate your marriage this evening, and she'll need my help, especially with her headache."

"She doesn't need to do that," Brandje protested.

"That's what I said," he nodded. "But once you meet her, you'll understand. The Richelieu Family is big on parties, and my wife is no exception."

"Yes, I learned that at Chinon last week." She squeezed Nate's shoulder. "Goodbye, then."

"What time are we supposed to be at the hospital?" Nathan asked, as he unloaded suitcases from the trunk.

"At one this afternoon. It doesn't give you much time," Nate said, putting the car in gear. "I'll see you this evening." Then he drove away.

Nathan put the last suitcase on the asphalt, and waved goodbye while Brandje climbed the cement steps and onto the wide porch. She pressed her nose against a window, anxious to see inside, curious about Nathan's decorating skills. If he was as talented at interior decoration as he was at writing novels, she would have nothing to do to improve the graceful country home.

Nathan unlocked the door and opened it. Brandje stepped forward. "I'll carry you in properly, Mrs. Duncan," he protested at once.

He scooped her up and carried her into a spacious hall with hardwood floors that shined as though they'd just been buffed.

Standing her up next to an oak carved staircase he asked, "Well, what do you think?"

Brandje reserved judgement until she'd finished inspection. Upstairs were four large bedrooms and two bathrooms. On the main floor there was a spacious living room, family style kitchen with formal dining room, a library with bay windows, and a half-bath. Off the kitchen, a staircase led to a large work room in the basement, and a well arranged fruit cellar.

The master bedroom, library and living room were the only rooms Nathan had restored so far. Brandje felt relieved. It would give her an opportunity to contribute some of her decorating flair. Ideas for the old fashioned kitchen immediately popped into her mind.

"Well?" Nathan asked again, after following her all over the house.

"It's perfect," she answered. "I couldn't have asked for anything better."

He gathered her close to him and whispered, "Whew, for a moment there I was beginning to think you didn't like it."

"I love it!" she reaffirmed. Then she remembered Nathan's horse. "Where's Dorsett?"

"Over in Mother's stable," he replied. "You'll have to meet him later. My parents' place is all he's ever known. I just couldn't move him away from his home."

"Oh, I'm sure Martin can persuade him," suggested Brandje, "when he arrives with Elisha."

"I hope so," Nathan said. "I don't have the heart to buy another horse when mine is only thirty miles away."

"May I see the rest of your ranch?" Brandje asked.

"Of course," he responded, "but it's not just mine anymore." He gave her a contagious smile, then he took Brandje on a brief tour of their property.

When they returned to the house, Nathan filled a sturdy four-footed tub with bath water so she could clean up and prepare for their trip to the hospital. He sensed that Brandje was a little uneasy about going to a new doctor.

He was uneasy for other reasons. He'd had a little time to study neuroendocrine carcinoma on the internet, and knew more of what they could expect at the hospital. It was entirely possible the doctors would want to do another liver biopsy and other tests that would necessitate

Brandje's staying in the hospital overnight. Nathan worried how he could possibly keep his promise to her.

The moment for their departure arrived and still Brandje hesitated. Nathan leaned against the door frame, watching as she examined her appearance in the oval mirror above a long maple dresser in the master bedroom. She wore a pair of cream colored, cotton slacks and a sunwashed blue blouse. The color she chose complemented her eyes, and he was pleased with her choice.

Dark cumulonimbus clouds had gathered since they arrived, threatening a terrible storm.

"Are you ready?" Nathan asked. "We're going to be late."

"I suppose."

"Don't you want to go?" he asked, crossing the room to gather her in the circle of his arms, and hold her against him.

Brandje toyed with a button on his shirt. "I'm frightened," she admitted.

"I'll do my best to keep my promise. You need to trust me." Even though he said the words, he doubted his ability to keep his word.

She leaned against him as she said, "I know."

Just knowing that she trusted him made the task ahead all the more difficult. He prayed that he would not disappoint her, then he lifted her chin, kissed her forehead, and tucked her arm through his to lead her downstairs.

After an initial examination at the modern medical center in Rochester, New York, Brandje was ushered into a tidy little office where Nathan sat waiting for her.

"Are you feeling all right?" he asked, taking her hand as she sat beside him on an overstuffed settee.

Brandje nodded. "All the poking and prodding was painful," she admitted, "but I've known worse."

"You're quite a rarity," said Dr. Finsen as he opened the door and walked over to the desk, tossing a folder on top of it. He was an older man, with plump pillow-cheeks beneath clear gray eyes. He leaned against the desk, half-sitting, draping one leg over the edge. "We see this form of cancer," he shrugged and pursed his lips together, "once or twice in a ten year period. I think that, given your age and general good health, it would be possible to transplant with excellent results."

One word came from Nathan. "When?"

"Possible, Mr. Duncan," Dr. Finsen corrected. "Not probable. We don't store livers in the deep freeze until the next patient arrives. Rather, the reverse is true, so to speak." He looked straight into Brandje's eyes. "I'm terribly sorry to disappoint you, but the probability of finding a suitable donor is remotely slim. Your blood type is extremely rare. It will be almost impossible to find a suitable liver for you."

"You're saying there's no hope?" Nathan questioned.

"I take a conservative approach, especially with patients who have the specific needs of your wife. I don't have all the answers you want. A donor could be brought through the ER tomorrow and prove me wrong. I've seen it happen a time or two. Unfortunately, it's been my experience that the opposite usually occurs first."

"I see," whispered Brandje in dismay.

Dr. Finsen nodded, then continued, "Dr. Gabe Rizner, a prominent specialist in this field, will be arriving this evening, per your father's request. He's on staff at Chicago Memorial, and has specialized in the transplant program for many years."

"Will I have to come back tomorrow?" Brandje asked timidly.

"No, I'm going to admit you today. We'll need to secure a current biopsy and run a battery of tests. You did realize that?" he asked.

Brandje cringed. She looked at Nathan, feeling desperate and forlorn.

"My wife hoped that she could have her tests done on an outpatient basis," Nathan said.

"That is quite impossible," said Dr. Finsen. "But, if she insists, we could probably release her in twenty-four hours. The liver biopsy is a risky procedure." He stood, indicating the interview was over.

Nathan looked over at Brandje and shrugged.

She stood up. "What's the point?" she asked both men. "Why even do a biopsy if the chances of finding a donor are so remote?"

Nathan stood and looked down at her, his mouth grim. "Because without the biopsy, they can't even look for a donor. Without the biopsy, there is no hope at all."

"They did one in England," she persisted.

"England does have some excellent facilities," Dr. Finsen said, "and very good tests. But even if the biopsy had been done here, it's been two months since then. We need current information. We need to know how the cancer is affecting your liver now, so we can determine how best to proceed."

Brandje sighed. "Will Nathan be able to stay with me?"

"Certainly," said Dr. Finsen. "We can arrange for a private room, and bring a cot in for him."

Reluctantly, Brandje agreed with a nod of her head.

"Good," Dr. Finsen said. "If you'll report to Three West, I'll have the nurses prepare you for the biopsy. In the meantime, Mr. Duncan, why don't you go over to admitting, on this floor?"

Nathan walked her to the elevator. "We'll still be together," he said with a withered sigh that sounded as desolate as she felt.

Brandje nodded, but the ache in her heart did not allow for a smile at the moment. She entered the elevator and pressed a button marked three. Before the doors whisked shut, she saw Nathan shrug.

Her mind raced with concern. Dr. Finsen wasn't the least bit encouraging. No guarantees could be offered. The operation itself could be fatal. She didn't want to stay overnight here. People die in hospitals. Her father died in hospital. For that matter, so had her mother.

The elevator stopped at level three, but Brandje couldn't force herself to get off. Almost without giving the matter another thought, she pushed the button marked Lobby and waited for the doors to whisk shut.

Within seconds she was on the main level once again, walking toward the automatic doors.

As she went outside, gusty winds whipped at her hair, sweeping it in front of her. She pulled a golden strand away from her eyes and felt the cool sting of raindrops as they pelted against her face. Ominous thunderclouds collided, making the sky rumble above her.

Brandje, oblivious to the elements, was struck with a paralyzing fear more real than her impending death. She would not be put in hospital unless they had a donor. She hated it when she'd had the appendectomy. No matter how hard she tried, she couldn't break the chains of fear that prevented her from staying in the hospital before it was actually time for her operation.

By the time she reached Nathan's car, she was thoroughly drenched. Her blue blouse clung to her curves, her hair dripped straight and wet. She pressed the latch, but the car was locked. The rain, relentless now, pelted against her with unleashed fury.

Brandje pressed the latch again, but it would not yield. She beat her fists against the window pane, her actions releasing the pent up emotions instilled within her since her visit with Dr. Finsen. But her assault on the defenseless automobile served no other purpose.

Rain splattered against the roof and splashed upon her face. She leaned against the car, rested her head on her arms, and wept.

After several minutes of self-pity, Brandje straightened and wiped the tears from her cheeks with her fingers, only to find that her effort was useless. There were more raindrops than tears on her face.

Really, Brandje, what a spoiled woman your husband married! she scolded herself silently. *Nathan deserves much better. Now straighten your act before he thinks you're nothing but a sniveling, selfish brat.*

Just as these thoughts formed, she felt warm hands upon her shoulders. Forcing the tears to stop overflowing, she turned into the circle of Nathan's arms and gazed up into his dark eyes.

"The song is *Singing In The Rain,* Brandje," he said with a tender smile. "Not crying."

"I know."

He looked deeply into her azure eyes and said, "Come on, let's take you home. We'll have Gabe Rizner stop by the house in the morning to visit you. Does that sound better?"

She gave him a lopsided smile for an answer, then wrapped her arms around his chest. "Thank you," she whispered.

A few hours later, Brandje woke up from a luxurious nap to hear Nathan conversing with someone downstairs. She slid out of bed and pulled on her husband's blue robe, knotting it at her waist. Their voices carried easily to Brandje's ears.

Tiptoeing down the stairs, she crossed the hall and stood just outside the arched entrance to the living room. Nathan sat next to a woman with fawn brown hair whom Brandje assumed was his mother. Nate sat on the other side of the woman.

"How do you know she didn't seduce you into marriage so she could hold you responsible for all the hospital bills?" the woman asked Nathan. "You said she was raised on a farm. Did you ever think that possibly she couldn't afford this type of surgery?"

"Mother," Nathan answered, his voice stern, yet gentle. "This discussion is pointless. Brandje and I love each other. Will you once consider that?"

Brandje took a step forward, her eyes on the threesome in the living room. She did not notice the antique hall table with a vase of artificial flowers displayed upon it. She bumped the table and knocked the vase over. Immediately she reached out and grabbed the vase before it could fall to the floor.

"Nice save," said Nate as Brandje put the vase back.

Nathan stood up. He went to Brandje immediately and put his arm around her. "Mother," he said, "I'd like you to meet Brandje Rebecca Fulton-Duncan, my wife." The smile of pride and love that wandered across his handsome face spoke volumes to Brandje.

Nicole Duncan stood. She was dressed immaculately in a tailored cream taffeta, mid-length skirt and jacket. A full, beige scarf was tied tastefully, and tucked under the neckline of the jacket. She also wore beige gloves and matching stack heel pumps.

"My dear," said Nicole, walking across the room to offer Brandje a limp handshake. "I'm so happy to meet you. I hope you can forgive us for not attending the ceremony. It was unexpected and we just couldn't get away. But I can certainly see why Nathan chose you. She's lovely, isn't she, Nate? I was just telling Nathan how surprised we were when he phoned to say he was getting married. We'd waited so long. Goodness, his sisters were all married before they were twenty-four."

Nicole's sentences flowed together so rapidly that Brandje could scarcely tell where one ended and another began. The older woman nodded her head as she spoke and gave a pretentious smile.

"Actually," said Brandje, setting the record straight, "I heard what you said to Nathan."

Nicole paled visibly. She glanced from husband to son, as though hoping one of them would bail her out, to no avail. An awkward moment passed before Nicole finally whispered, "I ask your forgiveness, Brandje."

"You have good cause to worry," Brandje continued. "If I had a son as handsome, wealthy and intelligent as Nathan, I'd want to keep him under lock and key. Now that he's my husband, I may anyway."

"I didn't mean to imply —"

"You didn't," Brandje interrupted. "You said exactly how you felt, no implications intended. I like that. It shows honest concern. It's true that Martin and I are not wealthy. However, my brother has sold our farm, securing enough to pay for most of the hospital expenses. What is left owing beyond that could be paid out of the life insurance left us by our father. So you see, I didn't marry Nathan because I need surgery. I married him for the same reason you married Nate."

"But I —"

"Nathan told me about your courtship," Brandje continued. "I found it fascinating that two completely opposite people could fall in love so quickly. Isn't it marvelous that Nathan and I feel the same way about each other?" She remained silent, allowing Nicole time to recover her wits.

Brandje looked up at Nathan and watched admiration wander across his face. *Perhaps I acted hastily*, she thought, *but at least we're both on equal footing.*

"My dear," Nicole Duncan said. "You may call me Mother. I assure you I have not even allowed my sons-in-law to address me as such." She held her head high, her shoulders square, apparently recognizing that she'd been put in her place, yet relieved to know where she stood.

Brandje noted the deep brown eyes, a reflection of Nathan's. Nicole had a fine, straight nose and high cheekbones, both characteristics inherited by her son. She stepped into Nicole's open arms and said, "I intend to do just that, Mother." When she pulled back, there were tears in both women's eyes.

"The shooting match is over," Nate said, turning his wife back toward the living room sofa. "Perhaps you'd like to change into something a little less comfortable, Brandje?" he winked. "Then join us again for some party planning."

Brandje nodded, kissed Nathan quickly and rushed upstairs to change. When she returned, descending this time in mauve skirt and cream colored blouse, they visited amicably.

Although Nicole was disappointed when Nathan insisted she postpone the family party a few days, she relented graciously for Brandje's benefit. Friendships were established with scarcely a hint of hesitancy between Nicole and Brandje.

After Nate and Nicole Duncan left, Nathan prepared tuna sandwiches for supper, but Brandje ate very little.

Dr. Gabe Rizner arrived early the following morning. He was an energetic man in his fifties, with a firm handshake, no doubt from his roles in gospel leadership more than his role as an eminent surgeon. More important to Brandje, he empathized far beyond Dr. Finsen's capabilities. Although her chance of finding a suitable donor was slim, he reasoned that Dr. Finsen considered it best to discourage, in the event of an unsuccessful outcome.

Gabe Rizner seemed to understand Brandje's hesitancy completely, and felt that there would be ways they could work around her fears. It was agreed that Brandje would enter the hospital the following morning very early. She would have the biopsy immediately, and various other tests directly afterward. If all went well, Gabe would release her by evening so she could go home and stay with her husband.

Nathan invited Gabe to attend church with them, and meet with his parents later that afternoon. Since Gabe had spent his mission in France, he was anxious to rub shoulders with some of his fellow gospel brethren and sisters from the country that had won his heart many years earlier. To Nathan's surprise, Gabe accepted the invitation. Gabe Rizner not only earned their respect as a trusted doctor and inspired brother in the gospel of Jesus Christ, he became a dear and valued friend, as well.

Gabe told them he could perform the surgery in Rochester as easily as in Chicago. Should a donor become available, he had a private jet available to him, and could be in Rochester within ninety minutes, plenty of time to perform the procedure expeditiously.

Brandje liked Gabe's casual, easy manner, but she was even more grateful, and impressed by whisperings of the Holy Ghost, that Gabe Rizner was a spiritual giant in the gospel of Jesus Christ.

Although her day at the hospital was worse than she expected, and she was forced to spend the first three days afterward in bed, she was fortunate enough to recuperate at home, with Gabe Rizner's approval.

By the fourth day Brandje felt better and was eager to be with her husband in drawing up plans for the new kitchen. She discovered that Nathan planned to remodel one room at a time, until the house was completely finished. He gave her full authority on the kitchen, allowing her to select the perfect cupboards and counters, colors, flooring and appliances. They spent one full day with an interior decorator, drawing up plans together.

Friday morning they purchased white wicker furniture for the wrap-around porch, and made plans to build a large deck off the kitchen for dining outdoors, and summer entertaining.

On Friday night Nathan's parents invited them over for the Duncan family dinner party. Nicole Duncan, having mellowed since the encounter with Brandje, went out of her way to make Brandje feel welcome and loved. She was pleasantly cheerful throughout the evening.

Nathan's three sisters were charming and witty, as were their husbands, and they were easy to love.

Brandje especially liked Jill Duncan-Forsythe, who was only two years older than Nathan. It was obvious that brother and sister were close, and Brandje warmed to Jill immediately.

Before the evening ended, Nathan's entire family had clamored for her approval and attention. She had feared it would be the other way around. To her great relief, Brandje now felt that she belonged, that she was a beloved member of Nathan's family. The feeling gave her hope unlike anything else could have.

      arly Saturday morning Brandje awakened while it was still dark. She slipped on a robe and walked outside while Nathan slept. Sinking into a white wicker glider on the wide wrap-around porch, she rocked back and forth, her mind deep in thought. She felt immensely better than the past few days, and recognized the remarkable ability her body had to heal. It gave her a sense of hope that seemed to permeate her entire being. She closed her eyes and felt the gentle morning breeze against her skin, warming her long before sunrise began.

    Her heart and mind turned to her Father in Heaven. How grateful she was for all the blessings that He had so generously given to her. She recalled the vision she'd been given, and realized that she had not been doing her part in keeping a bright and cheerful attitude, as she'd promised she would. She asked the Lord to strengthen her, to help her overcome the tendency within her to become despondent. Recognizing that only God could help her, she pleaded with Him to allow a donor to be found for her. Again, she felt the whisperings of the spirit, telling her that God was still in charge, that He was watching over her, and was ever mindful of her desires and physical needs. Tears slipped down her cheeks, but unlike those during the past few weeks, these were tears of pure joy.

    Strengthened by the spirit of the Lord, Brandje vowed to herself that she would try harder. She would strive to be the comforter in her home, rather than the comforted. With renewed courage, she stood and walked across the porch to the steps.

The front door swung open and Nathan came through the doorway. "Good morning," she said, giving him a bright smile.

"You're not trying to replace me already?" he teased.

"Of course not," she insisted, reminding herself that he was now the sunrise of her life. She turned into his arms and hugged him.

Hungrily his lips sought hers. Brandje gladly responded, and he soon carried her back upstairs.

Beginning that same morning, Brandje's mood improved on a daily basis. Life took on a rich and more vibrant meaning. Savoring every moment became an intense part of her life, and Nathan shared that intensity with her. Every second was cherished, treasured, and tucked away in their memory banks to last forever. Nothing was ever taken for granted.

They watched each sunrise together. Filling the sky with shades of pink and orange, the sun often ascended like a fiery red ball. These were sunrises unlike any she'd ever seen before. Together they thrilled to every flower blossoming anew each morning, and listened to every cricket chirping at night.

Sheltered in the circle of Nathan's arms, they shared every breath, every heartbeat, every kiss. The intensity of their love brought them closer, not only in lovemaking, but in the touch of their fingers together as they walked across the meadows holding hands, and ate picnics in the early evenings, deep in the surrounding forests.

Nathan refused to write at all for a while, until Brandje's health problem was resolved, he told her. He spent every moment with her. They read scriptures together, did genealogical research for her ancestors, attended Temple sessions, kneeled together across the altar to act as proxy for her grandparents and great grandparents, uniting her family to her in eternal bonds that would enable her to find joy and peace on the other side of the veil.

Insisting she write her own personal history, Nathan helped Brandje remember many things she had forgotten since she was a young girl. He videotaped their history making sessions, audio taped them, and helped her prepare a suitable Book of Remembrance for her posterity.

The doctors, surprised that Brandje continued to do as well as she did, encouraged her to rest frequently, exercise moderately, eat well and wait. All these things Brandje did, pushing herself as much as she could. She still napped every day, and went to bed early in the evenings, but she refused to give in, or give up. The Lord had given her peace and now she waited, hoping He would show her why He wanted her name on that donor list.

It wasn't until late in September that all the legalities of bringing Elisha to America could finally be resolved. By then, Nathan had spoken with their little girl almost daily by telephone and e-mail. They had also exchanged videos of each other. Brandje knew Nathan felt a closeness with Elisha equal to her own. She hoped their daughter would share her love with Nathan as freely. Brandje was greatly encouraged that both would bring comfort to one another.

The morning that Martin and Elisha were scheduled to arrive Brandje could scarcely contain her excitement. As she watched Nathan storming through the house, making certain everything was in order, she realized just how much he already loved Elisha. The realization brought such joy to her heart that she couldn't imagine life any sweeter.

Although they arrived at the airport early, Martin and Elisha were already waiting for them in the lobby with their luggage beside them.

The moment she saw them, Elisha squealed! "Mummy, Daddy!"

She dashed toward them as fast as her little legs would take her, and threw herself into their waiting arms, hugging both of them tightly. Her strawberry blonde ringlets bounced freely as she shook her head. "I'm never going to let you go!" she beamed. "Never, never, never!"

"Does that go double for this little doll?" asked Brandje. "I found her for you in Croix de Vie." Brandje held the doll out, and presented it to Elisha.

"She looks just like me!" Elisha exclaimed.

Brandje nodded. "I thought so, too. Do you like her?"

Elisha grabbed the doll and hugged it tightly. "I love her almost as much as you and Daddy and Uncle Martin!" Elisha declared.

Nathan lifted Elisha up into his arms and held her while Brandje gave Martin a big hug. They pushed a cart stacked high with suitcases out to the car. Nathan asked if Elisha wanted to walk, but she wrapped her arms around his neck and wouldn't let go.

Elisha talked non-stop all the way home. Her excitement was contagious. Martin and Brandje could scarcely get a word in, so they waited for a more opportune time. Sometimes little girls have to come first.

When they arrived at the red brick house with the wrap around porch, Elisha's eyes widened. She jumped out of the car the moment Nathan secured the brake. "It's a real home," she gushed. "Now I have a real home and a real family!"

After they took her on a grand tour of the house, they carried in the luggage and put all of Elisha's clothing in a chest of drawers and in the closet. "Is this room big enough for you?" asked Nathan.

Elisha nodded. "It has a big bed, and I don't have to share it with anyone but Rosebud, do I?"

"Who's Rosebud?" Brandje asked with a smile.

Elisha held up the doll Brandje had given her. "That's what I named my doll," she said, "because when I look at her, she reminds me of you, Mummy!"

"Mummy reminds you of rosebuds?" asked Nathan with a quick smile.

Elisha nodded. "Whenever she came to see me at the orphanage, she always brought me a rosebud," she explained.

Nathan smiled. "Then Rosebud is the perfect name for your doll. Do you think she'll like your bedroom? It's not very pretty right now. We wanted you to decide exactly how you wanted it."

"What's your favorite color?" asked Brandje.

"Orange," Elisha replied.

"Do you like peach?" asked Nathan.

"They're yummy!"

Brandje smiled. "I think he means the color peach. It's a very soft, light orange, with just a hint of pink. Would you like that color?"

"I'd like that color a lot!" Elisha beamed. "Can I have green, too? I like green. I like grass and leaves and fat green caterpillars."

Nathan laughed. "You can have any color you want."

Later that afternoon, while Brandje napped, Nathan took Martin and Elisha on a tour of the property. As they approached the barn, Nathan asked Elisha, "Do you like horses?"

"Very much!" she said. "Uncle Martin had two horses on his farm, but he had to sell them because we were coming to live with you!"

"Were you terribly disappointed?" asked Nathan, arching an eyebrow and giving Martin a wink.

"I felt sad," Elisha pouted, if only for a moment. "But now I'm too happy!" she amended. "I'd rather have you and Mummy than a horse!"

"She nearly cried when I first told her about the horses," Martin whispered to him.

Nathan nodded, then picked Elisha up and pressed his nose gently against hers. "Do you think there's enough room in that big heart of yours to love Mummy, Daddy, Uncle Martin, Rosebud and . . ." He paused long enough for Martin to open the barn door. ". . . your very own horse?"

Inside the barn stood a Shetland pony, decked out in saddle and reins. Elisha squealed with delight. "For me?" she asked. "For real?"

"For real," Nathan agreed. He placed her in the saddle and took the reins. "But only if you can think of a suitable name. This horse doesn't have a name yet."

"Oh, that's easy," said Elisha. "We should call him Snuggles, because I could just hug him forever and ever!" She bent over and wrapped her arms as far around Snuggles' neck as she could reach.

The two men spent nearly two hours teaching Elisha how to ride, how to get in and out of the saddle by herself, and how to respect the back end of all animals. When they finally put Snuggles back in the stall and left the barn, Elisha exclaimed, "Look, Daddy! We've got company!"

"That we do," grinned Nathan

"Lots of company!" said Elisha. "Look at all the cars!"

"Can you count them?" asked Uncle Martin.

"One, two, three, four, five!" she grinned and sprinted down the pathway ahead of them.

When they reached the house, Elisha sprang through the open front door and rushed inside, where she found balloons floating everywhere, and presents stacked high on a table in the living room. There were lots of people she didn't know, men and women, and several children. "Surprise, Elisha!" Everyone yelled.

"Who are *they*?" Elisha timidly asked her mother.

A matronly woman said, "Welcome to the family, Elisha." She bent down and offered her hand to Elisha. "I'm your new grandmother."

Elisha looked over at her new mother, uncertain how to respond. "For real?" came her tiny voice, now just a squeak above a whisper.

Brandje stood waiting nearby, her hands clasped together as though she was praying. She smiled as she reassured young Elisha. "Yes, Pumpkin. You have a grandmother, grandfather, aunts, uncles, and lots of cousins!"

Elisha looked into the dark brown eyes of the woman in front of her, who was still waiting for Elisha to take her hand. The woman's eyes were friendly, with sparkles in them, just like her new father's eyes. "You have eyes like my daddy's," she observed shyly.

"That's because I am your daddy's mother," said the woman with a wide, pleasant smile.

Elisha saw her daddy's smile in Grandmother's face, as well. She hesitated no longer, but threw herself into her grandmother's arms, hugging her for all she was worth! In her loudest, brightest voice she exclaimed, "This is my most happiest day in my most happiest whole life!"

And with those words, Elisha won the hearts of everyone within the Duncan house that day.

The very next morning, Nathan and Brandje appeared in Children's Court with Elisha, where a judge signed the adoption decree. They were not satisfied, however, until the following day when Elisha was sealed to them in the Palmyra Temple. Accompanying their eternal family unit in the sealing room were all of Elisha's aunts and uncles from the Duncan clan, as well as her new grandparents.

The only legality left for Elisha and Brandje was to receive their American citizenship, and they applied for permanent residency immediately upon their return from Palmyra, to begin the process.

For the next few weeks their lives settled into a pattern. Martin remained with them, so he could be on hand to help with Elisha in case Nathan would need to take Brandje to the hospital for her transplant. It turned out that Martin was, as Brandje insisted, very good at moving horses from one place to another. Within a week, with the assistance of a fine little filly, he had Dorsett happy and content at Nathan's ranch. While Elisha was in school, Martin worked outdoors, tending the horses, tilling the gardens in preparation for winter, and planting tulip bulbs and daffodils for spring.

Nathan gave Brandje the mornings with Elisha, letting her get their daughter ready for school. While they were busy, he helped Martin feed the horses and brush them down. Then they would take Elisha to school in the car. She could have taken a school bus that would stop down their lane, but Brandje was cheerful and energetic in the mornings, and she wanted every moment she could have with their little girl.

Each day after Elisha was delivered to her teacher, Nathan and Brandje returned home, where Brandje crocheted on the afghan she'd started for Nathan in France, while Nathan talked with her.

Brandje was a good listener. She gave Nathan quite a few good ideas regarding his novel, which she encouraged him to go back to each day while she napped. Although he had begun to write again, she knew there were still times when he would leave the computer and sit in a chair next to their bed, to watch her sleep.

Regardless of his protests back in London, Martin seemed genuinely happy to live with them. He picked Elisha up each afternoon, when she got out of school, and brought her home. If Brandje was still sleeping, he and Elisha would ride horses together.

Martin told Brandje that he'd read the Book of Mormon back in London, and though it was interesting, he still had many questions: He wasn't quite convinced about families being together forever. It was a principle he couldn't understand. She supposed he had too much practical farmer in him, and he seemed relieved when Brandje and Nathan didn't pressure him about his religious convictions. Truth be known, Brandje wasn't sure he had any.

She felt that Martin wanted to believe as Brandje and Nathan did, that families could be together forever, and she knew that he missed their parents keenly, perhaps more than Brandje herself. Perhaps he dared not hope for any reunion in Heaven; perhaps he feared the keen disappointment he would feel if it were not true. Regardless, Brandje and Nathan both expressed their understanding and empathy to his way of thinking, and let the matter rest for a while.

Elisha, Nathan, Brandje and Martin wasted no time in decorating Elisha's bedroom just the way she wanted it. Grandmother Nicole also helped, by taking Elisha and Brandje shopping for curtains, bedspreads, toys, dolls and other girl-things to complement the room once the painting, wallpapering and carpets were finished.

When the kitchen remodeling was completed, Nathan and Martin began building a greenhouse. They hoped to plant and grow gardenias for Brandje, to bloom for her year round. It was their way of saying they still believed a miracle would happen. At all costs, the two men tried to maintain hope. However, by late October, when the leaves were turning yellow, orange and red, hope became an elusive dream that started to slip away from all of them.

Brandje found it more difficult to function. Her mind felt like it was in a fog half the time. Dr. Finsen still offered no chance of finding a donor, and she had resigned herself to maintaining a cheerful, positive outlook, regardless of the outcome. One of her big disappointments was that she could scarcely wake up at dawn anymore. Her body and mind were in a downward spiral, and there was little she could do to force herself back up, regardless how hard she tried.

Having overslept on the sixth of November, Brandje rushed about trying to get Elisha ready for school. She was pale, in terrible pain, and the effort exhausted her.

Martin offered to drive Elisha to school by himself. Brandje didn't want to agree, but Nathan nodded and gave her a gentle smile, so she relented. It was difficult to admit that she couldn't function as well as she wanted to.

When Martin left, Nathan helped Brandje load the dishwasher. She loved the new kitchen and always wiped the shining counter tops with pride. When they were finished, she suggested, "You'll need to feed the horses, Nathan. I'm going to sit on the sofa and crochet for a while."

Nathan nodded, gave her a quick kiss, and said, "I won't be long."

Brandje went into the living room, gathered the basket of handiwork and began to crochet once again. She wanted to finish the last row on the afghan she'd been making for Nathan.

When Nathan came in from feeding the horses, he found Brandje asleep on the sofa, wrapped up in the afghan she'd been working on for the past two months.

He stood there, entranced momentarily, his heart joyful and hollow as he looked upon her. Wonder filled him as he realized that both feelings had entered his heart somehow. He felt joyful, because while she still lived, there was reason to hope; hollow, because her strength waned and she slept more than he thought one human being could sleep. He knew the sleepiness was due to the cancer as much as to the increases in her medications. She was now on several oral prescriptions, and morphine shots, when needed, which Brandje insisted on giving to herself as long as she could. This past week Nathan realized that her life was winding down, and she was taking his heart with her. If it were not for Martin and Elisha, he doubted he could endure what was happening to his wife's body while he sat idly by, unable to do anything to help her.

When Nathan heard the front door close, he turned around to see Martin tiptoeing in, apparently afraid he would awaken his sister.

Whispering, Martin said, "She's getting worse, isn't she?"

Nathan grimaced. But he had to nod in agreement.

"I can't bear it," said Martin as tears spilled over the rims of his eyes. He pivoted around and fled from the house. Nathan knew how Martin hated to let anyone see him cry.

"Nor can I," choked Nathan in a whisper that no one heard but himself. He watched Brandje sleeping, peacefully it seemed. If they didn't find a donor soon. . . .

Stubbornly, he refused to let that thought creep into his mind. He stepped across the living room and sat beside his wife as she slept on the sofa. Brandje stirred, so Nathan gathered her into his arms. "Sleepy today?" he asked tenderly.

"Mmm," she snuggled against him.

He loved the feel of her next to him.

"Very," she finally answered, looking up at him.

The azure blue color of her eyes that he loved so well was gone completely, replaced by a sad gray blue. "Should I carry you to bed?"

"Not yet," she murmured, as though savoring the moment of tenderness between them. "I finished your afghan." She held it up for his inspection.

Nathan's eyes filled with tears, but he blinked them back. "Thank you," he whispered. "I will always treasure it."

"I need to tell you something very important, Nathan," said Brandje.

"What is it?"

She looked up at him and tears filled her eyes. "I've reconsidered the promise I made you give me back in London."

"You have?" he asked, worried where his sweet wife was going with this line of reasoning.

"Yes." She nodded. "I understand, finally, why Martin tried so hard to protect me from seeing Father die. I feel the same way about Elisha. She's much younger than I was, and this will not be easy for her."

"Are you asking me to take you to the hospital?" he asked, his voice filled with fear.

"Not yet," she whispered. "But you'll know when."

"Oh, Brandje!" he moaned, holding her close, wanting to crush her against him as he had in the past, but fearing he would hurt her, she'd become so thin and fragile. "Brandje, I love you so!"

"Then don't give up hope," she said. "Last night I dreamed we were at the villa together. It was a wonderful dream, Nathan."

Wearily he asked, "You haven't given up hope?"

"No!" She shook her head defiantly. "Never! Until I take my last breath, don't you dare give up hope, either! Promise me!"

He didn't want to discourage her, but the stark reality of her condition, coupled with their inability to find a suitable donor, had waned his belief that she would be allowed to remain with him. He sighed as he relented. "I promise."

"No matter what it takes," she persisted. "No matter how hard it gets for you. Every time you see me, even if I can't speak or move or hear you, please tell me that you still have hope."

"Brandje —"

"Promise!"

He nodded, unashamed as tears filled his dark brown eyes and slipped down his rugged face. "I love you," he said softly. "I'll always love you."

"And I'll return that love a hundred fold," she whispered moments before she fell asleep in his arms.

Brandje slept most of the afternoon and could hardly awaken for supper. Nathan brought her a bowl of soup and spoon-fed her.

When Elisha came in to say goodnight with Rosebud, Brandje

mustered all the strength that she could to hold her little girl next to her and stroke her cheek.

Elisha became quiet and thoughtful. Timidly she asked, "Mummy?"

"Yes, pumpkin."

"When your daddy died, were you sad?"

"I was very sad," whispered Brandje.

"Oh."

Brandje sensed her daughter's uneasiness and comforted her by explaining, "But now I know that he lives with Heavenly Father, with Jesus and with my mummy. He's very happy to live in Heaven with them. Someday we'll get to live with them, too."

"Even me?" came the hopeful question.

"Especially you," said Brandje. "Remember that day when we went to the Palmyra Temple together?"

Elisha giggled. "Lots of people were there!"

Brandje smiled. "Yes, that's right. Well, that day we were given a great promise, do you remember?"

Elisha nodded sleepily. "The angel man said we could be a family forever."

Brandje kissed Elisha's forehead. "Forever means, even after our bodies die, we still get to live together in Heaven."

"Then you're not really sad about your daddy, are you?" Elisha asked softly.

"No, pumpkin, I'm not sad anymore."

"I'm not going to be sad either," promised Elisha.

They were both silent for a few minutes, then Brandje sang a lullaby to her daughter, a special song the two of them had created together. By the time she had finished singing, Elisha was sound asleep. Brandje pulled her daughter closer and gazed upon the precious child with tenderness and love, committing to memory every freckle, every eyelash and every ringlet of Elisha's strawberry blonde hair.

Right after doing the supper dishes, Nathan found his wife and daughter sleeping peacefully together, with Brandje's arm beneath Elisha's head, and Rosebud tucked under Elisha's arm. He was reluctant to separate them. Instead, he snuggled up behind Brandje and held them both until after midnight. Finally he carried Elisha to her own bed and tucked her in. Like her mother, she was a sound sleeper and did not awaken.

When he returned to their bedroom, Brandje was in the same position she'd been in earlier. He slipped beneath the quilt and pulled her gently into his arms. It seemed like hours before he fell asleep, and then only after she had turned away from him, as though she was uncomfortable in that position.

Just before sunrise the following morning, Nathan awakened and rolled over, wanting to take his wife into his arms. She did not respond to his nudging, nor his tender kiss. He turned on the lamp and shook her, but she remained as limp and lifeless as a rag doll.

He placed his hands upon her head and gave her a husband's blessing, anguish filling his heart and soul. Evoking the powers of Heaven in her behalf, he found that his final words of prayer could only be uttered as, "Nevertheless, Father, not my will be done, but thine."

Chapter Twenty-Three

"I'm sorry, Nathan," said Dr. Finsen. "If we cannot secure a donor within the next week or two . . ." He shook his head, realizing words were no longer necessary.

The two were sitting in a private waiting room outside the intensive care unit. Nurses and doctors rushed by the open door, unnoticed.

"I see," Nathan heard his voice answer. It sounded strange, almost like it came from someone else. A terrible ache inside his body had come with him that morning. It seemed so long ago, and yet, was it really just this morning?

"If you'd care to visit with your Bishop, he telephoned and said he would arrive in an hour or so. I'm sorry we can't give you any more hope than we have."

Nathan nodded. "Thank you."

"Gabe Rizner is en route as we speak. He. . . wants to make his own assessment."

"He doesn't trust you," Nathan tried to joke.

"Probably," agreed Dr. Finsen with a smile.

Nathan glanced at his watch. It was six-twenty in the evening. "I'll go in and sit with Brandje for a while," he said wearily.

He turned away from the window where yellow and orange leaves fell in tune to a brisk November breeze. The scene reminded him of the vibrant life his wife once had, and how she was slowly withering away, like these autumn leaves. Then he walked down the hospital corridor to the Intensive Care Unit. Silently he counted every step he took, trying to focus his mind on anything but what he faced in Brandje's room.

When he reached the ICU, he scrubbed his hands and put a hospital gown over his clothing before entering.

The door behind him whisked shut and he stopped several feet from her bed. Tubes and machines performed their life-preserving miracles as she lay sleeping. Her face seemed even more sallow this evening than earlier in the day.

A silent prayer seemed to chant in his heart. *Father in Heaven, why take her away from me? She could survive if she had a donor. Why haven't you sent her a donor?*

As though mesmerized by the quiet beauty of his wife, Nathan paid no attention as two nurses chatted at the main desk, while others performed their routine duties, taking vital signs, checking intravenous flow, drawing blood. For more than half an hour he stood by Brandje's side, as though riveted to the spot, his eyes transfixed upon her still face.

It saddened him to see Brandje so heavily sedated. But at least she wasn't screaming out in pain. When they first arrived at the hospital that morning, she had revived long enough to scream. The pain must have been terrible. Yet nothing the doctors gave her for it had helped. Finally, in an effort to preserve her strength, the doctors had induced the coma-like condition in which she now lived, where she could neither see nor speak.

Their entire relationship, from the moment he first found her sleeping upstairs at the villa in France, to that very moment where she lay in her hospital bed, passed before his eyes, in memory.

With a sad smile, he recalled the many times they'd spoken angrily with one another. Then it occurred to him that they had not quarreled since they created an eternal family unit, in the London Temple more than two months ago.

What he would give, right now, to have her sit up and yell at him! The thought surprised him, and he pushed it away, realizing that he may have to wait a long, long time to hear her voice again.

Before tears could well up in his dark eyes, he kissed her cheek.

Praying she could still hear him, he whispered next to her ear, "Brandje, I have hope for us. Don't give up on me, honey. We're going to get through this together. Do you hear me?"

When she did not respond, he pivoted and left the ICU in great haste, and sought privacy in the small hospital chapel, where he sank wearily onto a bench and placed his hands over his face, forcing his emotions to settle.

After a while, he felt a hand on his shoulder. Glancing up, he saw the warm smile of his bishop and home teachers.

They shook hands and offered condolences. Then they knelt together in prayer, each man taking his turn, asking the Lord for guidance, for understanding, and if it was His will, for a miracle.

Suddenly the door was pushed open and Dr. Gabe Rizner entered. His expression was firm, his stride quick, decisive.

"Gabe!" Nathan stood up, surprised to see Gabe dressed in surgical attire. "You made it."

Gabe Rizner shook Nathan's hand vigorously. Then, with a hint of sadness in his expression he said, "We have your donor, Nathan. Will you come and sign the necessary papers?"

Confused, Nathan said, "I've signed her papers. I thought everything was in order."

Dr. Rizner hesitated, his eyes searching Nathan's cautiously. "I'm afraid the papers are not for her," he said quietly. "They're for her brother . . ." He let the word trail off, hoping Nathan would understand.

"Martin?" Nathan questioned. "Martin?!!!" He gasped, and would have collapsed if his home teachers hadn't supported him at the elbows.

"Follow me," said Gabe somberly, nodding his head. "They need you in the emergency room."

A knot of apprehension grew tight in Nathan's stomach as he more fully realized what they would find in the emergency room that night. He drew back momentarily, unwilling to walk through the swinging double doors. If the priesthood brethren hadn't been right by his side, he wouldn't have been able to walk in at all.

Gabe held the door open for them. "I'll give you a moment alone," he said as they walked through. He directed them to the curtain and held it aside.

Nathan's feet propelled him toward a gurney where a gentle and familiar man slept silently, never to awaken in mortality again. Martin had given the ultimate sacrifice.

Another doctor opened the curtain and stepped inside the small holding area. "Are you the brother-in-law?" he asked.

"Yes," Nathan answered.

"I'm Dr. Carlton," said the man. "Apparently Mr. Fulton's car was stopped at a red light when a truck lost its brakes. The truck plowed into his car, forcing it into oncoming traffic. He was pronounced dead within a few minutes of his arrival here. We've done a brain scan, but the readout is flat. Although the respirator and heart pump are keeping oxygen flowing through his body, medically speaking, your wife's brother died shortly after the accident."

Nathan inhaled sharply and looked back at the still form beneath the sheet. Martin's chest rose and fell mechanically in tune with an accordion like tube that stretched from a machine to Martin's mouth, and pressed fresh air into Martin's lungs. Yet there was a peacefulness about the expression on Martin's face that was not dispelled by any of the paraphernalia connected to him.

How many times, Nathan thought, had Martin wished he could take Brandje's place? Perhaps he had sensed what lay ahead for him.

More importantly, what would Martin's death do, emotionally, to his beloved wife? Would she hate Nathan for signing the necessary papers?

Nathan promised her he would not give up hope, not until her last breath left her body. Had he known then what he must do now, would he have made such a promise?

He thought about Brandje's smile, her beautiful azure eyes, her long hair. He thought about her relationship with their daughter, her loving, motherly ways. He thought about her testimony and the vision that she had in France. The Lord told her to go on the donor list, to prepare her for this very moment. Nathan would not fail her now. She wanted his hope, and she would have it completely.

"Where do I sign?" he asked, forcing the anguish he felt for Martin behind him now, replacing it with a glimmer of hope.

Within a few minutes, Martin's body was wheeled away, and Nathan turned back to his companions.

"We're so sorry," said the Bishop. "Shall we wait with you?"

Nathan tried to smile. "No," he said, "but another blessing for Brandje isn't going to hurt her, if you don't mind."

"Not at all," came the immediate response.

Together, Nathan and the priesthood brethren returned to the intensive care unit where the nurses were preparing Brandje and her accessories for transport to the operating room.

"You made it just in time," said a nurse when she saw Nathan.

"We're going to give her a blessing," said Nathan. "Could we have a few minutes of privacy?"

"Make it quick," said the nurse, leaving them alone.

After Brandje was anointed, Bishop acted as voice while the other men assisted. He gave her a sweet and tender blessing. Nathan listened carefully to every single word. The doctors were blessed with divine inspiration, that they would be led by the spirit of the Holy Ghost as they operated on Brandje, that they would be able to perform the surgery according to their greatest skill. Brandje was blessed that she would be comforted, that the Lord was with her, and that He was mindful of her. Brandje's family was blessed with comfort and reassurance that the Lord was still in control.

But will she survive? Nathan asked the Lord silently. *Will she survive?* For that question, there were no answers.

Immediately following the blessing, Nathan leaned over, kissed his wife tenderly on the cheek and whispered in her ear. "I love you, Brandje. And I still have hope."

Then Brandje was whisked away on a gurney.

After assuring them he would be fine, Nathan's bishop and home teachers asked him to call them when Brandje was out of surgery.

When he was left alone, he had time to think about Martin. He felt certain Martin had been on his way to the hospital to see Brandje. No doubt he had dropped Elisha off at his parents' home before coming.

Then he realized he hadn't telephoned his daughter to tell her goodnight, or to tell his parents about the transplant. He made the call quickly, being careful not to say too much to Elisha, and asking his parents not to tell her about Martin or the transplant, at least not yet.

Then he waited and watched the clock. A short time later, Nate walked in unexpectedly and embraced his son. He insisted Nathan eat something after learning he'd not eaten all day. Afterward, the two men sat together, father and son, to wait and worry and pray and hope.

As Gabe Rizner prepared Brandje's liver for removal, Dr. Finsen prepared Martin's. Gabe had felt the still, small whisperings of the Holy Ghost several times that day. He prayed, as he worked, that God would direct his mind and his spirit to make the correct decisions for Brandje. He didn't want to leave Nathan with a double tragedy. Brandje and her husband had become dear to him. With absolute concentration, he silently entreated the Lord for guidance in performing the surgery.

Then Gabe noticed, if only for a brief moment, that Brandje's heart seemed to hesitate every few seconds. He worried that the spiritual impressions he'd received that day were, once again, the divine comforter telling him that he'd done his best and to leave the rest up to God. Too many times, in his battle to save human lives and mortal suffering, he'd lost. He prayed for divine intervention, knowing that in the final analysis the situation was not in his hands at all, but in the Lord's. Would this be one of those terrible, heart-wrenching times when he would have to tell the patient's family that his best efforts were inadequate?

A few minutes before both doctors were ready to transplant Martin's liver into Brandje's abdominal cavity, a beeper went off, and a worried nurse exclaimed, "She's crashing!"

A mad scramble to restart Brandje's weary heart began in the operating room. Syringes of medication were plunged into the IV lines, and conducting gel was smeared on Brandje's chest.

The surgery was put on hold while Gabe yelled, "Paddles!"

"Charging," said a nurse, as she turned a dial. Another nurse handed Gabe the defibrillator paddles just as the first said, "Go."

"Clear!" snapped Gabe. He placed the paddles on Brandje's chest and pulled the triggers. Then he watched the heart monitor as a flat line hummed across it.

"Nothing!" said a nurse in dismay.

"Again!" Gabe directed, listening only to the whisperings of the spirit within him, regardless of the fact that the monitor emitted a straight and unbroken line.

Brandje sat up, feeling vibrant and alive, unlike anything she remembered before. She wanted to go find Nathan, to tell him how much better she felt now.

Then, quite suddenly, she recognized Dr. Gabe Rizner, Dr. Finsen, and other doctors and nurses, who were scrambling around a woman on an operating room table.

"Is that me?" she asked.

But no one heard her, and no one answered her question. Everyone seemed completely unaware that she stood beside them.

Brandje turned away, not wanting to see the body stretched out on the operating table. She found herself floating toward the ceiling. Somehow the hospital disappeared and she was drawn toward a bright, intensely white light.

"Brandje," she heard Martin's tender voice beside her. He was dressed in white clothing, and he'd never looked so young and handsome before.

She reached out and took her brother's offered hand. Noticing the wrist length sleeve at the end of her arm, she looked down to see that she, too, was clothed in a pure white gown that reached all the way to her bare feet.

"Where are we?" he asked. "Is this Heaven?"

"I think so," she answered, but her next thought turned to her husband. "Where's Nathan?"

"I don't think he can come with us," Martin said.

Brandje held back. "Why not? Where is he?"

"I don't know where he is," said Martin somberly. "But I think he'll have to join us later."

Brandje felt a great sadness as she realized Nathan could not come with her. But the place where she and Martin arrived was such a pleasant place. She felt warmth and comfort within her, so much so that the thoughts of leaving her husband and daughter did not bother her as much as at first. Nathan would join her soon, and so would Elisha. For Brandje, the time would pass quickly.

"I think you're right," Martin observed. "I think we are in Heaven. I was in an accident and then . . ."

"I'm so sorry," she said. "Are you all right?"

"I must have died," he answered. "The doctors were operating on you, giving you my liver, and I stayed to watch."

"I think I died during the surgery," Brandje admitted. "I didn't want to die, Martin. I wanted to stay with Nathan and Elisha."

"Are you terribly sad?" he asked.

She thought about his question before she responded. "Yes," she began, "I will miss them terribly. And no, because I feel comforted somehow. But I worry that they'll be lonely without me."

Soon the white light dissipated and they found themselves walking along a path in an open meadow. Flowering plants grew everywhere. The green shades of the leaves were the most vibrant she had ever seen. There were all shapes, sizes and colors of blossoms, many they didn't recognize.

They walked along the path for only a short distance, until they saw a large white building ahead. It was a beautiful mansion with tall white pillars and a double door made out of gold. The building seemed to sparkle with a light of its own. Although the place in which they stood was bright as a summer's morning, they marveled that the brightness did not come from the sun, for there was no sun, and there wasn't a single cloud in the sky.

"So this is what Heaven looks like," said Martin wistfully. "You know, I think you were right about families being together forever."

The big golden doors of the building opened slowly. Soon a man and a woman stepped outside and motioned for them to come closer.

Immediately Martin dropped Brandje's hand and ran toward the couple. "Mum!" he cried joyfully. "Father!"

Brandje looked in amazement. Yes, she recognized the man as her father. But since her mother had died when she was an infant, Brandje did not recognize her immediately. Slowly she followed Martin, waiting her turn, thrilling as he was wrapped in the circle of his parents' arms. It seemed as though she could feel Martin's joy at being with his parents. Her spirits soared as she realized they could finally be a forever family, never to be separated again.

When it was her time to greet them, she embraced her father first. Then she turned and stared into the gentle face of her mother, Rebecca Fulton. Although they looked remarkably alike, it seemed strange that Brandje couldn't remember her. Suddenly, a small hole seemed to form in Brandje's mind, and memories of past events poured into her like sand in an hourglass. Brandje recalled her mother with vivid clarity, holding her as an infant, kissing her cheeks, and blowing bubbles against her neck, making her laugh with delight. The memories were so clear, it felt like they'd never been separated.

Brandje wiped at her eyes, surprised to find that she could cry in Heaven. "Mum?" she asked, her voice trembling with joy and love.

"Yes, Brandje," said Rebecca Fulton. She wrapped her arms around Brandje and held her for several minutes.

A warmth spread through Brandje unlike anything she'd ever known. She didn't want to let go, but soon Rebecca released her.

"Thank you," said Rebecca, "for doing our work in the temple. I've waited a long time to be with your father."

"You're welcome." Brandje laughed and cried all at the same time.

The big doors opened and the Savior, whom Brandje recognized immediately from her vision at the villa in France, motioned for them to come. As He did so, He smiled serenely at Brandje, filling her with peace and contentment.

Thoughts of Nathan and Elisha still troubled her. But, reluctantly, she accepted that she would have to stay. She took Martin's hand and began to follow her parents toward the open doors.

"No, Brandje," said her father. He gave her a tender kiss and put his arm about her shoulder. "You must go back," he counseled. "There are many here who are waiting for you to do their ordinances also."

"I can go back?" she asked. She was puzzled by this information. Then she recognized two emotions filling her with a sense of light and peace. She felt happy that she would be with Nathan and Elisha again, yet sad that she would have to leave her parents and Martin.

"It's peaceful here, and I have no pain anymore," she said, dreading the thought of going back to that body that had caused her so much anguish.

"You have a husband and a daughter who need you," her father reminded.

"I know," she said. "But Father, why show me all this only to take it away?"

"To help you understand why you must continue in the path you have chosen. There are many things you must do with your life before you can come back home with us."

"What must I do?" she asked. "Tell me."

"You must take care of your husband and daughter, keep your sacred covenants, and find your ancestors. You have much temple work to do. Continue your family history writing. Without your work, our grandchildren will never know who we are, or how much we love them."

When Brandje fully understood all that was expected of her, she hugged her parents and wept both for joy and for sorrow. She knew she would be homesick when she left this place.

When she hugged Martin, she said, "I'm going to miss you."

"But you'll be fine," he encouraged. "Because now you know where I am. Brandje, I'm glad that you'll have my liver, I have no regrets about that. But will you take my name to your temple? I want to be with Mum and Father forever!" He gave her a crooked grin.

"Of course!" Brandje laughed and cried all at the same time.

"We'll be watching over you," Rebecca said, "as we always have."

"And waiting for you," said her Father.

"Gabe," said Dr. Finsen, "it's time to call."

Gabe listened, but not to Dr. Finsen. He listened, as he had on a thousand such occasions, for the Lord's voice . . . for the Lord to tell him what he should do. It only took another second. Then a familiar feeling hit him like a bolt of lightning. "No!" He snapped belligerently. "One more time! Clear!"

He placed the paddles on Brandje's chest and pulled the trigger. Electricity shot through her body once again.

Everyone waited, holding their breath in silence. The monitor picked up a faint twitch, then another, and another. Suddenly the screen lit up with an increasingly steady heart rhythm. A dozen sighs of relief followed.

"It seems I was wrong," admitted Dr. Finsen with a smile. "You have an uncanny ability there, Gabe. Perhaps you should consider a vocation in which you could use it."

His remark diffused the tension in the room and most of the attendants laughed with him.

But Gabe could only look heavenward and offer a silent, yet intensely personal prayer: *Thank you, Lord! Thank you!*

Then Gabe Rizner nodded to those around him with profound gratitude. "Let's get this show on the road!"

It took six days before Brandje was able to talk again. The doctors kept her fairly sedated. When at last they removed the respirator and nose tube, the relief she felt was immediate. She hadn't imagined it could be so difficult.

A nurse cleaned her face and brushed her hair. "Better?" she asked.

"Much," said Brandje. "My throat feels parched, though."

"That's normal," said the nurse. "But the doctor says if all goes well today, you can be moved to a regular room this evening."

"Good," said Brandje. "Where's my husband?"

"Are you ready for him?" she asked with a gentle smile.

"I am!"

While the nurse went to get Nathan, Brandje closed her eyes. She didn't care to look at all the paraphernalia that accompanied a person in the intensive care unit. It frightened her. She turned her thoughts to her Father in Heaven and whispered a silent prayer in her heart, asking that He help her be brave and able to comfort others around her.

Within a few minutes, Nathan walked into the room. He hadn't found a way to tell Brandje about Martin yet. She'd been too sedated. However, she seemed much better today, when he looked on her. Relief swept over him as he noticed she no longer had the respirator or NG tube connected to her.

He leaned over and brushed her lips tenderly with his.

She opened her eyes, and for the first time in weeks, he realized the azure color he loved had returned. She had her sparkle back.

"Hi," she whispered. "Are you all right?"

"Better than you." He slipped her hand into his.

"You look terrible," she said. "Haven't you slept?"

He smiled. "It seems to me that you're the one who likes to sleep so much," he teased. When Brandje did not smile, he realized she was in a serious mood.

"Nathan, you have to sleep. How are you going to take care of me when I come home if you don't?"

He sighed wearily and sank into a chair beside her bed. *She's lucid today,* he thought to himself. *And that means I'll have to tell her about Martin.*

When Brandje saw the look in Nathan's eyes and the expression on his face, she knew instinctively what he was thinking about. "It's all right," she comforted. "Nathan, I understand."

He stood up and turned his back to her, but somehow Brandje sensed the concerns troubling him. He still thought she didn't know that Martin had been killed, that Martin's liver was now inside her, sustaining her life. And he was likely worried, now that she was recovering, that she might relapse if he told her about Martin. Perhaps he worried that her body would automatically reject the liver because of the stress Martin's death would place on her.

"Nathan," she whispered. "Come back here."

He turned around, his lips in a tight line. Sitting back down, he held her hand tenderly in his and kissed it over and over again.

"I walked through a beautiful meadow back to Heaven," she whispered. "It was when my heart stopped in the operating room."

Nathan lifted his head quickly, his eyes focusing on hers, his ears pricked. He arched an eyebrow in dismay. "They told you your heart stopped during the operation?" he questioned. "I asked the doctors not to tell you that until you were stronger."

"No one told me," she whispered. "Listen to me."

Nathan gave her his full attention.

"My heart stopped," Brandje explained. "And Martin was there, on the other side. He held my hand and told me about the accident. He and I . . . we thought that I died, also."

Tears pooled in Nathan's brown eyes and dripped effortlessly down his face. He shook his head for a moment, but she reached out and placed a finger on his lips.

"Yes, I know. But let me tell you about my vision. Martin and I walked through a beautiful meadow to a spacious building that seemed to glow all of its own accord. My parents were there, Nathan. Both of them! Martin was so happy to see Mum and Father. I thought I had to stay with them and wait for you to come later on. But Father said I could go back. He said I had things to do."

"What things?" Nathan asked, astonishment etched onto his rugged face.

"I'm supposed to take care of you and Elisha, keep my covenants, and find our ancestors in order to do their temple work," she answered.

Nathan searched her face, then bowed his head, as though offering a prayer. It seemed to Brandje that she heard him ask God to confirm that what Brandje had seen was real, though Nathan's lips never moved.

"Of course it was real," she answered. "Otherwise, how do you think I already know that Martin is gone?"

A feeling of warmth, light and energy coursed through her when he gave her a smile that indicated he was totally convinced of the validity of her words.

"I was supposed to go on that donor list for a reason," she explained softly. "Martin knew it long before I did."

Nathan kissed her hand, and held it to his face while he wept. With her fingers, Brandje wiped his tears away.

When he finally stopped, she stroked his face with her hand, admiring and loving him. *Do you still love me, Nathan, like you did before?* she wondered to herself.

"Of course I love you, Brandje!" he exclaimed, as though answering her question. "I love you with every ounce of strength I have."

"I didn't ask you," she smiled. "At least, not out loud."

Their eyes locked in surprise as they realized the importance of what had just occurred between them . . . twice!

They had truly become one, as the scriptures suggested!

Finally, though it had taken grave hardship on both their parts, husband and wife had formed a bond between them that could never be separated. They both realized, once and for all, that when God commanded Adam to leave his father and mother and cleave unto his wife and become one with her, He was not just talking about senses of the flesh or procreation of the human body. He was talking about their spirit selves, as well.

The spiritual bonding that takes place between husband and wife has eternal consequences far beyond the scope or imagination of mankind. It is the very glue that holds the mortal family together.

In the Spirit World, where millions of couples who lived and loved in mortal form now linger, spiritual bonding gives them hope in their posterity.

Looking forward to that bright day when they could resume the work of the Lord in fulfilling their roles as caretakers of sacred temple ordinances, Nathan and Brandje sealed that moment of eternal perspective with a tender, yet divinely spiritual kiss.

*I*n early July, twenty months later, while Grandpa Nate and Grandma Nicole took Elisha to Chinon to spend a week with the Richelieu clan, Nathan and Brandje found themselves back at St. Gilles Croix de Vie on the Atlantic coast of France.

Long before dawn, yet in the light of a full and glorious moon, they descended the stairs leading to the bottom of a tall cliff. The bluff was overgrown with fragrant gardenias that year, more than they had ever seen. Soon they climbed Timbal's Point and sat snuggled up together on a flat piece of rock almost exactly in the center of it.

The salt air cleansed their lungs. The scent of gardenias surrounded them with special memories.

In their hearts soared the promises they'd made to one another last July, a year ago, that they would journey to France every year thereafter and watch sunrise from Timbal's point, and spend the summer with Elisha in the stomping grounds of her ancestors.

As the sky gathered light, and changed from blackness to soft gray, to pink, Nathan watched as his beloved Brandje waited for the exact, perfect moment to tell him a secret. She had hinted about it a few times, but since he knew her so well, he also knew that Brandje's secrets were only shared when she felt it was perfect and right to disclose them.

"Are you ready?" she asked, just as the sky changed from pink to fuchsia and then to a brightening purple.

"Are you?" he questioned, hoping beyond all hope she would tell him that for which he had been praying steadfastly for months.

She nodded and rested her head upon his shoulder. "Gabe gave me a clean bill of health," she said. "I'm taking less anti-rejection medication than any of his other patients. He wants me to decrease it even lower. He hopes I can give it up altogether by the end of summer. He said to tell you that he sees no reason why I won't live another fifty years."

Nathan sighed as a spirit of divine contentment filled his heart and soul. "I've been praying that was your secret," he admitted. "You can't imagine how happy that makes me."

"There's more," she confessed. "It's a good thing you're sitting down." She leaned back and gave him a mischievous grin.

"What is my sweet, impish wife up to this time?"

"Gabe says I'm healthy enough now to carry our child."

"For real?" asked Nathan, using his daughter's phrase deliberately, and realizing the marvelous effect Elisha had on both their lives.

"For real!" Brandje stated.

Then Nathan stood up and lifted Brandje onto her feet. He swept her up in his arms and whirled her around as easily as if she were a young child.

Brandje laughed with him until he finally stopped twirling and let her stand beside him.

"Do you think we'll be able to have children?" he asked after a few moments of reflective silence. "Dr. Finsen said some couples don't ever conceive following organ transplants. Do you think it's wise to get our hopes up too high?"

"I have something else to tell you," she confessed as she gazed up into his dark brown eyes. "I had forgotten all about it until after my appointment with Gabe."

"What is it?" he asked.

"Do you remember during the surgery, when my heart stopped and I walked with Martin back to Heaven? My father told me why I had to return to you."

"Yes," he answered. "You're supposed to take care of me and Elisha, keep your Temple covenants, and do your genealogy."

"There was something else Father told me that day," she confessed.

"What was it?"

"He told me that I should write my family's history, that without my work, their *grandchildren* would never know who they are, or how much they love them."

He pulled her tight against him and inhaled the sweet fragrance of her hair. "Grandchildren?" he mused aloud. "That would mean —"

Brandje nodded, tilted her head and kissed him hungrily.

When she finally let him up for air, Nathan grinned. Then he suggested, "Maybe we'd better get busy creating those grandchildren."

And they did.

Sherry Ann Miller's first novel, *One Last Gift,* placed third in the national **Beacon Competition for Published Authors**. A sequel to *One Last Gift* is in progress.

Sherry Ann Miller

A Biography

*S*herry Ann Miller, the mother of seven and grandmother of twenty, is an optimist by choice, a genealogist by addiction, and a writer by genetic composition.

Her writing credits include two Latter-day novels, several full-scale musical productions (most of which she also directed), four published family histories, numerous one-act plays and road shows, and three screenplays (two were semi-finalists in competitions, and one was optioned).

One Last Gift (Granite Publishing & Distribution/July 2000), Sherry's first novel, placed third in the Beacon Awards for Published Authors. Sherry enjoys writing LDS fiction, and is currently working on a sequel to *One Last Gift*, in order to satisfy numerous reader requests.

While Sherry resides in North Ogden, Utah, her sailing vessel, the *Shoosey-Q*, resides in the NW where she and her husband spend as much time as possible sailing and fishing.

In addition to other LDS novels in the development stage, Sherry has several books in progress, including the ancestral history of her maternal grandfather (non-fiction); a narrative regarding her father's unique role during the 1963 Presidential Campaign (novel based on fact); and an account of the inspirational experiences she's had while researching more than 26,000 names for her family history files (non-fiction).

Sherry welcomes reader response. Please write to her in care of Granite Publishing and Distribution, or e-mail her at FDMEnt@aol.com.